Dostoevsky and the Novel

Dostoevsky
and the Novel

—

Michael Holquist

Northwestern University Press
Evanston, Illinois

Copyright © 1977 by Princeton University Press

Northwestern University Press Paperback edition published
1986 by Northwestern University Press, Evanston, IL 60201
by arrangement with Princeton University Press.

Printed and bound in the United States of America

Publication of this book has been aided by a grant
from the Paul Mellon Fund of Princeton University Press

This book has been composed in VIP Bembo

Library of Congress Catalog Card Number: 86-061251
ISBN: 0-8101-0729-5

This book is dedicated to my sons:
Peter, Benjamin, and Joshua

Acknowledgments

The peculiar anxiety that comes with the conviction that there is no past to learn from or to lean on is what this book is "about." Perhaps that is why its author is more than ordinarily conscious of the debt he owes to the institutions, books, and people who constitute the enabling history of his own volume. If it has been overlong in its preparation, it has not been for shortage of the scholar's most valuable resource—time, generous gifts of which were made by Yale University's Morse Fellowship, the International Research and Exchanges Board, Wesleyan University's Center for the Humanities, and the Australian National University's Humanities Research Center. The Paul Mellon Fund helped to defray printing costs of the book. Parts of Chapter 2 appeared in *Canadian-American Slavic Review* (summer 1972).

I am grateful in a variety of ways to my fellow *Dostoevskovedy* in the United States, particularly Donald Fanger, Joseph Frank, Robert Louis Jackson, and Victor Terras. Had I been able to incorporate more of their suggestions, this would have been a much better book than it is. If I have succeeded in saying anything that is valid about Russia, it is because I have been gifted with extraordinary friends there: Vadim Kožinov (whose efforts on behalf of M. M. Baxtin [Bakhtin] deserve the gratitude of all serious students of literature), Sergej Bočarov, and Genja Gačev. Thanks also to my former colleague Vadim Liapunov, whose erudition is matched only by the patience with which he suffers impetuous American friends. The students and teachers (they will know which was which) of the Literature Major in Yale College, particularly Alvin Kernan, Peter Brooks, Walter Reed, Margie Ferguson, Donald Freeman, Tom Doyle, and David Dammrosch were particularly resourceful in dramatizing the ways in which friendship can be an act of mind. I am grateful to Mrs. Gianna Kirtley for aid in the final stages of the manuscript's preparation. Thanks finally to Katerina Clark, wife and colleague, who made the completion of this book (among many other things) possible.

August 1976   *Austin, Texas*

A Note on the Transliteration System
Used in This Book

The IPA system is used where actual Russian words have been quoted and for citing editions published in Russian. Familiar Russian names ("Dostoevsky") or borrowings ("dacha") are given in their more usual spelling.

Preface

This book consists mainly of detailed readings of specific works. These interpretations, however, are based on certain assumptions of a more general nature, the most important of which should at least be mentioned. The interpretations that follow are grounded in a dilemma shared by a genre, a nation, and a man. Each of these three categories has its own line of development. This book looks at what happened when the three strands became intermixed. The novel, Russia, and Dostoevsky may each be seen as characterized by particularly urgent problems of self-identification, may be said to have a biography. At the center of each such biography stands the question, "who am I?" Each in its own way strives to answer the question of what it is by finding a story that will somehow explain how it came to be. Thus, while the task is necessarily different in its implications for each, the novel as a genre, Russian historiography, and the man Dostoevsky all appeal to narrative as the royal road to knowledge of what they are.

The notorious difficulty of defining the novel, the problem of its identity, stems from the fact that individual representatives of the genre differ so radically from each other. Each great novel is more unique in its class than examples of other genres in theirs. Each contains a multitude of specific details that differ from those in other novels. They tell the lives of individual persons. Each seeks to define the distinctive features of its own characters—what makes them unique, why they are what they are and not something else—therefore, a tendency toward idiosyncrasy inheres in the genre itself. As soon as a new definition for "the novel" is coined, at least three new ones are written or rediscovered that subvert such a generalizing impulse. Something like this assumption that idiosyncrasy is at the heart of what might be called novel-ness is what Viktor Shklovsky had in mind when he said of that most peculiar of books, "*Tristram Shandy* is the most typical novel in world literature."[1] The paradox consists in the

[1] *O teorii prozy* (Moskva, Federacija, 1929) p. 204

uniqueness of its members defining the class to which they belong. The novel is not only *about* problematical identity; its characteristic theme of selfhood and the ways in which it pursues the topic in narrative put its own formal identity into constant question.

The central role of anomaly in the novel as a genre is what insures that it will be the most characteristic cultural expression of nineteenth-century Russia. Russia, too, labored under the necessity of defining what *it* was. A major preoccupation of its people during that period was somehow to come to grips with their own peculiar status in the family of nations. Excluded from such defining categories of West European history as the Renaissance and Reformation, to name only two, they were just as anomalous when judged by the reigning historiographical norms as the novel was when measured according to the standards of traditional poetics. Russia, too, was forced to meditate its own identity. It sought the answer in history, in a coherent story the logical end of which would be a definition of the national essence.

The motivating assumption of this book is that the generic impulse of the novel to problematize identity, on the one hand, and the national quest of the Russians for an identity of their own, on the other, met and fused in Dostoevsky's works. The shape of his career as it is charted by the works he wrote, as well as the shape of the individual novels themselves, may be understood as morphological answers to the same existential questions. The characteristic dilemma animating a Dostoevskian novel is how a character finds, or fails to find, a story he can live as his own. The novels are quests for a proper biography, attempts to fit the contingency of individual lives into the form of pre-existing life narratives.

The book is laid out in a series of chapters that it is hoped outline a shape of their own. The first chapter sketches the Russian historical background—or rather the absence of it— that everyone during Dostoevsky's lifetime sought to fill. The next chapter concerns itself with *Notes from the Underground*, the text of which sets up the problem that dominates all the others following it: if there is a difference between living and telling, how can I tell a story about my life, myself, that is nevertheless somehow true? There follow a series of readings that show Dostoevsky's various experiments for sealing lives with story. The emphasis in the readings, then, will be on plot in the Dostoevskian novel, but plot conceived as including the metaphysical implications of narrative structure as well.

While this book contains readings of most of Dostoevsky's fiction from the "major phase" and some too, of the earlier texts, it does not include an interpretation of *The Adolescent* (or, as it is sometimes translated, *A Raw Youth*). I have not touched on this novel for two reasons: one, it seems less interesting in its own right,[2] when judged by the very high standard of Dostoevsky's other late works; and, two, its functional role in the structure of my argument is preempted by the utopian aspects of *The Possessed* and *Dream of a Ridiculous Man*, on the one hand, and, on the other, by the pattern of son-evolving-into-father that is present in *The Brothers Karamazov*.

[2] But see Horst-Jürgen Gerigk's book devoted exclusively to this novel: *Versuch über Dostoevskijs "Jüngling": ein Beitrag zur Theorie des Romans* (München, Wilhelm Fink, 1965).

Table of Contents

Dostoevsky and the Novel

══ *Chapter 1* ══

The Problem: Orphans of Time

I

Russia is always being discovered, or at least since the six-teenth century, when disputes arose in Europe as to whether von Herberstein or Sir Richard Chancellor could claim the honor of what Hakluyt was to call "the strange and wonder-ful discovery of Russia." For Milton in the seventeenth cen-tury and Voltaire in the eighteenth, Russia was still resistant to symmetrical English or French models of time and space, linear history, and binary (occident/orient) geography. One of the reasons Westerners still find it difficult to classify Russia is that the Russians themselves have never been quite sure where and when they are.

For most of Europe, January 1, 1700 was the beginning of a new century. For the Russians it was an even more momen-tous occasion. By decree of Peter I, it was the end of an old chronology that dated events from the creation of the world, and the first day of a new epoch that was to be calculated ac-cording to the Julian calendar. The new calendar was another of Peter's attempts to break down the differences between Russia and the West, and its adoption is perhaps the most comprehensive symbolic act of his reign. It is an emblem of Peter's intention to Europeanize not only Russian culture and space—to change the course of history, in other words—but to change the native sense of *time itself*.

The fact that in Peter's reign the year 7208 was supplanted by the year 1700 is a metaphor for much subsequent Russian history. It is first of all ironic that the Julian calendar should have been adopted as a progressive measure at a time when most of the rest of Europe was gradually going over to the even more accurate Gregorian calendar. Thus while Peter brought Russian time more into congruence with Western time, there would still be a gap (depending on the century) of twelve or thirteen days between Russian and European dates.

3

It remained to the Bolsheviks finally to wipe out this discrepancy when they introduced a new calendar to mark their revolution, as Peter had for his. But if the difference between a French, say, and a Russian calendar in the nineteenth century was only a matter of days, the difference between the historical development of French and Russian culture was felt to be considerably greater. For the Russians after Peter the clock—or calendar—was always West European, with the consequence that they felt out of phase at any given moment. Their history did not seem to parallel that of those privileged states in the West which shared a Roman Catholic Middle Ages or Renaissance Humanism, to mention only two defining ages that were absent in the Russian past. This problematic relationship of the Russians to their own antecedents may be seen as one of the reasons why it is not until the nineteenth century that a culture arose that Russians and West Europeans alike would define as being uniquely Russian, distinctive, but no longer exotic.

It is not, then, the blind prejudice of Westernizers alone that maintains that "Russian literature . . . starts with Derzhavin (1743-1816) and Pushkin (1799-1837) and all but one or two significant figures in it lived within the life-span of a single man, Leo Tolstoy (1828-1910)."[1]

While this may be merely curious or strange to West Europeans, it is a matter of the profoundest concern for the Russians themselves. Long before Sartre, they were forced to ask "What is literature?" as they strove to answer the question, "Can we have one?" In thinking this problem through, they repeated the pattern of Peter's calendar reform as they compared the West European literary past with their own. They were chagrined by the poverty and peculiarity of their native tradition in the face of developments in France or England. Since they began, as had Peter, by assuming that Western models of development were privileged, their problem was somehow to create a national literature that would be similar to those in Europe. At the same time they felt they could not

[1] Andrew Field, *The Complection of Russian Literature* (London, 1971), p. xi.

draw on the long heritage that already (by the nineteenth century) supported those literatures.

The very recognition of this dilemma was late in being made. One reason for this tardiness may be found in that fastidious disregard for history as a proper subject of reflection that eighteenth-century Russian *lumières* shared with the French thinkers they sought to emulate. As Frank E. Manuel has pointed out:

"For many eighteenth century *philosophes* history was either entertainment, a moral homily of a secular order, or an ugly spectacle of human vice and idiocy, the unlovely prolegomenon to the Enlightenment. It was difficult to discern philosophical sense in a combination of acts whose human motivation was overwhelmingly bestial and self-seeking. If men were driven by their uncontrollable lusts, how could their history be rational or subject to exposition in scientific terms? There was a fundamental cleavage between philosophy and history. . . ."[2]

Another reason why national identity was less of a problem in the eighteenth century than it was to become later can be traced to Neo-Classicism, the reigning literary ideology in the West, which had built into its theory (if not its practice) a means for overcoming—or at least avoiding—difficulties raised by unique national traditions. Tredyakovsky (1703-1769), Sumarokov (1718-1777), even Lomonosov (1711-1765), the men who define Russian literature in the eighteenth century, could exploit the *internationalism* implicit in Classicist theory; if you rigorously applied the normative requirements for writing an ode or an epic, as they were formulated by Horace and transmitted by a Gottsched or a Boileau, you were making literature. There was, in the strict generic definitions of such a theory, a conception of literature so abstract and yet so normative that it could be used to certify texts *as*

[2] *The Eighteenth Century Confronts the Gods* (N.Y., Atheneum, 1967), p. 152. A good example of the philosophical status of history in the Enlightenment is Kant's statement: "It is hard to suppress a certain disgust when contemplating man's actions upon the world stage." (Quoted in Bruce Mazlish, *The Riddle of History: The Great Speculators From Vico to Freud*, N.Y., Minerva Press, 1968 [1st paperback ed. orig. pub. 1966], p. 103.)

literature, without raising the sticky question of national traditions (or, for the Russians what was more to the point, about the *absence* of such traditions). Simply stated, this meant that Lomonosov was free to be less anxious than Russian writers in the next century would be about the status of his odes as *literature*, even though there was only a very poorly and recently developed tradition of the ode in Russia. He could experience confidence because he was imitating a model more ancient than the Russian (or, for that matter, the French or any other West European) state itself. If he could not—as Italian, French, or English poets in the eighteenth century felt they could—draw on sixteenth- or seventeenth-century examples of the ode in his native language, he could appeal to the example of Horace himself. There was a tradition he could turn to that would ensure the literariness of what he was doing as long as the validity of Neo-Classicist poetics was not called into question.

All these factors tended to obscure the meaning that Peter's reform might have if Russia was to possess its own unique cultural identity. It was not until the first years of the nineteenth century that concern for such an identity made itself widely felt. But when it did, it did so with particular urgency. During the reign of Nicholas I (1825-1855) the quest for a cultural personality of their own led Russians to ask questions so radical that they were called cursed. Of these *"prokljatye voprosy"* "the most widely debated . . . during Nicholas' reign was the meaning of history . . . in 1804 the society of History and Russian Antiquities was founded . . . the defeat of Napoleon and the reconstruction of Moscow created a broad, popular interest in history and Nicholas I contributed to it by encouraging the activities of a large number of patriotic lecturers and historians: Ustryalov, Pogodin and others. Between Pushkin's *Boris Godunov* (1825) and Glinka's *Life for the Tsar* (1836) historical plays and operas dominated the Russian stage. . . . Historical novels dominated the literary scene . . . [and there were] 150 long poems on historical themes . . . written in Russia between 1834 and 1848."[3]

[3] James H. Billington, *The Icon and the Axe* (N.Y., Alfred A. Knopf, 1966), p. 314. For accounts of the interaction between secret police and liter-

This is also, of course, the age of "Official Nationalism," when Nicholas was doing much more than merely "encouraging the activities of a large number of patriotic lecturers." The emperor, through such men as Uvarov in the newly redesigned Education Ministry and Benkendorf in the Secret Police, forced Dostoevsky's generation to confront in the most immediate, as well as the most insidious, ways, what it meant to be Russian. Faddej Bulgarin, who was an employee of the Secret Police, ran the most widely read newspaper of the day (*Northern Bee*); Senkovsky, another notorious government sympathizer, was editor of the period's most widely read journal (*Library for Reading*). Grech, a publicist who worked closely with both these men, constituted the third member of what was known as "the triumvirate." This unholy trinity never let an opportunity pass to further explicate the government's triadic motto, "orthodoxy, autocracy, nationalism."

The ubiquitous activity of these men—who were not ungifted as propagandists—forced not only their friends but also their enemies to turn to the one source that all felt was an adequate ground for supporting—or for de-mystifying—the litany of orthodoxy, autocracy, nationalism: history. History "in one form or another became the center of attention and controversy. 'The historian represented,' in the words of Pogodin (a leading historian of the period) 'the crowning achievement of a people, for through him the people came to an understanding of itself'."[4] The conception of the historian

---

ary figures see: Sidney Monas, *The Third Section: Police and Society in Russia Under Nicholas I* (Cambridge, Mass., Harvard U.P., 1961) and P.S. Squire, *The Third Department: The Establishment and Practices of the Political Police in the Russia of Nicholas I* (Cambridge U.P., 1968).

[4] Nicholas V. Riasanovsky, *Nicholas I and Official Nationality in Russia 1825-1855* (Berkeley and Los Angeles, U. of California Press, 1969), p. 102. This exalted conception of the role historians could play in forming national consciousness was so widely felt in Europe at the turn of the nineteenth century that it became almost a Romantic cliche: even the great Niebuhr, who with Ranke is generally considered to be the father of modern critical historical methods, admitted that "the evil time of Prussia's humiliation (under Napoleon) had some share in the production of my history" (quoted in G. P. Gooch, *History and Historians in the Nineteenth Century* [Beacon Paperback, Boston, 1968, p. 17]). He agreed with the king that "we must make up by

as detective of a nation's identity derived, of course, from German Idealist philosophy. D. M. Vellansky, M. G. Pavlov, A. I. Galich, and A. I. Davydov had already lectured on Schelling and the group known as the "lovers of Wisdom" (Lyubomudry—a Russian calque, of course, for philosophers) had already been formed before the Decembrist's 1825 uprising. Hegel played an even larger role in creating a new sense of the importance of history.[5] Nicholas I was a notorious Germanophile; during his reign the German influence was felt as much in the academy as it was on the drill field. Such scholars as Haxthausen and Hilferding did much to investigate and popularize such distinctively Russian institutions as the peasant commune (*obščina*) and oral epic (*bylina*).

A new sense of the importance that historical study might play in building Russian national identity was not confined to Polish emigrants, such as Bulgarin and Senkovsky, or the Baltic Germans enumerated above. Native Russian scholars and publicists were at the cutting edge of the new historical consciousness. I. V. Kireevsky (1806-1856), who had studied philosophy and theology in Berlin and Munich and had met both Schelling and Hegel, felt he had thereby earned the right to his distrust of the West; he was able to convince many Russians who were otherwise disgusted by the jingoistic excesses of official nationalism, that there nevertheless *was* something unique and valuable in Russian history. S. P. Shevyryov (1806-1864) also travelled extensively in the West, where he met many leading thinkers (spending three months in discussions with Baader alone). He, too, came back to his homeland convinced that the future lay in it; he also helped to make intellectually respectable those conceptions of Russia's greatness that were the stock-in-trade of "official nationalists." His career is important, too, in showing the growth of new in-

---

intellectual strength what we have lost in material power." He set himself to "regenerate the young men, to render them capable of great things. . . ." (Gooch, *loc.cit.*).

[5] See two important books by Dmitrij Tschizewskij, *Hegel in Russland* (Halle, Inaug. Diss., 1934) and the collection *Hegel bei den Slaven* (Bad Homburg, Herman Gentner Verlag, 1961, 2nd ed.).

stitutions dedicated to discovering Russia's uniqueness: he was the first to occupy a chair of exclusively *Russian* literature, and the author of the first comprehensive history of that subject (in four volumes, 1845-1860). Before Shevyryov became Professor of Russian Literature, he had taught general (or world) literature; the same movement from a general subject into its specifically Russian aspect—a pattern present in institutions throughout Nicholas' reign—can also be seen in the career of the above-mentioned Michael Pogodin (1800-1875)ʹ. He defended his Masters dissertation on *The Origins of Russia* in 1825; but when—in the following year—he received an appointment of the University of Moscow, it was as a teacher of universal history. It was not until the following decade that Pogodin assumed what was the first chair in exclusively *Russian* history.[6]

This explosion of interest in history during the reign of Nicholas I can be explained not merely as an effect of the general European "discovery of history" during the early years of the nineteenth century. It has its own roots in distinctive Russian traditions, as well. German philosophy of history (more than German historical writing as such, even though the same period witnesses its scholarly golden age in such men as Niebuhr and Von Ranke) influenced Russian thinkers, led them to search for what was unique in the national past. But the same search had roots as well in the ancient belief that Russia was different from other nations because she was "Holy Russia." Before 1825 there was little attempt to locate this holiness in what we would now recognize as history. Explanations for Russia's status as a chosen people were as mythical as was the concept itself cloudy and unspecific. But with the new sense of history that develops under Nicholas, attempts were made to ground Russia's peculiarly God-bearing role not in legend, but in actual events and institu-

[6] For a translation of some of the more important texts by Russians influenced by German Idealism in their thinking about national identity, see: Paul Debreczeny, *Literature and National Identity* (Lincoln, Nebraska U.P., 1970). See also: Wsewolod Setschkareff, *Schellings Einfluss in der Russischen Literatur der 20-er und 30-er Jahre des XIX Jahrhunderts* (Berlin, Inaug. Diss.), 1939.

tions. "If Russia was holy, then it must have specific and unique qualities, and those qualities must be recognizable in its history; but more than this, if 'Holy Russia' was the essence of Russia, then at some time, in the past if not the present, this essence must have been explicit. . . ."[7] In other words, the peculiar intensity that characterizes attempts to understand Russian history during Nicholas' reign is explained by the essentially *religious* task that history was widely felt to be capable of performing. History was important because it could reveal the kairotic moment in which the distinctiveness of Russian chronology was grounded. But the distinguishing characteristic of Russian historiography during the years when Dostoevsky was growing to maturity was the attempt to wipe out the distinction between *kairos* and *chronos*: history was practiced as a kind of Russ-odacy.

The search for a past that exercises the Russian imagination in the early decades of the nineteenth century was not confined to historians. While the central role of poets and novelists in the late Slavophile debates is well known, it should be kept in mind that Russian literature was *always* at the forefront of the search for a national identity. In the various eighteenth-century arguments about the propriety of different levels of Russian discourse as they related to "high" and "low" literary genres, there can already be seen the first indications of that cultural anxiety which becomes so acute under Nicholas I. But the years that intervene between Tredyakovsky and Belinsky are marked by a constant intensification of the Russian concern about the nature of the national literary tradition as it represented the national character as such. This crisis of cultural identity ultimately led to doubts as to the very existence of an indigenous literature, and therefore of a valid national identity. It is as a gradually ascending peak on this fever chart that we should understand the debates that begin at the turn of the nineteenth century about whether old Russian liturgical forms could provide a proper basis for a Russian literary language.

[7] Michael Cherniavsky, *Tsar and People* (New Haven, Conn., Yale U.P., 1961), p. 161.

The debate was a pamphlet war that ultimately led the opposing camps to form their own clubs. The adherents of the arch-conservative Shishkov joined the Discussion Group (*beseda*) of Lovers of the Russian Word; their opponents formed Arzamas. The various skirmishes of the debate, which extended roughly from 1803, when Shishkov's first book was published, to 1818, when Arzamas broke up, are usually unified under the title "The Polemic about old and new style." But this should not obscure the fact that, while style and language were the operative terms of the debate's broadsides, its real subject was the conflict between two opposed views of what might constitute a valid source for Russian national identity, each of which presupposed its own historical model. Shishkov's book, *A Consideration of Old and New Diction in the Russian Language* (1803), was the first blow struck in the struggle, but the position he outlined in this work continued to be the definitive statement of his side's argument throughout the debate that followed. Shishkov, a political reactionary who was inimical to the "liberal" Speransky reforms (and who became a powerful Education Minister after Speransky's fall) because they were based on foreign (read "French") ideas of progress, felt that not only were native political institutions being undermined by such men, but Russian culture itself. Living during one of the great ages of rapid change in the Russian language, he ascribed what were probably inevitable accommodations of the language to new technical and literary demands for expression to the machinations of a younger generation that had willfully neglected its own traditions to whore after non-Russian innovations. Although he did not himself participate in the controversy, Karamzin was regarded as the great enemy because, as the most popular and influential representative of Russian Sentimentalism (or, in this context more precisely, Pre-Romanticism), he had experimented not only with new genres, but with new words, many of them calques of French words. Karamzin had from the beginning of his career been more conscious than most of the relative poverty of modern Russia's literary life; in a letter to Lavater (April 20, 1787) he admitted that there

11

were very few Russian contemporary writers, certainly not many of interest to a West European audience. Karamzin published a *Pantheon of Russian Writers* in 1802, beginning with the ancient (and probably legendary) bard Bojan and going up to the end of the eighteenth century, which included only twenty figures. One of the primary reasons, as Karamzin saw it, for the poverty of Russian literature was the poverty of the Russian language, and his career as author both of fiction and history was a long attempt to overcome the "inequality" between Russian and West European literature. Thus, in the degree to which Karamzin *is* the ideological opponent of Shishkov, the struggle between the two should be seen as a conflict between two kinds of patriotism.

After 1827 doubts concerning national identity became even more radical. In 1803 Karamzin could say that there was as yet no Russian literary criticism, because criticism is always a "luxury" and Russian literature was not yet a Croesus. Not many years later, after the death of Derzhavin and during the lifetime of Pushkin (as a matter of fact in a letter *to* Pushkin), Beztuzhev-Marlinsky would write that "We have a criticism, but no literature."[8]

Shortly thereafter we have the curious spectacle of the period's most influential literary critic opening his career by announcing the absence of his subject: "We have no literature."[9] This conclusion Belinsky bases on two premises: a national literature is defined by (1) the length of its history and (2) by the organic growth, the interconnections, in the progress of that history. Compared to West European literatures, the Russian heritage was very brief indeed, extending back only to Lomonosov, less than a century before Belinsky wrote his "elegy in prose" (1834). And what there was of that heritage was characterized by fits and ŝtarts, with little or no internal logic in the relationship from one period to another between its geniuses such as Derzhavin and Pushkin. Furthermore, in Belinsky's view, the simultaneous relationship of second- and third-rate authors to such geniuses in any given period was so

[8] *Polnoe* (St. Petersburg, 1847), vol. ii, p. 84.
[9] *Izbrannye*, (Moscow-Leningrad, Gos. izd. xud. lit., 1949), p. 4.

sketchy that it was discontinuous. Belinsky's judgment, then, was that Russians could boast of a few isolated works of genius, but they did not have a truly national literature. Belinsky would later modify this view, but a basic insecurity about the health of Russian literature never left him: he kept writing annual reviews of Russian literature, as if he were periodically taking the pulse of a precocious but ailing child. These reviews always began, as did many of his other articles (and the opening chapters of his Pushkin study), in an attempt once again to establish a model for Russian literary history, to place his particular topic into one or another kind of cultural continuum.[10] But none of them went back any further than Kantemir (1708-1744).

An expert on ancient Russian culture might, of course, dispute Belinsky's views, as did several patriotic critics in the 1830's and 1840's. But doubts about the existence of a national literature, not pious affirmations of Russian culture, carried the day in the early nineteenth century. As late as 1847 Belinsky would be writing: "The history of Russian literature . . . like that of Russia herself, does not resemble the history of any other literature. Therefore it represents a singular, exclusive spectacle, which is . . . rendered odd, incomprehensi-

[10] It is only now, perhaps, that we can appreciate as the radical experiments they were, Belinsky's various attempts to establish a model of Russian literary history. His constant emphasis on "organic" criteria may be read as a kind of rough attempt to deal with literature as a *system*, much as would the best critics of the 1920's in Russia, such as Tynyanov ("On Literary Evolution," *Archaizers and Innovators*) and Eikhenbaum ("Literary Environment"). While he never attained the rigor that characterizes the best work of the Formalists, Belinsky nevertheless anticipates some of their insights into the nature of how change comes about in literary history. He would, for instance, have found much to agree with in the following analysis from Eikhenbaum's 1929 article mentioned above. "It may be positively stated that [our] crisis involves not literature in and of itself, but literature's social mode of being. The writer's professional status has changed, the reader-writer relationship has changed, the customary conditions and forms of literary endeavor have changed; a decisive shift has occurred . . . bringing to light a whole series of facts concerning the dependence of literature and . . . its evolution on conditions forming outside literature." (As translated by I. Titunik in *Readings in Russian Poetics*, ed. L. Matejka, K. Pomorska [Cambridge, Mass., M.I.T. Press, 1971], p. 58). See the excellent book by Victor Terras, *Belinskij and Russian Literary Criticism: the Heritage of Organic Aesthetics* (Madison, U. of Wisconsin Press, 1974).

ble, and almost meaningless when treated on the same plane with any other European literature."[11]

II

The most dramatic confirmation for this view is contained in Chaadaev's "First Philosophical Letter," which appeared in the same journal in which Belinsky had begun his career two years earlier. It seems an irresistible irony that the journal was called *Teleskop*, for both men seemed to view Russia from afar, as if their own homeland were not just another country, but another planet. This fact may, perhaps, give some idea of how distinctive Russia appeared to members of her own intelligentsia, raised as they were to respect West European traditions and perforce contrasting what they knew of their own reality with them. Chaadaev, whose importance has yet to be recognized in the West, cut to the heart of all doubts about the history of particular Russian institutions, political as well as cultural, by declaring, in effect, the Russians had no history at all: "Historical experience does not exist for us. Generations and ages have passed without benefit to us. With regard to us it is as if the general law of mankind had been suspended. . . ."[12] He goes on to speak of the Russians as "being somehow out of time. . . ."[13]

Now this sense of void in the past would be less painful if it were not accompanied by the prejudice that, "The mind feels at ease *only in an historical sphere* [emphasis added] . . . every minute it tries to lean on the past; it values the new forces only insofar as it can perceive them through a prism of reminiscences, of understanding of the past, knowledge of the factors which controlled its development through the ages. . . ."[14] In other words, it is at just that point when history seems most necessary to the Russians that they discover they do not have one, with the result that they have: "nothing durable, nothing permanent; everything flows, eveything passes without leav-

---

[11] "Vzgljad na russkuju literaturu 1846 goda" (Review of Russian Literature for 1846") in *Izbrannye Sočinenija*, ed. F. M. Golovčenko (Moscow-Leningrad, Gos. izd. khud. lit., 1949), p. 864.

[12] *Sočinenie i pis'ma*, ed. M. Geršenzon, vol. I, p. 84.

[13] *Ibid.*, p. 72.   [14] *Ibid.*, p. 97.

ing traces either outside or inside. In our own houses we seem
to be guests, in our families we look like strangers, in our
cities we live like nomads. . . ."[15]

Chaadaev has here stated what is perhaps the essential dilemma for the Russian imagination in the modern period: the
question "who are we?" asked as *"when* are we?" The rest of
the century is occupied by various attempts—institutional as
well as theoretical—to see who can give the Russians a history. The Slavophiles would seek it in the past, the Nihilists
in the future. The great conflicts in Russian intellectual life of
the past two centuries constitute a contest to see who could
give the Russians a history—a conflict that, of course, the
Bolsheviks won. History during this period was less, as Joyce
would say, a nightmare to awaken from than it was a dream
to realize.

Nineteenth-century Russian authors, then, felt an enormous sense of void in their own past. Henry James, in his
biography of Hawthorne, might complain about the difficulties American novelists experienced in a land where there was
no long-standing social matrix, no settings associated with
legends of their own. But his catalogue of absences—no
medieval castles, no old universities, no Epsom Downs,
etc.—while admittedly an ironic one, is a boast of plenty
when compared to the Russian sense of historical poverty. It
was not just philosophers and publicists such as Chaadaev
who dramatized this need, but—and to a greater extent—
Russian *writers*. Consider the following passage from Lermontov's *Hero of our Time* (1841):

"I returned home through the deserted alleyways of the sta-
tion: The moon, full and red like the glow of a fire, had begun
to appear from behind a serrated skyline of houses; stars were
shining calmly in the dark blue vault, and it amused me to
recall that at one time there were extremely wise people who
thought that the heavenly luminaries took part in our trivial
quarrels over a small plot of land or some fictitious rights.
And what of it? These lamps, which according to them, were
lit solely to illuminate their own battles and triumphs, still burn

[15] *Ibid.*, p. 78.

with their former lustre, whereas their passions and aspirations have long since been extinguished, together with them like a fire lit at the edge of a wood by a careless stranger. But at least that conviction that the whole sky with its innumerable inhabitants looked on them with a mute though immutable concern gave them some power of will! . . . But we, their pitiful descendants who wander over the earth without convictions or pride, without pleasure or fear—apart from the involuntary terror which grips one's heart at the thought of the inescapable end—we are no longer capable of great sacrifices for the good of mankind nor even for our very own happiness, for we realize its impossibility, and so we move indifferently from doubt to doubt—just as our ancestors .rushed from one delusion to another—having neither hopes nor even that vague but intense delight which the spirit gains in any struggle with people or fate, as they did."[16]

We should not let the conventions of Lermontov's Romantic rhetoric in this passage blind us to what is important in it: the degree to which it goes beyond Chaadaev's insistence that Russia *alone* has no history. Lermontov here universalizes this dilemma, makes it a condition for modern men, not just for Russians. It is an epiphany about the nature of history: there was a time when mythological cosmologies gave men a meaningful home, the order of the stars insured the significance of life lived beneath them; but that time has passed, there is no transcendent system for insuring order, men must now invent their own meaning, as they "wander the earth . . . from doubt to doubt." There is a bitter elegy here for the kind of system ("deception," religion, or astral mythology) that made life seem to have meaning. What is specifically

[16] Tr. Philip Longworth, Signet Classics, ed. N.Y. 1964, pp. 183-84. Compare this elegy on the death of meaning in the stars with the opening dithyramb of Lukacs' *Theory of the Novel*: "Happy are those ages when the starry sky is the map of all possible paths—ages whose paths are illuminated by the light of the stars. . . . The world is wide and yet it is like a home, for the fire that burns in the soul is of the same essential nature as the stars; the world and the self, the light and the fire, are sharply distinct, yet they never become permanent strangers to one another. . . . Thus each action of the soul becomes meaningful and rounded. . . ." *Theory of the Novel*, tr. Anna Bostock (London, Merlin Press, 1963), p. 29.

lamented in this analysis is that there is no longer any defense against history as flux; there is nothing to insure lasting values—with the result that the stars, as mere stars, seem to mock in their longevity the rapid passing, the may-fly transitoriness, of the lives of men. The stars still burn, but the men who worshipped them, "their passions and aspirations, have long been extinguisned . . . like a fire lit at the edge of a wood by a careless stranger" (by a *deus absconditus?*). What Lermontov is here doing, in effect, is announcing the death of God, decades before Nietzsche. But, like Nietzsche, he emphasizes that it was an event that occurred *in time*: there was an era when men believed in forces larger than themselves that gave shape and significance to their lives, to history—but they no longer believe.

The distinction between eternity and history is known to most religious systems (the *locus classicus* in Christian theology is, of course, chapter eleven of Augustine's *Confessions*). Lermontov points out the disparity between the two as the peculiar temporality that defines modern man. He here confronts " 'historical man' (modern man) who consciously and voluntarily creates history, with the man of the traditional past [or in contemporary times, so-called 'primitive'] civilizations who . . . had a negative attitude toward history . . . [and who] accorded the historical event no value in itself; in other words did not regard it as a specific category of [their] own mode of existence."[17] History, if it is merely a succession of events without something superior to it that can give it meaning, becomes its *own* meaning, or historicism: "every historical event finds its full and only meaning in its realization alone."[18] It was against this "terror of history" that traditional societies defended themselves: "either by periodically abolishing [history] through repetition of the cosmogeny and a periodic regeneration of time (as in New Year rituals, for example) or by giving historical events a metahistorical meaning, a meaning that was not only consoling but was above all

[17] Mircea Eliade, *The Myth of the Eternal Return*, Bollingen/Princeton U.P. paperback ed. (Princeton, 1971), p. 141.
[18] *Ibid.*, p. 150.

17

coherent, that is, capable of being fitted into a well consolidated system in which the cosmos and man's existence had each its *raison d'être.*"[19]

It is the absence of such a system in the Russian past against which Chaadaev had earlier railed. We have "nothing durable, nothing permanent, everything flows. . . ." The myths that the West developed to make its history cohere were all forged without Russia, which had yet to find its own myth.

But in the works Chaadaev wrote after his arrest (especially the 1836-1837 *Apologie d'un Fou*) he retreats from this position to the much less radical stance of a Russian Westernizer: "Yes, there was an exaggeration in . . . the charge [that they had no history] brought against a great people, whose entire guilt, after all, lies only in the fact that it was thrown by its destiny to the last confines of all the civilizations of the world, that it lived far away from the countries where by a gradual process culture had been accumulated, far away from the hearths, where this culture had been shining for ages."[20] Nevertheless, Russia, no matter how tentatively, is still part of this culture: "We live in the East of Europe—this is true, but we nevertheless never belonged to the East."[21] Chaadaev's pessimism had always been limited to the Russians alone: he subscribed to ideas of progress, the Enlightenment, the optimism of West Europe. His only complaint was that Russia was left out of this development. "[Russia] is not guided by a feeling for anything that lasts [*la durée permanente*], it finds itself gone astray in the world. There are a few lost beings in every country; but with us it is the general condition."[22]

In 1837 Chaadaev re-evaluates the achievement of Peter the Great, whom he now says succeeded in getting Russia back into history, thus securing her role in the happy drama of the European Enlightenment. "No people ever achieved more glorious triumphs on the field of progress" than had the Russians under Peter.[23] Chaadaev, who had stated the Russian historical dilemma in its most radical and pathetic terms,

[19] *Ibid.*, p. 142.
[21] *Ibid.*, pp. 226-27.
[23] *Ibid.*, pp. 222-23.

[20] *Sočinenie*, vol. ı, p. 232.
[22] *Ibid.*, p. 82.

could not ultimately live with the "terror of history" implicit in such a "modern" view. He immediately retreated to a reassuring myth system (human progress with a strong admixture of mysticism) that would guarantee that time *did* have a transcendent meaning.

It is against such a retreat, by one of the most unflinching minds of the age, that Lermontov's achievement must be gauged: in *A Hero of Our Time*, we have an example of the same temporal homelessness present in *The Philosophical Letters*, but Pechorin does not (beyond vague gestures toward a modish fatalism) retreat from the dilemma, the living effects of which constitute his story: he equates the deceptions that made history bearable for mankind in its youth (anthropomorphized stars) with the self-deceptions of his own youth. History becomes *his story* as he recapitulates in his own biography this movement from myth to historicism. Pechorin, the "hero" whose thoughts these are, goes on to equate the self-serving legends of mankind's youth with the false idealism of his own adolescence: "I entered on this life having already lived it in my thoughts, and I became bored and disgusted, like one who reads a poor imitation of a book he has known a long time."[24] He can only, as he has earlier said, "move from doubt to doubt"; there is nothing to insure value, certainty, outside that "time" of which Pechorin is "hero."

As a consequence, Pechorin is cut off, alone. But, as critics very early saw, his solipsism was, paradoxically, widely shared in Russian literature. He was assigned by literary genealogists to that very large family of other characters who also flaunt their uniqueness, the rupture between themselves and their times. Such characters as Aleko,[25] Onegin,[26] Chatsky,[27] Rudin[28] constitute a literary type now traditionally referred to as the "superfluous man" (*lišnyj čělovek*). The term has become a cliché, frequently used, rarely

[24] *Hero*, p. 183. [25] In Pushkin's *The Gypsies*.
[26] In Pushkin's *Evgeny Onegin*. [27] In Griboedov's *Woe from Wit*.
[28] In Turgenev's novel of that name (see also his *Diary of a Superfluous Man*).

examined. To *what*, then, are these characters superfluous? Russian society, is the usual answer: Russian society, which, due to its repressive politics and unwieldy civil service hierarchy, determines the exclusion of such types, for it offers no adequate scope for their energy and ambition. With no meaningful outlet for their gifts, they turn inward, strike vaguely Byronic poses that are often at variance with their iconic attribute of indecisiveness.

This is valid, of course, as far as it goes, but in order to understand what Dostoevsky will do with *his* "superfluous men," it is necessary to go a bit further, and Lermontov will help us here. Pechorin, when he sets out to analyze his dilemma, does not invoke the specific Russian social conditions, the historical *chez nous* of Chaadaev. Rather, as we have seen, he ascribes his diminished capacity to act to the absence of a supportive cosmology: in the past "the whole sky with its innumerable inhabitants looked down on [men] with a mute, though immutable, concern [which] gave them some power of will! . . . But we, their pitiful descendants who wander over the earth without convictions of pride . . . we are no longer capable of great sacrifices for the good of mankind, nor even for our very own happiness. . . ." Pechorin sees that he is not merely alienated from a particular society at a particular time, but that he is cut off from *any* system that will guarantee that his existence has meaning. He has become superfluous to his own being, and insofar as this is the case he is a forerunner of Dostoevsky's Underground Man.

III

Lermontov's conventionally Romantic rhetoric opens the possibility that his historical insight will be dismissed as having more to do with a period style than with a particular place and its distinctive problems. But Lermontov's sense of void and alienation is also present in the life and works of the man who most immediately influenced Dostoevsky's early career, Nikolai Gogol (1809-1852), a man whose idiosyncratic style is adequate to the constant concern he manifested for Russia's idiosyncratic role in history.

Gogol's last words, as he lay dying from the effects of a self-inflicted fast (and the brutality of his doctors), were: "a ladder, quickly, a ladder." It may be argued that he was once again—and finally—seeking a means to climb out of this world of flux and imperfection to that higher realm of static beauty he devoted his life to seeking. As his dying words indicate, he never did succeed in connecting the two levels of reality that determined his view of the world.[29] It is this sense of an ontological crack in the surface of existence that accounts for so much of the grotesque and the pathos in Gogol's work. Gogol, so unlike such other Russian masters as Pushkin and Tolstoy, nevertheless shares with them an overriding interest in the subject of history. The study of history was one of the means by which he sought to overcome the gap between such contradictions as dream and reality, Russia and the West, Russia as it was, and Russia as he felt it should be. Gogol actually taught history for three years (1831-1834), with disastrous results, although he could still claim, in a letter to M. A. Maksimovich as late as November 9, 1833, that, "Nothing *calms* one as much as history." Beginning with a plan to write a history of his native Ukraine, he soon moved on to a grander design: a *universal* history that would overcome his sense of schism in the world, bringing together all the scattered pieces. As he said, such a work "should gather into one all the nations of the world, divided by time, accident, mountains, seas, and unite them into one harmonious whole, forming out of them a majestically perfect poem."[30] But the unifying story of the nations was never written. What we get, rather, is a series of stories about the impossibility of such unifying stories. And at the heart of some of the more extreme of these tales is the recurring metaphor of Russia's anomalous place in European history.

The one story that more than any other of Gogol's stories recapitulates the Russian sense of historical dilemma is *Notes of a Madman*, concerned explicitly as it is with the

[29] See: James M. Holquist, "The Burden of Prophecy: Gogol's Conception of Russia," *Review of National Literatures*, III, i (Spring, 1972), pp. 39-55.
[30] Quoted in Leonid I. Strakhovsky, "The Historianism of Gogol," *American Slavic and East European Review* (Oct., 1953), p. 363.

psychological implications of being out of step with the times; his hero makes specific attempts to solve his existential dilemma by appealing to the potentially more ordered chronology of West European (Spanish) history. Although written in 1833-1834, it was first published in the 1835 collection *Arabesques*. The very make-up of this volume is an indication of Gogol's confusion; it is a miscellany of fiction, ancient history, and essays, with very little if any connection between them. This inability, or unwillingness, to accept the conventional distinctions between history (facts), essay (opinion), and story (fiction) is characteristic of the ontological-cocktail quality of Gogol's world view. It is his strength in the tales as it was a weakness in his life.[31]

The story itself is an exercise in the use of distancing techniques: first, as the split grows between its "hero" and the world, and, then, in the gap between the reader's original perception of the story and the one that Gogol forces upon him in the tale's conclusion. The overriding metaphor for all these ontological and psychological dis-connections is *temporal* discrepancy of one sort or another: being late, missing appointments, etc., at one level; and, in its highest expression, being out of joint with the irresistible sweep of history.

Poprishchin is also a superfluous man. The opening lines of the story show him, whose diary this is, to be late for work. But even when, later on, he does show up at the office, the director pretends not to see him. Poprishchin's temporal absence is confirmed spatially; he is *not there*. The cut-off between what he conceives himself to be and what society insists he in fact is, is also caught in his title, which does not reveal what he would *choose* to believe is his essential self: he is a *Titular* Councilor, very low in the Russian table of fourteen ranks. But his title is valid to the extent that it accurately fixes his situation, like it or not: he is a "councilor" in title only. Even the job that goes with the title is injurious to any valid

[31] It is also one of the many ways in which Gogol foreshadows Dostoevsky, even in the latter's mature phase: *Arabesques* and the notorious *Selected Letters from a Correspondence with Friends* (1842) are about as close to generic antecedents for that miscellany of essays, stories and "history," *The Diary of a Writer*, as one can find.

sense of identity: Poprishchin merely copies the documents of *others*; there are no words of his *own* in his work. He is further cut off from the discourse of the society he longs to join in that he does not share any of that society's foreign languages (the ability to speak that defined a man as being *salonfähig* as surely as his uniform). As he is working in the study of his superior's apartment he notices all the French and German books the director owns, none of which he can read—further evidence of a world from which he is excluded.

All of these discrepancies between the self-image Poprishchin seeks to erect for himself and that which is forced upon him, have a basis in the social distinctions of the time. These also permeate the "erotic" line of the story, Poprishchin's involvement with Sophie, his director's daughter: "her little hand is fragrant with the rank of general."[32] "Love" is what precipitates the ultimate divorce between him and sanity. Instead of union it promotes displacement. The knowledge is too painful for him to accept directly, and so he resorts to a bizarre means for letting the recognition seep into the cracks of his over-strained perceptual mechanism: he begins to "intercept" letters exchanged by two dogs, Madgie and Fidèle.

In other words, Poprishchin, in his attempt to write an autobiography he can live with, resorts finally to the old rhetorical trope of metonymy, which in its simplest expression is merely the name of an attribute that is substituted for that of the thing meant, i.e., scepter for authority.[33] But Poprishchin's experiment in substitution is more involved. Madgie, who lives in Sophie's house, stands in for her mistress; Fidèle has a demeaning and ridiculous name that Po-

[32] It was Donald Fanger who pointed up for me the degree to which Poprishchin's passion is drenched in rank-consciousness, one of the more important specific ways a sense of *difference* permeates the tale's whole structure.

[33] His defining attribute—an inappropriate response to society—is caught in the metonymic pole of aphasia, as it has been defined by Roman Jakobson: "Two Aspects of Language and Two Types of Aphasic Disturbance," in *Fundamentals of Language*, with Morris Halle (s'Gravenhage, Mouton, 1956). A good survey of the various meanings that metonomy has held will be found in Heinrich Lausberg, *Elemente der literarischen Rhetorik* (München, Huber, 1967 3rd ed.).

prishchin himself comments on, thus suggesting a relationship to himself, the bearer of another such name. The parallel is extended: Fidèle lives in the Zverkov building, where poor civil servants, like Poprishchin himself, live "on top of one another like dogs." Poprishchin cannot, in his own right, accept the fact that Sophie finds him absurd, but he lets Sophie (as Madgie) tell himself (as Fidèle) what the true situation is. Madgie describes her horror of an earlier suitor, a Great Dane. But now she has, in a certain Trésor, found her real love. She then describes Sophie's amused reaction to Poprishchin, as well as the fact that the girl is now in love with a young Guards officer who is courting her. The movement here is from Madgie and Trésor to Sophie and Guards officer, a parallel that, when it becomes explicit, is the ultimate rejection of Poprishchin.

It is too much, even when cushioned by metonymy. While reading the letters, Poprishchin interpolates "nothing, nothing—silence!" (or, less literally, "never mind") several times at those points where a bit more of the truth is about to emerge. He has repeated the same words earlier in the tale, when thinking of a vaudeville actress. Women force him into silence; there can be no sharing, no discourse with them. In the dog letters, it is written that "sharing feelings and impressions with another is one of the main blessings of life." But when such communion is nowhere possible, the frustrated desire for it becomes a curse. It is this which leads Poprishchin to canonize his loneliness. If he cannot exist with others, he must find a way to exist alone. Thus is born his mad conviction that he is the King of Spain. Some background is necessary in order to understand why Poprishchin—in his attempt to legitimize his identity—should have turned precisely to Spain.

Just as Gogol was beginning *Notes of a Madman* (1833, a year in which he was still officially a teacher of history) the Bourbon King of Spain, Ferdinand VII, died, leaving the throne to his infant daughter, Isabella II. This precipitated the first Carlist war, as supporters of Ferdinand's brother fought to establish Don Carlos on the throne. Thus Poprishchin, before he goes completely insane, reads in the newspapers that there is no king of Spain. This is the dynastic squabble he refers to, and Isabella II is the Donna he mentions. Now this is only one of *three* cases of disputed authority alluded to by Poprishchin. He also comments on events in France, specifically mentioning Polignac, the ultra-conservative statesman under Charles X, whose excesses led to the July revolution of 1830. And the last line of the story, concerning the Dey of Algiers, contains in it a reference to another fallen monarch, Hussein Pasha, who was deposed by the French invasion of 1830, which was launched while Polignac was still prime minister.

In the case of each historical incident alluded to in the story there is an end to *legitimacy*. Questions are raised about who is the real ruler. These problems of political legitimacy constitute a metaphor for the dilemma of existential authenticity in the case of Poprishchin. His career, too, has its revolution: when, as Titular Councilor Poprishchin, it finally becomes apparent to him that he cannot exercise hegemony over his own identity, cannot legitimize his claims to a self, he becomes Ferdinand *VIII*, the *rightful* heir, who has a true home in history.

But of course in order to do so he must use history against *time*: the movement from petty clerk to king is a transfer from one kind of temporality to another, from the change and flux of shared historical (even when it is experienced personally) time, to the lonely timelessness of insanity. Just as Poprishchin enters into his own space (the Spain of which he is ruler), he goes over to his own unique time as well, an aspect of his condition that is underscored by the breakdown in the chronology of the diary's notations. The date for the last entry when Poprishchin is still merely pondering newspaper accounts of the Carlist war is December 8, an extension of the temporal sequence with which the story began (the first entry is dated October 3); but the entry that records Poprishchin's discovery that he is Ferdinand VIII has the date: "Year 2000, April 43." And the other dates that follow are increasingly nonsensical. There is no *sequence* in them; there is no meaningful system back to which change can be referred: the role of king comes to Poprishchin from history, and he seizes it as a means to opt out of time.

Those are the distances built into the story, but there is also play with distancing techniques that Gogol clearly sought to incorporate in the act of reading the tale. The whole story is based on a strategy of indirection. The point of view in most stories told in the form of diary entries is usually described as being in the first person, or *Ich-Erzahhung*. But Poprishchin *has* no self to which an "I" can be attached. Terms other than pronouns must be sought to describe the point of view in this story, which is about the failure of their lived significance. We will get closer to the story if we see that just as Poprishchin's main mechanism for dealing with the world is metonymy, so is Gogol's for dealing with Poprishchin.

The very title of the story is a direction for how to read it. These are the notes of a "madman"; therefore the reader is warned that he must distinguish for himself the meaning of Poprishchin's experiences, independently of the interpretation Poprishchin will give events: dogs do not really write letters to each other, the insane asylum is not in Spain, the attendants are not minions of the Inquisition, etc. Reading the story with double vision, as he must, the reader is *forced* to keep his distance from Poprishchin, for at every point he has to be at variance with what Poprishchin says is happening. He is (insofar as he is mad) alienated not only from his environment within the story, but from the reader as well. What is more, the alienation is cumulative, it grows as Poprishchin enters deeper and deeper into his fantasy.

Until the very last entry of all. Here the language changes abruptly. Poprishchin recognizes what has befallen him, that he is being treated like a caged animal in the madhouse, and he cries out for pity. The momentary return to a sanity nowhere else present in the story is emphasized when he calls out to his mother to save him. He is, in other words, appealing to his actual parents, not the false genealogy of the Spanish succession. And just as he closes the distance between himself and reality at this juncture, so, simultaneously, does

26

Gogol (as manipulator of the narrative, if not the narrator) close the distance between Poprishchin and the reader, for whom Poprishchin ceases at this point to be merely a category—a madman, a foreigner from the time and space of *insanity*.

The difficulties and dangers of temporal aloneness, the condition that underlies Poprishchin's inappropriate responses vis-à-vis society at large, may arguably be read as a personal metaphor for the Russian historical dilemma under Nicholas I. The sense of cut-off between Russia and the rest of Europe that characterizes so much of Russian thought in the nineteenth century is more often than not valorized in the same way as the cut-off between Poprishchin and the rest of society. Accepting Western chronology as normative forced Russians to condemn the incongruities between their own past and that of "the others" (France and England) or to reach in the opposite direction by over-evaluating the role Russia might play in Europe's future (much as Poprishchin will save the future of "Spain" because of *his unique* legitimacy). In either case, Poprishchin's attempt to enter the Spanish succession contains in it the psychological tensions of being unhoused in time, as it was called by Chaadaev. The tragedy of Poprishchin dramatizes how pervasive, how deeply emotional, the problem of historical entrance was in just those years when Dostoevsky made *his* entrance.

IV

"Entrance" is invoked here in the sense that word is used by the historian of "things," George Kubler. In trying to define the use and limitations of biography in art history, he writes: "Biography is a provisional way of scanning artistic substance, but it does not alone treat the historical question in artists' lives, which is always the question of their relation to what has preceded and to what will follow them." Thus, in trying to define Dostoevsky's uniqueness, we must appeal to a tradition, keeping in mind that:

"The life of an artist is rightly a unit of study in any biographical series. But to make it the main unit of study in the history of art [or the novel] is like discussing the railroads of a country in terms of the experiences of a single traveller of several of them. To describe railroads accurately, we are obliged to disregard persons and states, for the railroads themselves are the elements of a continuity and not the travellers. . . . Each man's lifework is also a work in a series extending beyond him in either or both directions [past and future], depending on the track he occupies. To the usual coordinates fixing the individual's position—his temperament and his training—there is also the moment of his *entrance*, this being the moment in the tradition—early, middle, or late—with which his biological opportunity coincides."[34]

My argument is that Dostoevsky's distinctive place in the series of the modern novel is a function of his entrance at a particular moment in the series of Russian literary history. That is, he comes to consciousness as a thinker during those years when Russian national identity is conceived as a problem *in time*, of historical theory; and he matures as a writer at a time when literature is defined in Russia as the paramount source of insight into identity. We have seen that a central preoccupation of the Russian imagination under Nicholas I was to find a legitimate relationship between Russian and European temporalities, to fit the Russian moment into the European sequence. History was more often than not in Russia equated with *literary* history, as in Belinsky and Chaadaev, where the void in the national past is defined as an absence of a literature similar to the European model, therefore, as an absence of culture. Russian authors in the nineteenth century, for better or worse, labored under the responsibility of being the privileged source of national identity. Inscribed into Dostoevsky's biographical dates (1821-1881), then, are forces at work in the series of Russian history that will aid him in achieving his place in another series, that of modern literature. Dostoevsky is in the Russian tradition of Gogol and

[34] *The Shape of Time: Remarks on the History of Things* (New Haven, Conn., Yale U.P., 1962), p. 6. See also Boris Tomaševskij, "Literature and Biography," in Matejka and Pomorska, *Readings*, pp. 47-55.

Lermontov—and other native authors whose texts are narrative templates: problems of national (historical) identity. Dostoevsky appears at that moment when such problems begin to lose their parochial, national overtones and to assume the proportions of a dilemma facing all men in the modern period.

Of course Dostoevsky, the man, is more than a mere instrument of external forces in this process:

" 'Good' or 'bad' entrances are more than matters of position in the sequence. They also depend upon the union of temperamental endowments with specific positions. Every position is keyed, as it were, to the action of a certain range of temperaments. When a specific temperament interlocks with a favorable position, the fortunate individual can extract from the situation a wealth of previously unimagined consequences . . . thus every birth can be imagined as set into play on two wheels of fortune, one governing the allotment of its temperament, and the other ruling its entrance into a sequence."[35]

What, then, we may ask, are those particular aspects of Dostoevsky's biography which would make him more able than others to expand the significance of the Russian obsession with moment versus sequence?

There are, first of all, those key "moments" in his own life each of which seemed for a time to determine the meaning of the sequence of all the other moments. The best known of these is, of course, that moment on December 22, 1849 when Dostoevsky, standing in the snow of the Semyenovsky parade ground, clad in the white robe of the condemned, waited his turn to be executed for conspiring with other "revolutionaries" against Nicholas I. At the last moment the retreat was sounded and the true sentence was read out: four years of hard labor in Siberia, and then four years of exile in the ranks of the army. But up until the last moment Dostoevsky was actually convinced he was going to die in the next minute, and in the letter to his brother Michael describing the mock execution (on the evening of December 22) he writes: "Never till now have such rich and healthy stores of

[35] Kubler, p. 7.

spiritual life throbbed in me. . . . I am being born again in a new form . . . I'll be reborn to the better." For the rest of his life he sought to endow the often plodding progress of his day-to-day existence with the inspiration of that moment of resolution on the Semyenovsky. In the constant battle to relate that *kairos* to his biographical chronology, he learned those strategies of existential narrative that would permit him to fully exploit (and finally transcend) the wider significance of Russian nationalism. The years of prison and exile taught him aspects of the time/identity equation unsuspected by other writers who made their entrances at the same time. As Dostoevsky wrote (in his notebooks for *A Raw Youth*): "I pride myself that I have been the first to portray the real man of the Russian majority, and have for the first time revealed his distorted and tragic side. *The tragedy lies in the consciousness of his deformity* [emphasis added] . . . I alone have exhibited the hero of the tragedy of the underground. . . ."

What Dostoevsky is here calling "consciousness of deformity" is an awareness of the cut-off between *kairos* and *chronos*, utopia and reality. *A Raw Youth* is but one of many novels and stories (such as *The Possessed* or *Dream of a Ridiculous Man*) in which the dream of a static golden age (always set in an arcadian Greek archipelago) exists as an ahistorical affront to the flux of time, in which each of the characters must work out his own temporal contract between significant moment and meaningless sequence. It is Dostoevsky's emphasis on the *felt* quality of such contrasts, on their necessity and their variety, that makes him so important to the history of history.

Vasily Rozanov, in his 1891 essays on the Grand Inquisitor, was probably the first (other than Dostoevsky himself) to recognize that by conceiving Russian historical doubts as existential scenarios, Dostoevsky had initiated something new in world, as well as Russian, literature. Rozanov dwells on those elements in Dostoevsky that other critics would call cruel (Mikhailovsky) or sick (Gorky). But while such critics had used these traits as evidence for Dostoevsky's position on the periphery of what they conceived to be the literary and historical tradition, Rozanov advances them as arguments for Dostoevsky's central place in an anti-tradition. The gloom and disease, whores and axe murders, far from indicating that Dostoevsky is an exception, prove he is typical of a new age. Rozanov's book[36] is a *catalogue raisonné* of what have become clichés for the modern predicament. It is the age of alienation ("No common idea binds the nations together any longer, no common feeling guides them—everyone in every nation works only at his particular job" [p. 188]); of pessimism ("Everything sad and gloomy attracts contemporary man, for there is no longer any joy in his heart" [p. 189]); the death of God ("For more than two centuries the people of Europe have been acting directly counter to the Saviour's great precept 'But seek ye first the Kingdom of God' " [p. 187]). The book is permeated with a Yeatsian gloom: "Life dries up at its source and falls apart" (p. 189).

Rozanov believes that as other geniuses had revealed the essential meaning of their epochs, so does Dostoevsky for his: "The Legend of the Grand Inquisitor, so far as history is concerned, can be regarded as a great and powerful reflection of that peculiar post-Christian spirit. . . . When Alyosha tells his brother: 'Your Inquisitor simply doesn't believe in God,' the latter answers, 'You've finally guessed it.' *And this determines the Legend's historical position*" (pp. 168-70 [emphasis added]). Rozanov is working with a specific historical model: there has been a steady decline in all that was healthy and certain until, in "our historical life the 'legend' is the most poisonous drop ever to fall to earth after having finally separated itself from that phase of our spiritual development through which we have been passing for two centuries already" (p. 208). What Rozanov most wants from Dostoevsky is something to tell the time by: he conceives temporality not as a clock that keeps moving, but as an hourglass that is about to run out. Dostoevsky is the last grain of sand ("the most poisonous drop") to fall from the hemisphere of history into the hemisphere of

---

[36] *Dostoevsky and the Grand Inquisitor*, tr. Spencer E. Roberts (Ithaca, New York, Cornell U.P., 1972).

apocalypse, the signal that we are now in an *Endzeit*. Dostoevsky's status as religious prophet is in fact merely a subfunction of his historical role as Rozanov conceives it.

It was said long ago that all novels contain clocks; why, we may ask, does Rozanov insist that Dostoevskian time is necessarily chiliastic? In order to answer this question we must take into account spatial as well as temporal considerations. Although the *Legend* is set in the past, "the transference of contradictions that were revealed only in the nineteenth century to a conversation taking place in the sixteenth does not make a bad impression at all . . . to the foreground come features only of what is deep and eternal in man, so that the mixture in it of past, present and future—as it were, a combination of all historical time in one moment— [seems] . . . necessary" (p. 131). In other words, argues Rozanov, Dostoevsky's revelations are about *Man*, his significance is for everyone; the *Legend* tells not just Russian, but European, standard time as well. The sense of excitement in Rozanov's rhetoric derives from his conviction that it is finally a *Russian* historical model that is about to define European history:

"The race last to enter the historical arena and to which we Russians belong has in the peculiarities of its mentality the greatest capacity for [bringing harmony into 'life and history']. Instead of the forcible tendency of the Latin races to unite everything . . . without considering the individual spirit . . . and instead of the stubborn tendency of the Germans to . . . withdraw into an endless world of details, the Slavic race enters . . . into the most diverse and apparently irreconcilable contradictions" (p. 201).

Dostoevsky's Inquisitor who "simply doesn't believe in God" is seen as the greatest contradiction any man has been able to conceive at any time; it is an ultimate discontinuity, "the only synthesis in history of a most ardent thirst for religion with a total incapacity for it" (p. 190).

In the Heraclitean prejudice that the death of one God is the death of all, Rozanov seeks to convince that such doubts as these prove that time is running out. By questioning *Heilsgeschichte* in so radical a way, Dostoevsky threatens any kind of

Geschichte. The reason why Rozanov is less gloomy about the prospect than otherwise he might be is because it is, after all, Dostoevsky—most Russian of Russians—who has announced the apocalypse for all: "In world literature, we find frequent attempts to deny the existence of God, but here we feel that we are approaching something special, something that has never before appeared in any literature, a point of view that has never been taken by any man" (p. 85). In the same section Rozanov takes up the Grand Inquisitor's metaphor of non-Euclidean geometry, "which is now being worked out by the best mathematicians of Europe" (p. 86). At the same time Dostoevsky was going beyond God, Lobachevsky was going beyond Euclid, and Europe was about to be given a new sense of order by both Russians. Rozanov, as he uses this image, clearly has in mind a particular set of parallel lines that converge. He means the lines of European and Russian history, so long separate, but now, at the end of time, about to meet. By announcing the end of history the Russians shall enter it; there is just enough time left for the Europeans to realize, in an ultimate turnabout, that *they* have been discovered by the Russians. Rozanov's desire to make the ticket Ivan returns to God Russia's ticket for entering a common history with Europe is pathetic evidence of how deeply Russian exclusion from Western historical models was felt.

Dostoevsky has, of course, become an obligatory item in the catalogues Modernism invokes to define itself as a period. If we understand Modernism as something more than the particular concerns of a specific age, but see it rather as the latest name given to an ancient and recurring pattern in the history of imagination, it soon becomes clear that Dostoevsky is a "Modernist" not because of any new themes he introduces—alienation, the death of God, the transvaluation of values, etc. When those who believe with Virginia Woolf that "On or about December, 1910 human nature changed," cite Dostoevsky, they do so—often unwittingly—because they recognize in his work an obsessive meditation on the opposition that generates *all* such preoccupations, the structure—and its transformations—that underlies all "modern" themes: the

33

conflict between moment and sequence, between modern and historical. As Paul de Man has pointed out, "Modernity exists in the form of a desire to wipe out whatever came earlier in the hope of reaching a point that could be called a true present, a point of origin that marks a new departure."[37] While most Modernisms could be so understood, the problematic relationship between past and present that has obtained in Russia since Peter I (but that becomes acute only in the nineteenth century) provides a further twist to the meaning of the opposition between modernity and history. Because Russians labored so long under the fear and shame of not possessing what Sartre called "that proprietor's luxury, a past," they experienced modernity as a state forced upon them by West European historical models that excluded their presence. Each generation had to seek a "point of origin that marks a new departure." Thus Dostoevsky is the inheritor of a particular historical tradition—a tradition of radical doubt about history itself.

[37] "Literary History and Literary Modernity" in *In Search of Literary Theory*, ed. Morton W. Bloomfield (Ithaca, New York, Cornell U.P., 1971), pp. 245-56.

Chapter 2

The Search for a Story: *White Nights*, *Winter Notes on Summer Impressions*, and *Notes from the Underground*

I

It is customary to regard *Notes from the Underground* as a key to understanding the thematic concerns of the novels Dostoevsky wrote in his subsequent career, as a kind of Rosetta stone for such hieroglyphs of the major phase as *Crime and Punishment* or *Brothers Karamazov*. While there is much to recommend such an approach, it is perhaps no less interesting if we try to focus on the work from the other end of the telescope: that is, if we regard it in the light of works *preceding* it in the Dostoevskian canon. One of the preconceptions of what follows is that *Notes from the Underground* differs from Dostoevsky's earlier work—and is therefore significant in interpreting his later work—insofar as it makes use of a new basis for the various conflicts out of which all the fiction, early and late, is spun. In such works as *Poor Folk* or *White Nights* the characteristically Dostoevskian dichotomies of self/other, dream/waking, validity/self-deception, etc., are already present. But the scope of such conflicts is—relative to his own post-1864 phase, at any rate—comparatively narrow: what is often advanced as the best argument for Dostoevsky's importance—that he is a great psychologist—is perhaps most true of these early works, where he is frequently *only* a psychologist.

The Double, that extraordinary inscape of schizophrenia, may be regarded as the early text that arguably comes closest to the novels of the major phase; it nevertheless ultimately avoids the metaphysical dimension present in the later period. At the heart of such early fictions is a conception of character that is more limited (or "merely personal" in the sense of that late neo-platonist, Jay Gatsby) than it will be later. Another difference is that, while Dostoevsky already knew in these early works that St. Petersburg was a fantastic city, the how and why of its ontology have not yet been grasped by him in such a way that he can use it as a cosmological space, a very special sort of planetarium, as he will do in *Crime and Punishment* or *The Idiot*. In the early work St. Petersburg is still one of those countries of the mind, of which there are so many in the nineteenth-century novel that one frequently has the sense of reading psychological gazeteers (Balzac's "Paris," Dickens' "London"). The space of Dostoevsky's earlier works is more confined because it is cut out of a bolt of temporality differing from that extensive sense of time which gives shape and locality to the later novels.

I am assuming that the central concern of all Dostoevsky's work is a series of questions about identity; not only "who am I?" but "how can I be?" or "if I am *that*, who, then, are others?" It is further assumed that such questions are grounded in time. Thus the difference between earlier and later work springs not from a change in themes but rather from a different structuring of the same questions that results from Dostoevsky's increasingly complex sense of time and history. The specific way in which the experiences of mock-execution, Siberian exile, and his first trip to Western Europe affected Dostoevsky's work from 1864 on, was more and more to exacerbate those questions of identity he had always asked, as he more and more deeply explored that relationship between self and time which can be grasped in something like the following terms: "Man first existed in space, but he first became aware of himself in time. Thinking is an activity performed in time, for it is only in terms of time that thought becomes conscious of itself. *The discovery of the self and the experience of temporality occurred simultaneously since it is the self that posits, separates, and mediates the dimensions of past and future*"[1] [emphasis added]. The sense of time is more complex in Dostoevsky's later novels, and, therefore, so is the sense of self. Such a statement should not be let to stand on its own, so be-

[1] John G. Gunnell, *Political Philosophy and Time* (Middletown, Conn., Wesleyan U.P., 1968) p. 11.

36

fore plunging into an interpretation of *Notes* itself, I will first contrast it with a pre-exile story, *White Nights*.[2]

II

White Nights (1848) was one of the last pieces Dostoevsky wrote before his arrest on April 23, 1849. Its subtitle, "From the Reminiscences of a Dreamer," is significant: this is a tale about *dreams*, and not about nightmares. The organizing contrast is one between a conventional conception of dreaming, on the one hand (the distinction between night or day dreams is lost in the mysterious half light of St. Petersburg's midsummer white nights) and a conventional conception of reality, on the other, symbolized in the contrast between the soft nights of the poet's *past* that are used to divide the various sections of the tale ("1st night," "2nd night," etc.) versus the harsh morning of his *present* ("morning" is the title of the final section, when the poet must face the fact that Nastenka has gone off with her boarder). Thus, instead of probing for reality in a quotidian (a modifier that must in this context have a special resonance) waking experience that is more fantastic than dreams, as he will in his later works, Dostoevsky in 1848 assumes an opposition between unexamined dream and unquestioned reality that limits the frontiers of both. However, insofar as its basic contrast is one of conflicting ontologies, *White Nights* is similar to *Notes from the Underground*, where such a conflict, intensified and re-structured, is crucial. In this and other ways we must now explore, the earlier work reads like a sentimental parody of the later work (and in this its other subtitle "A Sentimental Novel" is justified).

[2] Since I make so much of the difference between the pre- and post-Siberian phases of Dostoevsky's career, it should be noted that "White Nights" was published, in addition to its initial appearance in *Fatherland Notes*, T, LXI (pp. 357–400), three more times during Dostoevsky's lifetime; each of these editions (in 1860 and twice in 1865) was published during Dostoevsky's later phase. Although Dostoevsky changed the 1848 text (especially in the 1860 version), none of his changes radically affects the interpretation offered here.

Both tell the tale of a duel between lonely, unhappy men who seek to capture young women by means of a self-consciously "literary" eloquence. Both are told in the first person, in the form of notes, with the eccentric dreamers making frequent asides to the reader. The poet in *White Nights* begins by admitting he is "prey to a peculiar melancholy. I suddenly fancied that everyone was forsaking me in my loneliness, that everyone was casting me off. . . . It frightened me to be left alone, and for three whole days I wandered up and down the streets in deep dejection. . . ."[3] Like the underground man, too, he is a *boulevardier-voyeur*, who walks about the city studying others: "Of course they don't know me, but I know them" (p. 11). His room has many of the characteristics of the underground: "green, grimy walls hung with cobwebs" (p. 13). And the awful rigidity, the fear of change that the underground represents is also here: "If I see a single chair standing differently from where it had stood the day before, I grow restless; I gazed at the windows, but all to no avail . . ." (p. 11). The suggestion of prison here is another parallel with the later story, as is the vexed relationship between the poet and his servant: "It even occurred to me to summon Matryona and give her a fatherly scolding about the cobwebs and the untidiness generally, but she only looked at me in surprise and left the room without a word, and so the cobwebs remain undisturbed to this day" (p. 14).

Like the underground man the poet *"has no story (istorija—* an, ambiguity Dostoevsky will not in the 1864 work neglect) *of [his] own"* (emphasis added, p. 32). He calls himself a "Type" (p. 33), meaning individual, but it is clear he is also a "type" in the sense of a generic example. Since he has no story that is his to *experience*, he makes up stories about himself to *tell*—referring to himself in the third person. He quotes the poet Zhukovsky (p. 42), his speech is always lofty, taken from books. Just as Liza says to the underground man that he

[3] Citations are from: *White Nights*, tr. O. N. Shortse (Moscow, Foreign Languages Publishing House, no date). The passages used here have been checked by comparison with the original text as published in the *Polnoe sobranie* (Leningrad, Nauka, 1972), vol. ii.

"sounds like a book," so Nastenka tells the poet: "couldn't you somehow make your speech less splendid? Because you sound as if you were reading it out of a book" (p. 40). He depends on literature in this way for two reasons, both similar to those which explain the underground man's literariness. First, because it is part of his—hesitating—campaign to win Nastenka, to seduce her with words: just after he tells her a pathetic story about himself, he admits: "I shivered with pathos, having come to the end of my pathetic utterances. I remember how hard I strove to bring myself to laugh just then, for I could already feel some hostile imp stirring in my heart . . ." (p. 50). He knows the girl feels "a certain respect for the pathos of my speech and my lofty style" (p. 50).

Second, he needs literary clichés to provide him with a plot, things to *do* and *say* in the absence of any more substantial ground for action: "I am a dreamer. I have so little actual life, moments like this [his meeting with Nastenka] come to me so rarely that I cannot but live through them again and again in my dreams" (p. 27). Later he says "Do you know what I have come to, Nastenka? Do you know that I now have to mark the anniversary of my past emotions . . . this anniversary, too, has to be observed according to the same foolish, incorporeal dreams; I am driven to it because the foolish dreams themselves are no more, for *I have nothing to support them with*" [emphasis added] (p. 54).

Beyond likenesses between the character of the two major protagonists of *White Nights* and *Notes from the Underground* there is an even more convincing structural parallel between the two plots. Each is a collection of notes, focussing on an encounter with women in the past. The poet looks back over fifteen years to his meeting with Nastenka; the underground man writes sixteen years after his duel with Liza. Thus, in the case of each there is an attempt to understand the present by interpreting a key moment in the past, a moment that has had the effect of shutting the one in amidst his cobwebs, for the other of sealing his underground forever. Just as the underground man's fine words of Part I are undercut by his actions in Part II, so the conclusion of *White Nights* serves to indict the dreamer: "The vista of all my life to come stretched before me so bleakly and so sadly, and I saw myself the way I am now, exactly fifteen years since, an aged man, in the same old room, as lonely as ever, with the same old Matryona . . ." (p. 110).

But he immediately resorts to his habit of not facing the truth, of obscuring it with fine words and "exalted emotions," as if he were a bookish squid surrounding himself with inky rhetoric as he addresses the memory of Nastenka in the best Sentimentalist tradition: "that I should ever mar your pure and blissful happiness with a cloud of sorrow . . . that I should ever crush a single one of those exquisite flowers you wore in your dark curls when you walked up to the altar with him . . ." (p. 112), etc. This purple patch, following as it does his recognition of the prison erected around him by his dreams, adds an unintended pathos to the poet's last question (and the tale's last line) "Good Lord! A Whole Minute of Bliss! Why, isn't it enough, even for a lifetime?" The answer for the dreamer, of course, is that it is *not* enough for a lifetime, and we can see the genesis here of all those characters in Dostoevsky's later novels who will seek to correct the poet's error, will seek to find a moment that *will* be enough to guarantee a lifetime.

Up to this point we have emphasized parallels between *White Nights* and *Notes from the Underground*. However, each of the similarities listed contains also, on closer examination, a difference. The character of the poet in *White Nights* is that of a merely embryonic (or so we should say were we to forget that the latter springs from a test tube) underground man. We remarked on the poet's melancholy, his loneliness; but, as he says himself, the reason he feels cut off from others is merely because it is summer and everyone else has left town to go to their *dachas*: "And finally, only this morning [of the tale's first night], I understood what was the matter. Why, they were skipping from me into the country" (p. 14). He recognizes his proclivity to dream rather than to act is potentially dangerous ("A new dream—a new dose of happiness! A new dose of poison, subtle and sensuous," he says [p. 34]); but his analysis of why this should be so never gets beyond the level of psychological common sense, beyond a received wisdom that is content to use such small change as "shyness" as a technical term for the farthest reach of its speculation. The most complex metaphor the poet succeeds in finding for his condition is a "miserable little kitten" tormented by thoughtless children, so that it must "spend a whole hour [under a chair] bristling and snorting, washing its hurt little face with both paws . . ." (p. 38).

The plot, no less than the character of the major protagonist in both stories, differs not so much in details as in the *scope* of their various contexts. The poet reflects on his personal past, the one moment of potential change in an otherwise uninterrupted stasis, in order to insure the present out of which he writes his notes. The underground man also, of course, reflects on a past encounter with a woman, but the interest has shifted from the encounter itself, from a *personal* event, to the very act of analysis. Thus the underground man must ultimately combine not just two moments cut out of his own biography; he must re-think the possibility of "past" and "present" as it has traditionally been understood in the European historical imagination.

While the grammar of Dostoevsky's concerns—the morphology of character-type and in large measure even the syntax of plot-shapes—remains surprisingly uniform in works written before and after his decade of prison and exile, the semantics of those elements go through an enormous change, as he constantly expands the context of his novelistic gestures. *White Nights* is limited by the generic possibilities of the feuilleton. Dostoevsky wrote a series of these for the *St. Petersburg Gazette*, beginning in April, 1847; it is out of these sketches that *White Nights* developed. The parallels between the story and the *Petersburg Chronicle* (generic name for the feuilletons Dostoevsky wrote during this period) have been pointed out often enough not to need comment,[4] except to remind the

---

[4] For the easiest available account in English of the text's history see Konstantin Mochulsky, *Dostoevsky: His Life and Work*, tr. Michael A. Minihan (Princeton U.P., 1967), pp. 67-70, 92-98. The best interpretative account

41

reader that whole chunks of the feuilleton material are present, virtually unmodified, in the short story.

The feuilleton had, by 1847, become, under the influence of Eugene Sue's example in *Les Mystères de Paris* (1842), a complex literary form in its own right. But the emphasis was overwhelmingly on *description* rather than on analysis, a distinction caught in the very name of what became its most influential form in Russia, the physiological sketch. It was the journalistic equivalent of time-lapse photography; the typical author of such a piece would find a perspective point on the city (for Nekrasov, *The Corners of St. Petersburg*, for Krestovsky *The Squares of St. Petersburg*, for Butkov *The Upper Stories of St. Petersburg* [all in 1845]) and then describe what went on in his chosen *tranche de ville*, usually, over a twenty-four hour period, as in Kovalevsky's *Petersburg by Day and Night* (also in 1845), or in the opening discourse on Nevsky Prospect in Gogol's story of that name. The aspect of the city such an author would choose had as its ultimate function much the same purpose that monuments of nature or antiquity had for sentimental travelers—such as Karamzin—in the eighteenth century; their importance was in proportion to the degree they could spark an emotional response. They were, in effect, essays in the rediscovery of what already was there, and therefore occasions for demonstrating the writer's sensibility or wit. Thus such feuilletons had built into their generic presuppositions a limited sense of time and personality. As the titles above suggest, they were overwhelmingly *local*.

In order for the *Problemstellung* of *White Nights* to become what it is in *Notes from the Underground*, in order for "Petersburg" to become the "underground," an analytical impulse deeper than that provided by an expansion of the feuilleton was necessary. And of course in the years between *White Nights* and *Notes from the Underground*, everything in Dostoevsky's biography was conducive to a deepening of that

---

of the relationship between Dostoevsky's novels and the feuilleton—French and Russian—is found in Donald Fanger's book *Dostoevsky and Romantic Realism* (Cambridge, Mass., Harvard U.P., 1965), esp. pp. 135-51.

impulse: imprisonment, "execution," hard labor in Siberia, exile. It is a decade of returns for Dostoevsky: return to the living after that day in 1849 on Semyenovsky Square when he was certain he would surely die in the next moment; return to Petersburg after nearly a decade of prison and exile; and, after his first trip abroad in 1863, a return to Russia. Each of these returns would give rise to at least one book: return from death and exile resulted in *Notes from House of the Dead*; return from Europe (after his first visit to the West), in *Winter Notes on Summer Impressions*. The first book is Dostoevsky's discovery of that particular *Russia* he will intend from now on when invoking that name; the second is his discovery of that particular sense of *Europe* he will deploy in his later writings. From 1864 on, these two poles will serve as major categories for organizing the shifting patterns of opposition that constitute the core of his subsequent works. In order to understand the underground notes (which were published in the following year) we must first take a closer look at these winter notes.

I I I

Winter Notes on Summer Impressions is the first sustained treatment of the contrast between Dostoevsky's "Russia" and his "Europe." It is an account, published first as a series of articles in his journal *Vremja* (*Time*, [1863]), of two months he spent in the summer of 1862 in several West European countries (Italy, Switzerland, Germany, as well as England and France). The whole emphasis of the book, however, is on London, and especially Paris. In Dostoevsky's portrayal of the French bourgeois, in particular, we can see him discovering the most extreme form of all that the West would come to mean for him. I mean by this not only the static characteristics of national type (egoistic, sanctimonious, materialistic, etc.) but the dynamic *temporal* model that explains such characteristics. That is, "East" and "West," in Dostoevsky's use of the terms, are merely convenient tags for two kinds of temporality; each stands in for a space where different conceptions of time have resulted in different anthropologies. Thus the opposition that generates all the others in *Winter Notes on Summer Impressions*, from the contrasting seasons of the title to the contrasting political and religious theories of the text, is one between a merely human time in which the end of history is contained *in* history (change and upheaval, the West), on the one hand, and, on the other, a transcendent time (slow evolution, Russia), in which the making of history is extra-historical, i.e., derives from a God outside time.

How does space, and the national character that is peculiar to it, function as a temporality? Consider the anecdote Dostoevsky introduces as a newspaper article that he had read under the headline, "Vestiges of Barbarism." The anecdote is also a good illustration of his humor, which often results from the contrast between a ridiculous or embarrassing event and a philosophical purpose in the service of which he immediately enlists the event. The anecdote tells of how a Moscow matchmaker was seen taking a package one morning from the apartment of two newlyweds, a package that contained the bride's bloody nightgown, proof of her virginity to be shown to the parents: "The newspaper indignantly, conceitedly, blusteringly reported this unheard-of barbarism 'existing even today, in spite of all the progress of civilization.' " Dostoevsky sarcastically agrees that this custom is "savage," "Slavic," possible only because "of ignorance of anything better, higher, European" (p. 69).[5] He contrasts this unconscious Russian concern with the "dainty garments" and "minute calculation" of society women as they "add padding to a certain part of their enchanting European clothing."

In other words, the difference between East and West, Russia and Europe, is not that the one is more advanced than the other; by questioning such a possibility Dostoevsky points to what he feels the real difference is: "Are these cares, these worries, these *conscious* [Dostoevsky's emphasis] preoccupations about additions of padding—are they purer, more moral . . . than 'the bloody nightgown taken to the parents of the

---

[5] Citations are from: *Winter Notes of Summer Impressions*, tr. Richard Lee Renfield (New York, McGraw-Hill, 1965), compared with Russian text in: *Polnoe* (Leningrad, Nauka, 1973), Vol. v.

bride'?" (p. 70). The word he stresses here, "conscious," is key to the differences: West Europeans are offended by the gown because the custom does not accord with their prejudices, prejudices that have been erected into a theory of history. Such "vestiges of barbarism" occur "even *today*, in spite of all the *progress* of civilisation." That is, the West sees itself as farther along toward a definite goal in history than the Russians, who are still trapped at a stage the Europeans have previously experienced, but have now gone beyond. Thus the Russians, in this view, exist in a brute chronological synchrony with the West, but in a *historical* diachrony. France and Russia may share the same continent, but each has a different time. The Russians have experienced less "history" than ˙he French during the same amount of time.

Dostoevsky is concerned to attack this historicism, choosing the French bourgeoisie as the supreme example of its power to corrupt. The first sentence of the chapter in *Winter Notes* he calls "Essay on the Bourgeoisie" is a question he spends the rest of the book answering: "Why are they ill at ease here?" [in Paris] (p. 101). Why should the nineteenth-century Frenchman—envied even by other Europeans as the heir of all the ages, secure in a rich culture, great wealth, and the trappings of imperial power—lack confidence? Because while he proclaims himself to be the most advanced product of human progress he must—insofar as he believes such a claim—recognize that he is, *therefore*, "alone on earth, that there no longer is anything superior to him, that he is the ideal" (p. 117). Dostoevsky presents him as the logical outcome of Abbé Sieyès' 1789 prophecy: " 'What is the third Estate? Nothing! What ought it to be? Everything!' Well, everything happened just as he said" (p. 109). But to have achieved "the perfect terrestrial paradise" (p. 103), to live at the *end* of history so conceived—is to experience its meaninglessness. It is to experience that which was foretold to be *everything*, actually to be, when realized, *nothing*. The Frenchman knows that while others may seek to re-enact his historicism, to achieve the end of progress the French already have reached is in fact a goal not worth pursuing. It is this knowledge that

45

defines his loneliness: all others are deceived; he alone knows the awful truth. What defines his unease is the need to keep up the appearance of paradise to which his progressive historical model condemns him. So the bourgeois is forced to labor mightily to deny the particular kind of meaninglessness his historically achieved paradise results in. Thus all the lies that are institutionalized in his government, sexual mores, newspapers, the very clothing (padded, deceptive) of his women: all are aimed at concealing the inadequacy of an historical scheme that posits bourgeois values as its supreme goal.

The various strategies for deception developed by the bourgeois grow out of his sense of void: "I do not exist. I absolutely do not exist. I have hidden myself!" (p. 101). He doubts his existence, not as did the dreamer of *White Nights*, but because he conceives it as a radical individuality: "In Western nature in general 'fraternity' is not present; you find there instead a principle of isolation, of intense self-preservation, of personal gain, of self-determination, of the I, of opposing this I to all nature and the rest of mankind . . ." (p. 110). As a result of this solipsism, language loses its power to communicate, to bind together, a condition Dostoevsky examines in his study of the bourgeois love of eloquence.[6]

Eloquence is conceived by Dostoevsky not as forceful expression, but as bombast; the characteristic trait of language so used is a disparity between event and expression: eloquence is a term used by him to indicate language's power to deceive; it is form put into the service of *concealing* content. A French politician will know that "nothing at all will come of his speech, that it is all one big farce and nothing more, . . . a masquerade. And nevertheless he speaks; he speaks for several years on end . . ." (p. 128). Together with his frequent references to French spies (see pp. 82, 85, 119, 125), it is the over-inflated language of the bourgeoisie more than any other aspect of their existence that Dostoevsky uses to condemn the

[6] He finds the origin of this love for *eloquence* in Louis XIV's statement "L'état c'est moi" (p. 126), a further indication of the fact that Dostoevsky is positing a relationship between radical insistence on the self and the—therefore—unstable language to which solipsism is reduced.

deceptiveness of the West. "The bourgeois is eaten up with eloquence to the very bone" (p. 132). Since the bourgeois defines his individuality as a radical uniqueness, he *is* alone: he cannot share language with others, and so language loses its ground of meaning. The only thing one bourgeois shares with another is the concern to cover up the void at the center of their existence; thus the dominant mode of their discourse is eloquence, hyperbole. And thus it is, too, that the dominant art form of the bourgeois in Dostoevsky's scheme is not—as later historians have argued—the novel; rather it is melodrama, institutionalized theatricality: the bourgeois "needs something lofty, he needs ineffable nobility, he needs emotion, and melodrama contains all of these. . . . Melodrama will not die as long as the bourgeois lives . . ." (p. 146). Just as eloquence (as Dostoevsky uses it in this essay) is conceived as something more than a particular situation demands of ordinary language, so is melodrama more extreme than ordinary drama. Between the norms of language and eloquence, between drama and melodrama, there is a distance, and it is that disparity which defines the space where the bourgeois has his being.

I V

In Dostoevsky's analysis of the French bourgeois one can see for the first time the particular meaning that "the West" will have in the works to follow. He has discovered a way to think about, to conceive—if not yet to novelize—that opposition of Russia versus the West that will fuel the dialectical structure of the later works. *Winter Notes* is an important element, then, in the development of the Dostoevskian mythology, if we assume that one of the major functions of myth is "to stabilize and extend classification itself . . . myth explains not so much what to think about events and objects, but in what directions and with what degree of force to think—and how precisely to situate the constituents of the thinkable."[7] That is to say that

[7] Warner Berthoff "Fiction, History, Myth: Notes Toward the Discrimination of Narrative Forms," in: Morton Bloomfield, ed. *The Interpretation of*

the major elements present in *Notes from the Underground* were
also present in Dostoevsky's earlier work. But the exercise of
Winter Notes has taught him into what directions such elements as past and present might be extended, with
what degree of force to analyze such topics as dreaming and
eloquence.

In *Winter Notes* Dostoevsky discusses the predicament that
will figure so largely in all his later works. It is given as the
unease of the French bourgeois who lives at the end of history. In *Notes from the Underground* that unease has become the
anxiety of modern man: the underground man is Dostoevsky's French bourgeois raised to the level of a phenomenolog-
ical type. The shape of the plot is itself a metaphor for the dilemma of the underground man, which is to live the unease of
a brutally over-simplified historicism: where there are no
supra-historical values, all values are merely historical phenomena that are valid only in a certain time in a certain place.
Since all order is relative, how create a system to live by? In
this scheme literary plot (or the underground man's use of
plot) equals history, and the plotlessness of the notes themselves is a structural metaphor for the failure of history, or at
least the failure of history understood as the principle that the
meaning of existence will come to light progressively in the
course of its own process.

In his analysis of the French bourgeois, Dostoevsky defined
the Westerner as a man who feels he has come to the end of a
history. The bourgeois, with his faith in progress, then, is the
telos of his own theory of history, and his intellectual de-
fenders, such as the Abbé Sieyès in the eighteenth century or
Henry Buckle in the nineteenth, try to convince their less re-
flective fellows that they should—as the crown stone in the
pyramid of time—feel happiness. It is what Nietzsche had in
mind when he wrote that, "the belief that one is a late-comer
in the world . . . frightful and devastating when it raises our
late-comer, by a neat turn of the wheel [*mit Kecker Umstül-
pung*] to the level of a God as the true meaning and object of

Narrative: Theory and Practice (Harvard English Studies I) (Cambridge,
Mass., Harvard U.P., 1970), p. 278.

all past creation and his conscious misery is set up as the perfection of the world's history.''[8] The pride of the bourgeois is a result of theory; their uneasiness is a result of experience. They do not *feel* like the end; therefore they resort, as we have seen in our reading of *Winter Notes*, to strategies for deceiving themselves and others that the theoretical conclusion—they are the end, the highest—is true. Thus the melodrama, with its overdone gestures, its appeal to the coarsest emotions, its insistence on nobility, is Dostoevsky's essential metaphor for the bad theater of their lives.

In the underground man we see both poles of this dilemma—the theoretical and experiential—being examined from the inside: that is, the underground man is conscious of the theoretical conclusion that modern man must be the pinnacle of history as it has come to be understood in the nineteenth century (its meaning will be revealed in its own process); but he is also aware that he does not *feel* like the heir of the ages. He not only, like the bourgeois, recognizes the incompatability of such a history with his own experience, but he goes beyond the bourgeois in seeing clearly what the implications of the conflict are. He does not try to keep the old, organic sense of history—history as guarantor of identity—alive by deception, as does the bourgeois. Rather, he abandons it as an inadequate source for understanding himself. And he does so because in his rejection of any system (science as well as history) as a means by which to understand himself, he abandons the primary assumption of older conceptions of identity based in history.

The old sense of history, the history that the underground man casts off, has been characterized by Michel Foucault as one in which it was felt that: "by ordering the time of human beings upon the world's development . . . or inversely by extending the principle and movement of a human destiny to even the smallest particles of nature . . . human destiny was conceived of as a vast historical stream, uniform in each of its points, drawing with it in one and the same current, in one

---

[8] "Von Nutzen und Nachteil der Historie für das Leben," *Kritische Gesamtausgabe*, ed. Giorgio Colli, Mozzino Montinori (Berlin and New York, Walter de Gruyter, 1972), iii, i, p. 30.

and the same fall or ascension, or cycle, all men, and with them things or animals, every living or inert being even the most unmoved aspects of earth."[9]

That is to say that all things were felt to be moving within the same all-encompassing sea of time. While nature had its own rhythms (rocks and stars, or insects with a life span of only a few hours), those rhythms shared with the rhythm of human life a *developmental* aspect. Everything had the same temporality: you could understand the present by viewing it as the sum of past developments. In this conception there is nothing—from the point of view of time—that will serve to distinguish the uniqueness of man's status in the universe (what Max Scheler has called his *Sonderstellung*). Laws proper to the explanation of physical phenomena, therefore, will be proper to explain the human phenomenon as well. What men shared with nature was an etiological time: the present came out of the past at different speeds, but, whether rock or man, each was to be understood historically, as the present product of a process begun in the past.

This prejudice is obvious enough in those works we conventionally call histories; but the connection such a temporality has with personal identity is perhaps more clearly charted in autobiography, which is, after all, a narrative of events occurring in time, a kind of history in its own right. At least since Rousseau, the historical bias has been particularly strong in autobiography, a genre in which "formal continuity is a principle of philosophic, not merely narrative, coherence. It is in some sense the real subject of the work, the gradual evolution of an always-identifiable self."[10] This is what John Stuart Mill means when he calls his autobiography a "mental history." That is, there is not only chronological continuity, but a conceptual continuity. The parallel with conventional his-

[9] *The Order of Things,* no tr. (New York, Pantheon Books, 1970), p. 366.
[10] John N. Morris, *Versions of the Self: Studies in English Autobiography from John Bunyan to John Stuart Mill* (N.Y., London, Bove Books, Inc., 1966), p. 12. Morris refers to nineteenth-century autobiographies here, but his insight is surely of broader application. And it is even arguable that it was precisely in the nineteenth century that the historical sense of self broke down.

tory is in this, "that there are at least two levels of interpretation in every historical work: one in which the historian constitutes a story out of the chronicle of events and another in which, by a more fundamental narrative technique, he progressively identifies the *kind of story* he is telling, comedy, tragedy, romance, epic, or satire. . . ."[11] This "more fundamental narrative technique" is what F. M. Cornford in his study of the tragic structure of Thucydides' history has called "mythistoria," history cast in a literary or philosophical form that was already inwrought in the structure of the mind, part of its unreflecting assumptive world, before the work was even contemplated.[12]

In what has been called the first biography, we can see both elements, the chronological and conceptual (E. M. Forster's "story" and "plot," the Russian Formalist distinction between "*fabula*" and "*sjužet*") separated off: Xenophon divided his encomium to Agesilaus ". . . into two parts. The first was written in . . . chronological order . . . the second part was a non-chronological, systematic review of Agesilaus' virtues. As Xenophon explains at the beginning of chapter three, after having given the record of the king's deeds he is now attempting to show the virtue that was in his soul."[13] In other words, Xenophon writes as if he can tell the life, and *then* explain it.

In subsequent biography, however, the need is felt to fuse the two elements—the chronology of a life *with* its meaning. The narrative continuity of the text asserts the unity of the self, and it does so by stressing a temporally continuous personality. We may call this self "historical," in that its basic premise—that its essence is contained in its temporal shape— is one that historians have always felt: the assumption that there is an elective affinity between the modes of explanation and the modes of emplot-ment, and that by means of such an affinity they may achieve a particular kind of explanatory ef-

[11] Hayden White,"Interpretation in History," *New Literary History*, Vol. IV, No. 2 (Winter, 1973), p. 292.

[12] *Thucydides Mythistoricus* (London, Edward Arnold, 1970). See esp. p. viii.

[13] Arnaldo Momigliano, *The Development of Greek Biography* (Cambridge, Mass., Harvard U.P., 1971), p. 50.

fect, an over-arching interpretive grasp of the historical field under study.

The historical self, then, is the subject of a biography whose events are arranged as a function of the author's attempts to *explain* those events. The belief that past, present, and future constitute a causal relationship is so deeply ingrained in historical accounts that historians have used this chronology even in societies and at times when philosophers were speculating on radically different conceptions of what might be the shape of time. Among fifth-century Greeks, for instance, philosophers might argue that time is cyclical, and even though contemporary religion tended to support this view, Herodotus—as a working historian—knew that, "on the human level there was real change. Later historians were quite aware of this fact. They also knew the present came out of the past; and . . . were aware of [the future] as well. . . . Historians move now, as always, in their own path with respect to time; perhaps this is inevitable inasmuch as history is [a discipline] . . . by which men account to themselves for their nature."[14]

While historians may have continued to operate with this sense of history, there were, of course, others in the nineteenth century who challenged the validity of such past-present-future models to "account to themselves for their nature," and the underground man is one. The bourgeois was still operating with an historical sense of self, not only in his individual life, but in his assumptions about the world at large. Just as he at age, let us say, of fifty was the sum of all his previous life, he *was* his biography, so was, let us say, France in 1863 the sum of the *world's* biography. That is why, in Dostoevsky, the French are said to be at the end of a history.

But in the nineteenth century, as Michel Foucault has recently reminded us, others were become aware of a separation between the history of things—the world—and men: "It was discovered that there existed a historicity proper to nature . . . it became possible to show that activities as peculiarly human

[14] Chester G. Starr, "Historical and Philosophical Time," *History and the Concept of Time* (Middletown, Wesleyan U.P., 1966), p. 31.

as labor or language contained within themselves a historicity that could not be placed within the great *narrative* [emphasis added] common to things and to men . . . [language, economics, etc.] have internal laws of functioning, and . . . their chronology unfolds in accordance with a time that refers in the first place to their own particular coherence. . . ."[15] It was seen that linguistic history had a shape that did not correspond to the shape of economic history, for instance, and, furthermore, that *none* of the subjects of these disciplines (what Foucault calls "positivities") had a privileged shape that could, in itself, define a history of man:

"Things first of all received an historicity proper to them, which freed them from the continuous space that imposed the same chronology upon them as upon man. So that man found himself dispossessed of what constituted the most manifest contents of his history: nature no longer speaks to him of the creation or the end of the world, of his dependency or his approaching judgment. . . . The human being has no history: or, rather, since he speaks, works, and lives, he finds himself interwoven in his own being with histories that are neither subordinate to him nor homogenous with him. By the fragmentation of the space over which classical knowledge extended in its own continuity . . . the man who appears at the beginning of the nineteenth century is 'dehistoricized.' "[16]

It is precisely the domains of classical knowledge (the sciences, even mathematics, as well as "history") that the underground man specifically rejects—and he does so in his attempt to find a history that is validly *his own*, and not simply a template superimposed upon the alien chronologies that such *other* histories represent. This is the "consciousness" that he identifies as his sickness, the consciousness that traditional ways of organizing histories and biographies no longer avail. He is conscious of the *myth* in mythistoria as merely a fiction. Previous attempts to organize chronology had behind them unexamined assumptions about what might properly constitute an explanatory model, such as "God," "Kingship," or "Science." Such authors either were *unconscious* that their his-

[15] Foucault, *Order*, pp. 367-68.   [16] *Ibid.*, pp. 368-69.

tories were a function of belief, of ideology or religion, or they consciously attempted to synchronize their narrative of events with a pre-existing conception of order, such as the ancient Chinese historians, who would "determine the facts or the dates, establish texts, lop off interpolations, classify works, not with objective detachment, but in the hope of rendering more acute and purer, in themselves and their readers, the consciousness of an ideal that history cannot explain, for it precedes history."[17] There was something out there that was *true* and events could be referred back to whatever it was—God or the clockwork order of the physical universe—for a valid order of reckoning. The underground man cannot find a way to order events because there is no ground back to which he can refer them, because there is *no* order he will bring himself not to question. The condition of history becomes for the underground man the condition of contingency.

V

Contingency is not only what *Notes from the Underground* is about—it is the condition that is dramatized in its own unique plot. Dostoevsky gives the illusion of contingency by systematically subverting the traditional literary expectation of a neat beginning, middle, and end. Almost all literary plots meet the conditions for plot outlined by Aristotle for tragedy, something that: "is an imitation of a whole, that is, it has a beginning, a middle, and an end. A beginning is that which does not itself follow anything by causal necessity, but after which something naturally is or comes to be. An end, on the contrary, is that which itself naturally follows some other thing, either by necessity or as a rule, but has nothing following it. A middle is that which follows something as some other thing follows it. A well-constructed plot, therefore, must neither begin nor end at haphazard, but conform to these principles."[18]

[17] Marcel Granet, *Chinese Civilization* (New York, Meridian Books, 1958), p. 2.
[18] VII, 2, 1450b in S. H. Butcher's tr. (New York, Modern Library, 1952).

The Search for a Story

The high degree of abstraction in such a definition permits endless interpretations of what might constitute a beginning, middle, or end. But two things are clear: Aristotelean plot is *ordered*, and it has *movement*. Later in the *Poetics* he says: "the tragic plot must not be composed of irrational parts. Everything irrational should, if possible, be excluded."[19]

The parallel between this view of plot, on the one hand, and what we have been discussing as a historical sense of self, on the other, should be clear. The order of events in Aristotelean plot is determined by its ability to define the whole; it, once again, is an *explanatory* chronology.[20] The principle that excludes the irrational is a principle of order pre-existing any attempt to give coherence to a specific set of events. The Aristotelean plot is achieved through rules of exclusion governed by the principle of the tale's unity; thus we begin by assuming the tale *has* a unity, and further that it is defined by its chronology in such a way that any *other* order will appear irrational. Plot, then, ignores what is gratuitous to itself, and in these terms its movement is logical. Now let us recall that the underground man is opposed to logic, the syllogism. It should come as no surprise that the plot in which he is caught, the plot that defines him, is itself anti-historical, is not *linear* or Aristotelean. It is, in fact, the underground man's twisted formula of $2 \times 2 = 5$ expressed in architectonics.

Aristotelean plot also has parallels with the metaphor, which is defined in classical rhetoric, since at least Quintilian, as also having three parts: a metaphor is a comparison of two things, based on a third element common to both, the *tertium*

[19] *Ibid.*, xxiv, 10, 1960a.
[20] It is no wonder, then, that Aristotle finds the perfect tragedy in Oedipus, since it is the story of a man whose downfall results from his *inability to choose the right chronology to explain his dilemma*. Oedipus, whose association with linear biography is made clear when he guesses the sphinx's riddle (man is the sum of his various ages), assumes he is the sum, the product, of *one* history (in which he is the child of one set of parents); but this theory—because it is linear and because it is based on a false genesis (a kind of genealogical *post hoc, ergo propter hoc*)—has the wrong consequences all along the line through Oedipus' life, and it is only the correct linearity that reveals the tragic truth. Thus, while *anagnorisis* and *peripeteia* constitute a movement from wrong to right biography, both are *historical*.

55

comparationis. By subverting the assumptive world of order behind classical plot structure, Dostoevsky put in jeopardy the neat proportional relationship of classical metaphor. As Bede Alleman has pointed out: "For Aristotle analogy is something easily expressed mathematically, that is by a proportional equation: the proportion of a to b equals the proportion of c to d. . . . But modern poetry no longer recognizes the essential prerequisite for this act of combination: namely the idea of a rational order of the universe that can be represented adequately by a network or relationship."[21] In the case of the underground man we can be more specific about the way in which this breakdown of "the rational order of the universe" stands in: it is not the breakdown of a single, ordered cosmology. Rather, what has collapsed is the idea of *order* itself. Thus the inability of the underground man to account for his self in historical terms; he cannot find a chronology that is *in itself* explanatory of what he feels he is. His dilemma is structurally dramatized in the collapse of linear plot (historical development) in the *Notes*, considered as a literary text.

Before turning to the text of *Notes from the Underground*, let me very quickly recapitulate what I understand to be the specific qualities of traditional plot against which Dostoevsky is working. Most dictionaries give four definitions of plot: it is (1) an area marked off on a surface, usually ground; (2) a chart, diagram, or map; (3) the plan of action of a play, novel, poem, short story, etc. (4) a secret project or scheme, a conspiracy. All of these meanings bear on the history of our subject. A plot is, above all, a thing marked off, something that has boundaries, that is distinctly itself and not some other thing. In order to achieve this quality of boundedness it must work by rules of exclusion; certain things must be left out. What plots leave out, of course, is various degrees of contingency, the state in which events may occur by chance, accidentally, fortuitously. This is the irrational against which

---

[21] "Metaphor and Anti-Metaphor," *Interpretation: The Poetry of Meaning*, ed. S. R. Hopper and Daniel Miller (New York, Harcourt, Brace, World, 1967), p. 114.

Aristotle inveighs, the messiness of ordinary lived experience with its confusions, its half-finished sentences, its daily eruptions of the absurd. Plots are a means to cut all that out, and are thus like maps, which turn stormy oceans into neat, still designs, or the chaos of a jungle into a geometric patch of green ink. Thus plot is bounded, purged of contingency, and therefore available to linearity.

It is the fourth definition that we must invoke in connection with *Notes*: a conspiracy. *Notes from the Underground* is in this sense a plot against plots, at least of the sort Aristotle—and the dictionary in the first three of its definitions—intended.

The basic pattern of the *Notes* is a cycle of well-made stories that—in themselves—make sense, have traditional, *literary* plots. The structure of these stories is then subverted, one by one, as they are shown in the face of reality, in the face of the very contingency they abjured to achieve their shapely form—to be just that: shapely forms. They are only *tales*, and nothing more. This configuration, which defines the *several* stories the underground man tells about the world and himself, is subsumed by the same pattern, as it is bodied forth in the movement from Part I of the *Notes* to Part II. In Part I the underground man makes himself a character in a philosophical parable, which, for all its acerbity, has the effect of turning him into an Existentialist hero. That is why Part I is included in Existentialist anthologies without Part II, because the Liza episode—reality, events, contingency—gives the lie to the rhetoric of Part I, which is merely talk.

This movement from Part I to Part II has the same function as the Scheherezade story in *The Arabian Nights*; it is the story of stories, the structural model for all the other stories it contains. And, like Scheherezade, the undergound man must keep telling stories in order to stay alive. As he says: "I used to invent my own adventures. I used to devise my own life for myself, so as to be able to carry on somehow."[22]

[22] All quotations are based on a comparison of the Garnett tr. as published in *Three Short Novels of Dostoevsky*, ed. A. Yarmolinsky (New York, Anchor Books, 1960), with the original text published in *Polnoe* (Leningrad, Nauka, 1973), Vol. v.

He must make up plots for himself to figure in, because none of the available systems used by others to structure their lives are for the underground man acceptable, believable. He specifically attacks Darwinism: "When . . . it is proved to you that you are descended from a monkey, then it's no use pulling a long face about it: you just have to accept it." Of course, he does *not* accept it. Darwin must be a special target for the underground man, Darwin who found a whole new system for shoring up the connection between the history of nature and the history of man; who posits a developmental theory for rocks and humans, each of which is to be explained by the shape of its chronology: "I look at the geological record as a history of the world . . . written in a changing dialect."[23] While attempts have been made to dissociate Darwin from the doctrine that has become known as "cultural Darwinism," it is difficult not to hear the voice of Dostoevsky's French bourgeois of the *Winter Notes* in such lines as the following (from *The Descent of Man*): "Man may be excused for feeling some pride at having risen . . . to the very summit of the organic scale."[24] The underground man rejects Darwin because the evolutionary plot is too neat, is too homogenous, for him. Darwin may, with his system, be able to write the biography of coral atolls and perhaps even of the human *species*—but he cannot provide a biography for the underground man; he cannot account for the sense of unique selfhood that is the underground man's curse and pride.

It is important here to grasp that the underground man is not merely objecting to the indignity of being descended from an ape—his capacity for self-disgust can absorb much more than this—what he is opposing is the attempt to employ *History* as an explanation: ". . . you can say anything you like about world history, anything that might enter the head of a man with the most disordered imagination. One thing, though," he says, "you cannot possibly say about it: you can-

[23] In a letter to Lyell, quoted in: Stanley Edgar Hyman, *The Tangled Bank, Darwin, Marx, Frazer and Freud as Imaginative Writers* (New York, Atheneum, 1962), p. 41.
[24] Quoted in *ibid.*, p. 52.

not say that it makes sense." What the underground man means by "world history" becomes more explicit if we keep in mind that he uses Henry Thomas Buckle (1821-1862) as his symbol of the historian par excellence. Buckle ascribed to the workings of time the rational order of a well-played game of chess (he was an internationally famous player before reaching the age of 20): "the progress of every people is regulated by principles . . . as certain as those which govern the physical world," he wrote in his *History of Civilization in England* (Vol. I, 1857; Vol. II, 1861). What Buckle shared with Darwin was the sense that the present grew out of, was explained by, the *past*; and thus while the present might represent a height not previously achieved by men, men could not be *separate* from those who had gone before, could not be radically *themselves*.

It is the need to attack the dependence of part to whole that also accounts for the underground man's rejection of mathematics: "Twice-two-makes-four is in my humble opinion, nothing but a piece of impudence. Twice-two-makes-four is a farcical, dressed up fellow who stands across your path with arms akimbo and spits at you. Mind you, I quite agree that twice-two-makes-four is a most excellent thing [*prevosxodnaja vešč'*]; but if we are to give everything its due, then twice-two-equals-five is a most charming little thing, too [*premilaja inogda veščica*]." The underground man rejects the formula $2 \times 2 = 4$ because it—like Aristotelean plot, like Darwin's conception of nature or Buckle's conception of human history—emphasizes the whole over the parts: four is seen as the product, the sum of what has gone before, 2×2. What is equally significant here is the way he turns the two philosophical systems represented by $2 \times 2 = 4$ and $2 \times 2 = 5$ into personalities: the diminutive used to evoke the latter system makes it almost a literary character. By making the conflict into a little tale he suggests that there is no ground for it, that it is therefore fiction, merely another story.

This insistence on the fiction-making process as the basis of all his understanding is extended in the same section. The underground man collapses the pet ideas of nineteenth-century positivism into a simple metaphor: the crystal palace. He then compares it to a musical comedy. But he does so in a particular way: "In vaudevilles, for instance, suffering is not permitted. . . . In the crystal palace it is unthinkable. . . ." Just as the invalidity of the French bourgeois was said, in *Winter Notes*, to have found its best representation in melodrama, here it is argued that the perfect order (the system of parts to whole) of the Utopian Socialists is no more related to experience than is the vaudeville: both operate by the law of plot; they achieve their shape by excluding contingency; each is systematic only to the degree that they exclude the pressure of events. Well might he say in the concluding section of Part I (p. xi) that he is pleased with the "*literary* quality" of his jokes.

The first movement from Part I into Part II is full of ironies. There is first of all the underground man's admission that (p. xi) "I assure you most solemnly, gentlemen, there is not a word I have just written I believe in!" That is to say, none of the various positions he has attacked *or* supported in the course of his long polemic on systems satisfied his needs to believe. They are *all* mere fictions—the system of mathematics, on the one hand, and the underground man's own plea for *freedom* from systems, on the other. It is programmatically necessary that he state at the outset of Part II its discontinuity with Part I: the structure he presents in his text is not sequential in the way $2 \times 2 = 4$ is, or a *progressive* history is, or in the way that most literary plots are arranged.

There is, of course, a central ambiguity in his use of literary plot: its neat order may be used as a damaging metaphor for systems that seek a neat order outside literature, and thus it is stressed that insofar as history or social reform or scientific thinking seek to impose a homogenous order on the world, they are *fictive*, like literature: the harmonious schemes of Utopian Socialists, for instance, have the ontological status of vaudeville. On the other hand, however, since he has abandoned the possibility of *any* system as a privileged source in which to ground his selfhood, he is condemned to a world where *nothing* is real, and therefore the strategies of fiction provide the only workable means of giving shape—if only momentarily, from story to story—to experience. Recognizing that the history of rocks, the history of things, does not suggest a shape for his self, he is forced into the recognition that time is not something we invent as a construct—it is, rather, what we are. But what *kind* of time are we? If "History is the systematic science of that radical reality, my life,"[25] what separates it from the "systematic sciences" of geology or physics and the histories *their* "radical reality" constitute? Or, as Foucault puts the question:

"Can [man's] history ever be anything but the inextricable nexus of the different times [of the positive sciences] which are foreign to him and heterogeneous in respect to one another? Will the history of man ever be more than a sort of modulation common to changes in the conditions of life (climate, soil fertility, methods of agriculture, exploitation of wealth), to transformations in the economy (and consequently in society and its institutions) and to the succession of forms and usages in language?"[26]

As we have seen, it is these systems which the underground man rejects; to accept them would be to chart a temporal course for himself by maps that pictured the wrong ocean. He seeks rather to evaluate his *own* progress of things. The uniqueness of what is human would be lost if humans were perceived as merely the nodal point for the various histories of things that are *not* human. If he is merely a way to tell the time of things, then, "in that case, man is not himself historical: since time comes to him from somewhere other than himself, he constitutes himself as a subject of history only by the superimposition of the history of living things [biology] the history of 'things' [geology, physics] and the history of words [linguistics]."[27]

But if the coordinates of these progressions will not serve to shape the life of an individual man, where may one turn to find a clock that will validly tell the time of self? The underground man's answer is to plots from literature, plots of several familiar kinds. He is attempting to forge a continuity for

[25] Ortega y Gasset, *History as System*, tr. Helene Weyl (New York, Norton Library, 1962), p. 223.
[26] Foucault, *Order*, p. 369. [27] *Loc.cit.*

his identity, to experiment with what would constitute a true history of his self. Therefore, as does any historian, he "must draw upon a fund of culturally provided 'mythoi' [or standard plot schemes] in order to constitute the facts as figuring a story of a particular kind, just as he must appeal to that same fund of 'mythos' in the minds of his readers to endow his account of the past with the odor of meaning of significance."[28] Such a view assumes that the power of history to explain things resides in its story, and, further, that there can be no story without a plot by which to make of it a story of a particular king.

We must keep these points in mind as we read the underground man's reasons for attempting a biography, a biography, moreover, he does not intend to be read by anyone else. He is attempting to write a biography, a history of continuous identity for himself—and the fact that his attempt breaks down into mere disconnected notes from underground is only one of the ironies he dramatizes. He quotes Heine, who "says that true biographies are almost impossible, and that a man will most certainly tell a lot of lies about himself. . . . But Heine had in mind a man who made his confessions to the public. I, however, am writing for myself. . . ." The form of biography is always false to the essence of life it tells; it gives that life a shape that is recognizable to *others*, but what others grasp as a meaningful form must be a *common* form, and insofar as it is common the uniqueness of its subject is lost. The underground man several times attempts to answer why he writes down his biography: "I am imagining an audience on purpose so as to observe the proprieties [*vesti sebja priličnee*] when I write . . . it will look more dignified on paper . . . the whole style will, I'm sure, be better." By imagining an audience, he can imagine what they will expect of a biography and he can in turn use those conventional demands as parameters for a self he cannot otherwise historicize. He cannot find his *own* mode of emplot-ment, so he will use the conventional one. He seeks to make a coherent story out of his life by imposing on it a literary pattern. The process is

[28] White, "Interpretation," p. 294.

dramatized in the closing lines of Part I as he seeks to create a bridge—to make a coherent connection—with Part II: "moreover, I may feel easier in my mind if I write it down. I have, for instance, been oppressed lately by the memory of some incident that happened to me long ago . . . it has been annoying me like some tune you cannot get out of your head. And yet I simply must get rid of it, I have hundreds of such memories. . . ." Like Max Frisch's Gantenbein, he "has had an experience and is looking for a story with which to match it; for one cannot live with an experience that has not found outlet through a story."

The predicament of the underground man is, stated simply, that the only way he can organize a self is through stories that fit into existing literary categories, shapes that pre-exist his own life, are as outside his experienced sense of self as the temporal shapes of Darwinian progressions or mathematical sequences. He writes his memoirs to achieve the coherent effect of literary plot for his biography. And yet he knows such plots are made up, fictive, have no ground: they can be manipulated by himself but are *not* of himself. We can see this dilemma in the structure of the story that makes up Part II, the encounter with the prostitute Liza.

The fact that what he is about to relate is a *fiction*, a story in the sense that the order of his plot is secured through the exclusion of *chance*, is revealed in two ways: one, the event that triggers the underground man's memory of the Liza episode is in itself fortuitous: "Snow is falling today, almost wet snow, yellow, dirty. It was snowing yesterday, too, and the other day. I think it is because of the wet snow that I remembered the incident which gives me no rest now. . . ." The second way in which the empty order, the bad literariness of the underground man's method is undercut, is in the epigraph to Part II that follows immediately. It is a passage from Nekrasov's 1845 poem "*Kogda iz mraka zabluždenja*," the story in verse of what happens when a "decent man" brings home a reformed prostitute. It is a poem full of the worst literary clichés, all served up with a mind-numbing sentimentality. Dostoevsky gives the lie to the whole thing by cutting the poem off at a particularly pathetic moment with a series of "and so forth and so forths."

It has often been pointed out that, in so doing, Dostoevsky has dramatized a contrast between Nekrasov's sentimental version of the prostitute and his own realistic picture. But the way in which Dostoevsky explodes the literariness of Nekrasov's poem in the last line is, more specifically, another structural metaphor for the pattern of the story—neat plot —which is then destroyed by contact with reality. In other words, the debunked sentimentalism of the poem catches the basic morphology not only of movement from Part I, "The Underground," to Part II, "Apropos of the Wet Snow," but for *all* the stories that the underground man makes up to give himself an identity and that are later invalidated by contingency.

The underground man has no organic coherence, no systems for ordering experience that he can believe in; existence does not come naturally to him. His life is an inversion of the Cartesian cogito: instead of, "I think, therefore I am," the underground man, whose sickness is an over-developed consciousness, thinks, therefore he is *not*. Sprung from a test tube, he must act like a man born of woman. But with no patterns to fall back on, he is forced to invent his own, with no rules to guide him except for those which derive from his reading. He is constantly making experiments in ontology, a mad scientist in the cluttered laboratory of his own identity.

At the beginning of Part II he says: "I even used to make experiments to see whether I could meet without flinching the look of one or another of my colleagues. . . ." This experiment is characteristic of several others the underground man makes. It is the first of several encounters that define the only way the underground man can confront other people or events in real life: he can do so only as *combat*, as an unending series of skirmishes. But these battles for existence are not the sort one encounters amid the unpredictability of actual warfare: they always have the choreographed, ritual quality of duels, which are all very literary, of course.

The initial section of Part II bristles with references to the underground man's wide reading: "At home I mostly spent my time reading," or "Apart from reading I had nothing to occupy me." His literariness operates at several levels. There is the obvious one of specific reference to well-known works by Pushkin, Lermontov, Byron, Balzac, and very frequently to Gogol. But the essential meaning of the underground man's literariness is the one we have already remarked in connection with plots: it is his way of establishing a continuous self, of giving shape to the events that constantly threaten to overcome him. Consider the first sustained story of Part II: one night the underground man sees some men quarreling in a billiard parlor. He goes inside, but is picked up and set down by an army officer, who wishes to get him out of the way in order to make his exit. The underground man is mortified, moved about "as if I were a piece of furniture. I would have given anything at that moment for a real, a more regular, a more decent, and a more, so to speak, *literary* [Dostoevsky's emphasis] quarrel." He considers haranguing the other men in the place who have witnessed his humiliation, but decides, "they would jeer at me if I protested and began addressing them in literary language. For even today we cannot speak of a point of honor . . . except in literary language." He himself recognizes the artificiality, the contrived "literary" nature, of the duel.

He does two things—he actually *writes* a story about his encounter and sends it off for publication, but it is rejected. So he falls back on his more usual literary variant: "At last I resolved to challenge the officer to a duel." He writes a "most beautiful, most charming letter" of challenge, but does not send it. Instead, he resolves on a duel of another sort: he will meet the officer on Nevsky Prospekt—and not move aside. "I shall only knock against him as much as he knocks against me." But he leaves nothing to *chance*—all must go according to the script he has prepared in his mind. And like a good actor/producer, he considers the setting and his costume. Of the former he says, "there was sure to be quite an audience there; a countess, out for a walk, Prince D. taking a walk," and then he adds what is even more important for him, "the whole *literary* world taking a walk." He prepares his costume by buying a new fur collar for his overcoat, plagiarizing here, as he does in other places, from Gogol's story *The Overcoat*. When all is prepared—two years after his first meeting with the officer—the underground man does confront his unwitting antagonist on the Nevsky, only to be ignored by him. But he is not daunted by this—*he* was true—if not to any generally held code of honor, then at least to his own plot. This shows another way that he uses his stories: not only as blueprint for future raids on reality, but as a kind of narrative therapeutic after life has squashed him once again—as he says so accurately of himself—like a fly.

This leads naturally into the opening of sub-chapter ii in the second half of *Notes*, where he reveals that he would dream "for three months on end, skulking in his corner." Freed from reality, he says, "I suddenly became a hero." It is at this point that he reveals one of the primary meanings of life as single combat: in life he is lowest of the low, in his dreams he is a hero. As he says: "Either a hero or dirt [*grjaz'*], there was no middle way." Which is to say that there is no middle way between his dreams and reality. His is an impossible either/or; the order of daydream, with perfect plots, is totally removed from reality, where there is only the complete chaos of contingency. It is this lack of dialectic, of a middle, that makes the duel so crucial a metaphor for the underground man: it too is a polar opposition, an either/or, you or me—to the death.

The underground, then, can be understood as a kind of literary space, that place in the mind where good stories can happen. The underground man reveals here some of his more imaginative plots: he will become a millionaire; everyone will love him; he will preach new ideas; a general amnesty will be declared; the Pope will agree to leave Rome and move to Brazil; Lake Como will be transferred to the outskirts of Rome, where, in the Villa Borghese, a ball for the whole of Italy will be held. This impulse to turn everything into a story is best expressed by the underground man himself: "Everything, however, always ended most satisfactorily in an indolent and rapturous transition to art, that is, to the *beautiful* forms of existence, all ready-made, snatched forcibly from the poets and novelists and adapted to every possible need and requirement."

It should be noted in passing, by the way, that the remarkable plot he hatches about the Pope's removal to Brazil, etc., follows the pattern of *all* his stories: it is marvelous, but it cannot last. The line that ends this particular story is: "this would be followed by the scene in the bushes, and so on and so forth—don't tell me you don't know it!"

We now move into chapter ii of Part II, in which the essential story of that whole cycle, the Liza episode, begins. The underground man invites himself to a dinner given by some former schoolmates, an occasion for revealing certain facts of his childhood, two of which are significant from the point of view we are pursuing here: one, even at a tender age he, not surprisingly, "was already reading books which [the other boys] could not read." More importantly, he says of himself "Whether it was because I was not used to change or for some other reason, all through my life I could not help feeling that any extraneous event, however trivial, would immediately bring about some radical alteration in my life." Precisely: since it lacks any coherence of its own, his biography is helpless to resist the effect of "extraneous events." That is why he makes up stories that are viable only when uncontaminated by reality. It is also why he cannot lift his glass when, at dinner, Zverkov proposes the toast: "To our past, gentlemen, and to our future!" The underground man cannot share in this toast because it presupposes a continuum in biography that he does not share—his life has no organic beginning, middle, and end.

He offends his friends, finally, challenging one of them to a duel. When the others scoff at this, he says "you can't possibly refuse me. I want to show you I'm not afraid of a duel. You can fire first, and I'll fire in the air!" It goes without saying that such nobility is one of the most overworked clichés of duels in literature, and another hint at the Pushkin story of a duel that the underground man mentions specifically, *The Shot*.

His schoolmates leave him as they go off to the bordello. The underground man decides to follow them. The duel mechanism is now extended: he says that everything depends on another encounter with his former friends, "my whole future. . . . Either they'll implore me for my friendship on their knees—or I'll slap Zverkov's face!" He creates a situation in which everything turns on one act—sets up an either/or; that is the meaning of the duel at one level. Its meaning at another is indicated in the underground man's words as he speeds to the confrontation: "So this is it—this is it at last—a head-on clash with reality." Once again it is literature versus life. As the sledge drives him to Olympia's he tells himself more stories about what will happen—he knows it all in *advance*, his compulsive making of plots evaporates reality. He sees himself as Pushkin's Silvio, but this tale, too, is debunked by events. When he rushes into the bordello, there is no one there, "everything had vanished, everything had changed!" as he says.

Now begins the real duel he is to fight at the bordello. He makes love to the prostitute Liza, and, as they are lying in the bed later, he starts telling stories. At first things are a bit jumbled. "The events of the previous day passed disjointedly through my mind, as though of themselves and without any effort on my part." But he very quickly works out a strategy, a story, a plot. He tells of a burial in Volkovo cemetery, of a grave that had a foot of water in it. It is all a lie, as he admits: "I had never seen [the ground] there, nor have I ever been in Volkovo cemetery." But he wishes to hurt his opponent, Liza. He embroiders his tale: the coffin buried in the marshy ground was that of a prostitute who had come to a sorry end. As he goes on, he says, "Suddenly something flared up in me, a sort of aim had appeared." He decides to incorporate Liza into the story of his own life; he seeks to gain power over her by getting her to act out a part he shall write. It is a plot *against* the girl that is advanced by means of the *plots* in the stories the underground man now tells her. The next tale—of a self-sacrificing father's love for his daughter—is cribbed from Balzac's *Père Goriot*. The underground man—whose considerable gifts for rhetoric have been demonstrated in the eleven chapters of polemic in Part I—now warms to his task; nobility shines in the scenes he draws for the girl. He introduces some more plots: he tells the story of how happy Liza would be "if she had a rosy little baby boy sucking at [her] breast"; he creates a touching domestic scene with an adoring husband. "It is with pictures, with pictures like these you will beguile her," he thinks to himself.

But his tone is so literary that even the prostitute recognizes it for what it is: "Why you—you're speaking as though you were reading from a book." This only spurs the underground man on to even more *complex* stories. He tells of how once, on a New Year's eve, he saw another prostitute turned out into the cold night, shrieking at the top of her lungs and beating the steps with a salt fish. He is a great author for details! Since his tale of Liza's future with a child and husband left her unmoved, he spins out another plot for her future: she will die a horrible death of consumption, and be buried in a grave of wet blue clay, covered with dirty snow. This, too, is a tale full of literary clichés: "I knew I was speaking in a stiff, affected, even bookish manner . . . but this did not worry me . . . for I knew . . . that this very bookishness would assist rather than hinder weeping." The underground man has his opponent at his feet, destroyed by stories just as surely as if she had been wounded by a pistol in a duel. He cannot resist one last, grand gesture of nobility—he gives her his address. He knows he has triumphed when she shows him her greatest treasure—a declaration of love from a medical student who did not know she was a prostitute. She has her stories, too.

But his sense of achievement is short-lived. Just as the Lake Como dream-story was destroyed by the scene in the bushes, this victory of fantasy is undercut as he thinks on the way home: "But the truth was already blazing through my bewilderment. The disgusting truth!"

The next day he writes a masterly letter of explanation to

the former schoolmates he had so offended at the dinner party. It shows again how the underground man is able to take chaotic events and force them into a neat pattern, flattering to himself: it is another of his plots, this time imposed on the past instead of the future. He knows it is all a lie, but "the main thing is that I got out of it."

At any rate, he has new worries. What if Liza takes him at his word and comes to his shabby apartment: once again one of his stories will be destroyed by life's refusal to accept his plots. At first he is angry at the girl for believing him. But, then, as days pass and she does not show up, he starts telling himself a different story of what would have happened had she, in fact, visited him. It is another idyll—he educates her, she falls in love with him, he is tender, noble. It is all, as he says, very "George Sandian." When he thinks her coming is a *reality*, there is no room for stories, and he is *angry*; when it appears she will *not* come, he is freed to make up a story about what *would* have happened *had* she come—and it is a much more Aristotelean tale.

But of course Liza does come to his room. He is thrown into a towering rage: he tells her he did not wish to save her; he spun those tales he told her for the sake of the telling. "For all I wanted was to make the few fine speeches, to have something to dream about." She is dream fodder. In other words, he was merely telling more of the stories that keep him alive, that give shape to the unconnected minutes of his disjointed biography.

However, instead of being crushed, Liza pities him, understands that he is unhappy. He cannot believe this at first: "I was so used to imagining everything and to thinking of everything as it happened in books, and to picturing everything in the world as I had previously made it up in my dreams, that at first I could not all at once grasp the meaning of this occurrence." But when he does understand her pity, he is even more furious: "our parts were now completely changed . . . she was the heroine now, while I was exactly the same crushed and humiliated creature . . . she had appeared to *me* that night—four days before. . . ." Because his capacity to

70

come to terms with the world outside his own plots has long
since atrophied, he cannot accept even the girl's selfless
love—accept, in other words, the thing for what it is. He
smothers this reality with another plot. She has refused to accept the role he has assigned her. Even more, by pitying him
she has turned the tables; he has been outflanked, *wounded* in
this duel. But even as she holds him in her arms, he forces her
back into his plot, that plot that says she is not a woman, but
merely a category, a prostitute. He has sex with her again—
that is, he insists she act out the attribute of her role, remain in
her dramatic *emploi*.

She becomes aware that he has used her for purposes of revenge, and is about to crawl away. For the underground man
she cannot leave soon enough—she has brought too much reality into his schematic underground. "I wanted her to disap-
pear. I longed for 'peace.' I wanted to be left alone. . . . 'Real
life' [*živaja žizn'*]—so unaccustomed to it was I—had
crushed me so much that I found it difficult to breathe." In
other words, he almost expires from reality.

As she goes out the door, he presses a five-ruble note into
her hand as the ultimate reminder that she is still the character
he has invented—only a prostitute. But just after she has gone
out he thinks, "This cruelty was so insincere, so much
thought out, so deliberately invented, so *bookish*, that I
couldn't stand it myself even for a minute." But he is too late
to catch the girl—who has disappeared into the wet snow that
is always, in the *Notes*, part of a semantic field associated with
death.

Returning to his room he discovers she has left the money
on a table—once again reality thwarts his plot. He dashes out
after her again, but she is gone. At first he regrets he was unable to apologize to her—but this emotion is soon surrounded
and devoured by the narrative pseudopod of yet another
story: it is all for the best that he did *not* catch her, what he has
done will help her somehow, his insult will purify her—he
has done a good deed, etc. Sixteen years later, as he is writing
all this down in his memoirs, it is the style of the story, not its
substance, he remembers: "I may as well add that I remained

for a long time pleased with the *phrase* about the usefulness of insults. . . ." This emphasis on style as language used in the service of concealment is only one more way in which the underground man reveals himself as an avatar of Dostoevsky's French bourgeois (who used "eloquence" in the same end) in *Winter Notes*.

In the closing lines of the *Notes*, the meaning of the underground man's literariness is made explicit. He presents himself as typical of modern man: "We have all lost touch with life, we are all cripples, every one of us . . . we have gone so far that we look upon 'real life' almost as a sort of burden, and we are all agreed that 'life' as we find it in books is much better." That is, since there is no dialectic between imagination and reality, what results is the either/or of neat plots in fantasy, on the one hand, and threatening chaos in real life, on the other. Since there is no middle, how can there be a beginning or an end that makes sense: there is no center in the underground, how can it have boundaries? Since there is no natural, no organic way to end, the *Notes* simply peter out: "But enough—I don't want to write any more 'from the underground.' " But of course he does *not* end, as the "editor's note" that Dostoevsky appends makes clear: "He could not resist, and continued further."

The underground man will continue to spin his web of stories until the ultimate contingency—death—puts a stop to them. Because there is *nothing to hold the stories together*: there is no plot of plots. Because there is no comprehensive *end* toward which each of the stories is directed, the story they comprise all together can have no ending: the breakdown of teleology in the plot of *Notes* is an attempt by Dostoevsky to expand the meaning of plot beyond what are traditionally thought to be merely literary bounds; it is plot understood as the problem of the possibility of a meaningfully coherent series at all. Thus the underground man's hostility to all that is merely literature. His position is the polar opposite to Matthew Arnold's exaggerated claims for the role of literature in an age of disbelief: "The future of poetry is immense, because in poetry our race . . . will find an ever surer and surer stay. There is not a creed which is not shaken, not an accredited dogma which is not shown to be questionable, not a received tradition which does not threaten to dissolve. Our religion has materialized itself in the fact . . . and now the fact is failing it . . . the strongest part of our religion today is its unconscious *poetry*"[29] [emphasis added]. Even *this* last hope is dashed by the underground man. For not only does he not believe in systems born of reason—logic, history, mathematics, science has been pointed out so many times; he *also* doubts systems born of fantasy—dreams, stories. Not only had the *adequati rei et intellectus*, the adequation of mind to things, broken down, but so has the adequation of imagination and things: the underground man knows that his stories are only stories.

But Dostoevsky's counterplot serves not only to characterize the underground man. It is a technique he will employ again and again: in *Crime and Punishment* he explodes that most syllogistic of all plot structures, the detective story; in *The Possessed* he subverts several plots familiar to all readers of utopian fiction; in *The Brothers Karamazov* he sets up the life of Zosima along the familiar lines of saintly biography, only to provide a most unhagiographic twist in the monk's stinking corpse.

The calculated inversion of plots familiar to readers from other books is a major structural device of the whole Dostoevskian *oeuvre*. It is this device which provides the illusion of that enormous contingency one senses in the Dostoevskian novel. This is why Walter Kaufmann has called *Notes from Underground* "the best overture for existentialism ever written."[30] He has in mind only the themes to which the underground man gives expression in Part I of the *Notes*. It has remained to another philosopher, who is also significantly a novelist, to locate the structural importance of the story, to isolate the meaning of Dostoevsky's attack on conventional

[29] Quoted in Richard Ellman, Charles Feidelson, eds. *The Modern Tradition* (New York, Oxford U.P., 1965), p. 913.

[30] *Existentialism from Dostoevsky to Sartre* (New York, Anchor Books, 1956), p. 14.

plot. Sartre, in his programmatic work *Nausea*, provides the theory behind Dostoevsky's structural practice. Roquentin says:

"I have never had adventures. Things have happened to me, events, incidents, anything you like. But no adventures . . . for the most banal event to become an adventure, you must . . . begin to recount it. This is what fools people: a man is always a teller of tales, he lives surrounded by his stories and the stories of others, he sees everything that happens to him through them; and he lives his own life as if he were telling a story. But you have to choose: live or tell."[31]

The underground man, too, is aware that man—whether he be scientist, politician, or historian—is "always a teller of tales." But his conclusion is less optimistic: there is no choice; perhaps it is the case that *in order* to live, men are condemned to tell.

[31] *Nausea*, tr. Lloyd Alexander (New York, New Directions, 1965), pp. 37-39.

74

Puzzle and Mystery, the Narrative Poles
of Knowing: *Crime and Punishment*

The best way to see the biographical dilemma in *Crime and Punishment* is to focus on the distinctive plot of that novel. At first glance it would seem to be the least complex of all Dostoevskian narratives (which is no doubt why *Crime and Punishment* is so frequently called Dostoevsky's "best-made" novel). It is divided into six parts (or books) and an epilogue. In the first part Raskolnikov murders two women; then, in the next five parts, everyone (including Raskolnikov) tries to figure out the crime; in the sixth part Raskolnikov confesses, is tried, and sent to Siberia. In the epilogue he repents of the crime (but only in the second part of the epilogue) and has a mystical experience; the novel ends with the narrator's assertion that "here begins a new story." The murder in the first book, and its consequences in the next five books, constitute *one* kind of time, a pattern made up of one kind of privileged moment and the sequence that flows from it. The conversion in the epilogue and the "new story" it results in constitute *another* kind of temporality, another moment-sequence design.

Dostoevsky stresses that Raskolnikov discovers "another reality" in the concluding pages of *Crime and Punishment*. The argument of this chapter is that the difference between this reality and that other which dominates in the rest of the novel can best be grasped as the difference between two patterns of moment-sequence that are dramatized as two different and opposing types of plot and the two different kinds of time, two different ways of understanding, two different modes of interpretation that their traditions presuppose. The uniqueness of *Crime and Punishment* consists in the dialectical (or in Bakhtin's sense of the word, the dialogic) structure Dostoevsky has created out of these oppositions.

It has often enough been pointed out that the essential trait of Dostoevskian characters is their duality, the synthesis of extremes present in all of them, which results in dialogic or polyphonic relationships of enormous complexity.[1] As John Bayley has recently said, "[Dostoevsky's] characters . . .[are] all involved in a dream, in a dramatic relation with their own self-awareness . . . [they are both] the insulted and the proud, the hated and the hater. In Dostoevsky the contract is dissolved: its partners become one flesh."[2] There is a sense in which all his characters are "doubles." But behind the psychological unity he creates out of his metaphysically split *characters* is the structural unity of his *plots*, which are also made up of elements that, in the hands of a more conventional novelist, would be clashing, disparate, even mutually exclusive.

As Leonid Grossman long ago pointed out: "The book of Job, the Revelation of St. John, gospel texts, the Epistle of Peter in the New Testament . . . are . . . combined in a manner peculiar to [Dostoevsky], with the newspaper, the anecdote, the parody, the street scene, the grotesque or even the lampoon. He daringly throws into his melting pot more and more new elements . . . the sensations of cheap thrillers and the pages of God-inspired holy books. . . ."[3] In another article, one devoted exclusively to Dostoevsky's frequent use of material from the Gothic (Radcliffe, Maturin) and adventure novel (Soulié, Sue), Grossman further documents his author's traffic with such questionable genres: "How did it happen that the lowest genre of [artistic prose] turned out to be the most convenient expression for the creative ideas of an artistic philosopher who was a genius?"[4] In Dostoevsky's novels you

---

[1] The masterwork on this—as on so many other topics in Dostoevskian criticism—is, of course, Mixail Baxtin's *Problemy Tvorčestva Dostoevskogo*, the second edition of which is now available in a superb English translation: Mikhail Bakhtin, *Problems of Dostoevsky's Poetics,* ed. and tr. Caryl Emerson (Minneapolis: University of Minnesota Press, 1984).

[2] "Character and Consciousness: *New Literary History* Vol. v, No. 2 (Winter, 1974), pp. 234-35.

[3] As translated in: Vladimir Seduro, *Dostoevsky in Russian Literary Criticism 1846–1956* (New York, Octagon Books, 1969), p. 206. The original is in "Put' Dostoevskogo," *Tvorčestvo Dostoevskogo* (Odessa, Vseukrainskoe Izdatel'stvo, 1921), p. 84.

[4] "Composition in Dostoevsky's Novels," *Balzac and Dostoevsky*, tr. Lena Karpov (Ann Arbor, Michigan, Ardis, 1973), p. 93.

get material "ranging from philosophical doctrines to puppet show effects out of the folk theater . . . philosophical dialogue expanded into an epic of adventure; it is the *Phaedo* put at the center of the *Mysteries of Paris*, a mixture of Plato and Eugene Sue."[5] We can, in the case of *Crime and Punishment*, be more specific about the terms of the plot contrasts Dostoevsky uses: what Grossman identifies as the Eugene Sue tendency is present in the six books that constitute the body of the novel as a detective story; the Platonic element is present as a wisdom tale in the epilogue.

I

E. M. Forster once said that "in a novel there is always a clock,"[6] by which he meant, of course, that just as clocks organize time outside of texts, so does plot within them. Forster later goes on to discuss various kinds of plot, among them one most easily apparent in the detective story:[7] "It occurs through a suspension of the time-sequence; a mystery is a pocket in time . . . half-explained gestures and words, the true meaning of which only dawns pages ahead."[8] The first six books of *Crime and Punishment* constitute a very complicated variant of this narrative type. In order to get at its complexity, some basic considerations about detective plots should be kept in mind.

[5] *Ibid.*, pp. 94–95.

[6] *Aspects of the Novel* (New York, Harcourt Brace and World [Harvest Book], n.d. [1st pub. 1927]), p. 29.

[7] Although he hesitates to use so lowly an example, taking instead *The Egoist*, rather than "Conan Doyle (whom my priggishness prevents me from enjoying)." *Aspects*, p. 92. For those who may find something anachronous in my suggestion that Dostoevsky uses detective-story techniques, I add an historical note: The first modern detective story, the one that immediately established all the conventions that have since become so familiar—the eccentric but brilliant detective, the admiring foil, the well-intentioned floundering of the police, etc.—was Edgar Allan Poe's "The Murders in the Rue Morgue," which appeared in *Graham's Magazine* of April, 1841. Dostoevsky knew many of Poe's tales, and in his journal *Time* (*Vremja*) he actually published translations. He alludes to both of Poe's Dupin detective stories: "The same power of imagination . . . characterizes his satires of *The Purloined Letter*, of the murder committed by an orangutan . . . and so on." *Vremja*, I, p. 230 (1861). Thus Dostoevsky would have been familiar—*before* he wrote *Crime and Punishment*—with the form of the classic detective story.

[8] *Aspects*, p. 87.

We may, first, extend Forster's metaphor by recognizing that the distinctiveness of such structures consists in their having not one but *two* clocks. There is a clock for the crime and another for the solution; one time for the criminal, another for the detective; and the action of the tale consists in the synchronization of the two clocks:

"We know that the [detective novel] is grounded in the tension between two stories: the missing story of the crime, and the presented story of the investigation, the sole justification of which is to make us discover the first story. One element of the story is in fact told to us at the outset: a crime is committed almost under our nose; but we have not learned the identity of the criminals nor the true motives. The investigation consists in reviewing incessantly the same events, in verifying and correcting the tiniest details until, in the end, the truth about this same initial story is revealed. . . ."[9]

When the detective's plot (in the sense of beginning, middle, and end) corresponds precisely with the criminal's plot (in the sense of conspiracy), the murder is solved. Another way to articulate this process is to appeal to a distinction often used by the Russian Formalists:[10] All plots can be broken down, or just as significantly, *cannot* be, into *fabula* and *sjuzet* (roughly corresponding to Forster's "story" and "plot"). *Fabula* is understood as the chronological sequence of events, 1, 2, 3, 4. *Sjuzet* is the way such a chronology is actually arranged in a particular text: 3, 1, 2, 4, for example. Thus it can be said that the distinctive feature of the detective story is that its *sjuzet* consists in the discovery of its own *fabula*.[11]

[9] Tzvetan Todorov, "The Two Principles of Narrative," *Diacritics*, Vol. I, No. i (Fall, 1974), p. 41.

[10] See especially: Viktor Šklovskij, *O teorii prozy* (Moskva, Federacija, 1929), esp. pp. 24-90, 125-42; Boris Tomaševskij, *Teorija literatury* (Moskva-Leningrad, Gosizdat, 1928), esp. pp. 131-57.

[11] Insofar as the detective's task is to re-assemble a story in its proper chronology, he is similar to the psychoanalyst. As Steven Marcus has written: "The difficulties [in Freud's presentation of a case history] are in the first instance formal shortcomings of *Narrative*: the connections, 'even the ostensible ones'—are, for the most part incoherent, obscured and unclear; 'and the sequence of different events is uncertain.' In short these narratives are disorganized and the patients are unable to tell a coherent story of their lives." "Freud and Dora: Story, History, Case History," *Partisan Review*, XLI, No. 1

The detective novel then may be said to have two clocks, *but they both tell the same time*. When the detective solves the crime he makes a past event present again, a situation that could be represented as 1, 2, 3, 4, 1' in which 1 stands for crime, 2, 3, 4, for the detective's attempts to solve it, and 1' as the crime reconstructed. For the reader, the end (as conclusion) is already present in the beginning; but the end (in the sense of *telos*) is in the *middle* of a detective novel for readers: its whole charm and purpose consist in the process of establishing the correct time (that is why there is usually so much "business" about timetables and diagrams in them). The question is whodunit, but the method is who-was-where-when. The time both of crime and solution, as well as process, in the detective novel, is all cause-and-effect, sequential.

Parallels between the deductive reasoning of detectives and physical scientists have often been noted:[12] both use historical method in the sense that in order to reach conclusions of the sort each desires, they "must treat the past as continuous with the present, and interpret the traces left by earlier events in terms of the same laws and principles as apply in the present. . . ."[13] As Toulmin and Goodfield have pointed out, in order to "solve" the origin of species or of other natural phenomena, the procedure was the same: "In each case, men grasped the structure of the past only when they took a genuinely historical view; which meant interpreting the present states of Nature and humanity as temporary products of a continuing

---

(1974), p. 91. Another scholar who has suggestively treated parallels between detective and analyst is Stanley Edgar Hyman in his chapter on Freud in *The Tangled Bank: Darwin, Marx, Frazer and Freud and Imaginative Writers* (New York, Atheneum, 1962), pp. 293-424. Perhaps the best single piece on the metaphysical implications of detective stories, one in which the parallel with Freud is also made, is: Ernst Bloch, "Philosophische Ansicht des Detektivromans," *Verfremdungen* (Frankfurt, a.M., 1962), Vol. I, pp. 37-63. "When Theodor Reik suggested [a] comparison with [Sherlock] Holmes (for Freud's technique, not his tone) in 1913, Freud said he would prefer a comparison with Giovanni Morelli, a nineteenth-century art scholar who specialized in detecting fakes." Hyman, p. 313.

[12] See, for instance: Régis Messac, Le *"Detective Novel" et l'influence de la pensée scientifique* (Paris, 1929).

[13] Stephan Toulmin, June Goodfield, *The Discovery of Time* (N.Y., Harper Torchbooks, 1966 [1st pub. 1965]), p. 244.

process developing through time."[14] In other words, the detective, like the scientist, assumes a homogenous time that is as characteristic for the *object* of his study as it is for the *method* of his study; what you get is a temporal democracy in which the past explains the present, which in its turn will one day in the future have the explanatory power of the past. This is a linear or horizontal conception of time and it stands over against another view of temporality that might, by contrast, be called hierarchical or vertical time.

If detective stories are the most elementary expression of horizontal time—horizontal, that is, in the sense that all events occur on the same level of reality—wisdom tales are the most basic index of a time that may be called vertical insofar as it presupposes a split-level ontology, a hierarchy of realities that are distinguished by the degree of stasis that attaches to each. Wisdom tales are understood here as a subdivision within the "simple forms" catalogued by André Jolles,[15] who identifies nine such forms, including proverbs, legends, riddles, etc., as well as the tale (*das Märchen*). Jolles stresses that the tale in its most basic expression is characterized by a strong ethical thrust: the world of which it tells is different from, better than, our own: "In the tale we are dealing with a form in which what happens, the course of events, is ordered in such a way that it entirely corresponds to the exigencies of naive or unreflexive morality; that is, events are good and just according to the absolute judgment of our feeling. As such the tale puts such events into the most pointed opposition to what we are accustomed to observe—to what, in fact, happens in the world."[16]

[14] *Discovery of Time*, p. 246.
[15] *Einfache Formen* (Halle, Max Niemeyer Verlag, 1930), pp. 218-46. In Russian tales the role of the other world (*inoe carstvo*) has been charted by Maria-Gabriele Wosien, *The Russian Folk-tale: Some Structural and Thematic Aspects* (Slavistische Beitrage No. 41) (München, Verlag Otto Sagner, 1969), esp. pp. 107-44, which is a study of the quest motif in the miraculous tale (Aarne-Andreyev, pp. 300-749).
[16] Jolles, p. 241. ". . . in dem Märchen eine Form vorliegt, in der das Geschehen, der Lauf der Dinge so geordnet sind, dass sie den Aufforderungen der naieven Moral völligentsprechen, also nach unserem absoluten Gefühlsurteil 'gut' und 'gerecht' sind. Als solches steht nun das Märchen im

Wisdom tales—Midrash, koans, parables from the Bible, Hassidic stories—set themselves off from tales as such in their emphasis on hermeneutics: the distance between the two worlds is affirmed in a structure of conflicting interpretations about what that distance means: the final, "correct" interpretation is superior to the others insofar as it insists on the degree of the cut-off between the two worlds. It is very close to what Jolles calls *Antimärchen*. Whether it is understood as the Augustinian distinction between the Logos of God as opposed to the mere words of men, or the aboriginal neo-Platonism that distinguishes between the Dream Time and everyday flux, such a view assumes that what is most real does not change. All that does change—all that is historical—is meaningful or real only in the degree to which it can be referred back to the privileging stasis. Thus interpretative tales that spring from such a world view tend to have structural affinities with detective stories in that they, too, are characterized by plots that have their end in their beginning. However, when beginning and end are conceived as a non-historical alpha and omega, the interest is no longer in the process, the middle. The solution to a detective story exhausts the meaning of what it sets out to understand because its defining act of interpretation is grounded in a temporality that is unitary; criminal and detective act in the same historical reality, and thus logic is the tool of both. That is why so much ingenuity is expended in such tales to establish the equivalence of both, the endless search for an adequate antagonist, a "Napoleon of crime" to test the titan of deduction.

But the wisdom tale, while it frequently has the problem-false-answer-followed-by-correct-solution pattern of detective stories, does *not* treat "the past as continuous with the present and interpret the traces left by earlier events in terms of the same laws and principles as apply in the present."[17] It seeks not to demonstrate a gradual progress unfolding in horizontal time, but to remind men again of the cut-off be-

---

schärfsten Gegensatz zu dem was wir in der Welt als tatsächliches Geschehen zu beobachten gewohnt sind. . . ."

[17] See above, fn. 13.

tween vertical levels of temporality, man's change and the Gods' stasis.

Consider an example from Midrash, the body of stories that evolved around attempts to interpret difficult passages in the Torah. Genesis 8:11 says, "And the dove came to [Noah] at eventide; and lo, in her mouth [was] an olive leaf freshly plucked." A gloss on this runs "Whence did she bring it? Rabbi Bebai said: the gates of the garden of Eden opened; she brought it from there. Rabbi Aibo said to him: if she brought it from there, ought she not to have brought something superior, like cinnamon or balsam? But with the olive [the dove] gave a hint to Noah, and said to him: Master Noah, rather this bitter thing from the hand of the Holy One, blessed be he, than a sweet thing from your hand."[18] The structure of this tale—making it typical of such stories—is: there is a problem to be solved; two wise men tell stories that seek to resolve the dilemma. First an answer is given (the olive branch came from Eden). This leads to an incorrect deduction: the dove should have brought cinnamon or balsam. Then the correct answer is given: better a bitter thing, etc. The first answer is logical, assumes that transcendent laws are coterminous with earthly laws, can therefore be solved by reason. But the "correct" answer points to the disparity between the two. The answer to such a puzzle is not a *solution*; rather, it is a reminder of another, and greater, mystery.[19]

The best-known example of this pattern is provided by the contrast between two mysteries in the Oedipus story, the question put by the sphinx and the question of who murdered Laius. Lest the accusation be brought that speaking of

[18] *Hammer on the Rock: A Short Midrash Reader*, ed. Nahum Glatzer (New York, Schocken Books, 1962), p. 31.

[19] Hundreds of examples of such a structure are provided by the Hassidic tradition, in which storytelling was highly honored. As two students of them have recently pointed out, "The form of the legends of the Besht [founder of the Hassidic sect] is fairly consistent. Customarily the plots begin with a puzzle or a dilemma or a calamity. This is often followed by an unsuccessful attempt to solve the problem by a physician, a sorcerer, or a lesser scholar. Then the Besht resolves the situation by means of his supernatural powers." *In Praise of the Baal Shem Tov*, eds. Don Ben Amos, Jerome R. Mintz (Bloomington, Indiana, Indiana U.P., 1970), p. 148.

Oedipus in connection with tales is to confuse forms, I remind the reader that Jolles himself points to the happy ending of *King Lear* as an example of the "simple form" of the tale once again reasserting its power over the human imagination. Jolles again and again points to the tragic aspects of the split between the ordered world of the tale and the disorder of the world in which it is told: "The tale opposes itself to a world of reality . . . what is tragic, here we may say, is the contention between a world that is naively felt to be moral and the naive ethical demands we make upon what happens."[20] It has been said that Oedipus is the first detective; and in Sophocles' *Oedipus the King* the tragedy opens with the chorus praising the hero for his ability to solve puzzles: you solved the riddle of the sphinx, and moreover, "You did this with no extra knowledge you got from us, you had no training for the task. . . . You are a man of experience, the kind whose plans result in effective action."[21] Oedipus, like so many private detectives, is an amateur (he had no training for the task) who gets results when the professionals (the police), like the seer Tiresias, fail. He sets out to solve the murder in a no-nonsense way, admonishing the chorus "You are praying. As for your prayers, if you are willing to hear and accept what I say now you will find rescue and relief from distress."[22] He attacks the solution Tiresias offers because it is not logical; it is mere priestly mumbo-jumbo: "When the sphinx chanted her riddle here, did you come forward to speak the word that would liberate the people of this town? . . . But you did not come forward, you offered no answer told you by the birds or the Gods. No I came, know-nothing Oedipus, I stopped the sphinx. I answered her riddle with my own intelligence—the birds had nothing to teach me."[23] The seers and their birds, the professionals and their methods, failed to solve the case of

---

[20] Jolles, p. 241. ". . . das Märchen stellt sich als einer Welt der Wirklichkeit gegenüber . . . tragisch, so können wir hier sagen, ist der Widerstand zwischen einer naiv unmoralisch empfündenen Welt und unseren naiv ethischen Aufordnungen an das Geschehen."

[21] *Oedipus the King*, tr. Bernard M. W. Knox (New York, Washington Square Press, 1971 [21st print.]), p. 3.

[22] *Ibid.*, p. 14.   [23] *Ibid.*, p. 27.

the sphinx, and Oedipus in this passage sounds very much like a detective, the genius amateur, boasting of the superiority of his solution (Poirot's little grey cells, Sherlock's repeated, "You know my methods, Watson!"). But the Laius case is more difficult, less amenable to logic. Jocasta says that he conducts the investigation as if he were no longer "a man in control of his reason, judging the present by the past."[24]

But it is just this historical, this deductive, method that assumes horizontal time that Oedipus is, at this point, pursuing: he is attempting to synchronize clocks, to bring past and present into a meaningful congruence. But this time the riddle—in marked contrast to the first problem Oedipus confronts—does not give itself to his reason. It is not Oedipus who solves the crime, but Apollo, as had to be the case because even when all the puzzles in horizontal time had been unravelled, when the story of Oedipus and his true parents and the story of the fight at the crossroads have been reconstructed by deductive means into a true history, the biggest question of all remains: why did these events occur in this way at all? The shape of the events—the chronological reconstruction of who-was-where-when that always is the solution in detective stories—does not in this case constitute an explanation. The historical resolution of the puzzle—it was Oedipus who-dunit—simply points to the greater mystery of why it all happened. And in order to answer that question, vertical, extra-human time needs to be broached. The Oedipus story, then, is similar to other wisdom tales in that it is not only about the mystery of fate but an insistence on the Completely Other.[25] Oedipus is taught finally to accept the incommensurability of mere ratiocination, logical deduction (and the historical sense of time that enables it), on the one hand, and, ultimate questions—mysteries not puzzles—on the other.

Lest the emphasis on two opposing grounds of interpretation in Oedipus seem strained it should be remembered that:

[24] *Ibid.*, p. 62.
[25] "Das ganz Andere." See Rudolf Otto, *Das Heilige* (München, Beck Verlag, 1963 [1st publ. 1917, esp. pp. 13-37, "Mysterium tremendum"]). There is an English translation: *The Idea of the Holy*, tr. John W. Harvey, (New York, Oxford U.P., 1923).

"The Greek word *Hermeneious* referred to the priest at the Delphic oracle. This word and the more common verb *hermeneien* [to interpret] and noun *hermeneia* [interpretation] point back to the wing-footed messenger-God Hermes, from whose name the words are apparently derived (or vice-versa). Significantly, Hermes is associated with the function of transmitting what is beyond human understanding into a form that human intelligence can grasp. The various forms of the word suggest the process of bringing a thing or situation from unintelligibility to understanding."[26]

Hermes, as the one who bridges the gap between the language of men and the language of Gods, is a translator. It is not surprising then that wisdom tales that seek to accomplish the hermeneutic task are so full of indirect, metaphorical expression (metaphor from *metaphoreien*, Greek verb "to translate"), even when the translation attempt is to find the one correct meaning for a word out of several that might be possible. Such is the case in Oedipus, where all agree that the ultimate source of meaning is in the Gods; it is Apollo who sends the signs. But the signs themselves are ambiguous, could mean many things. How is one to determine the *single* meaning the Gods intended?

It would seem that insofar as this is the major question in tales presupposing a vertical ontology, another analogue between seer and detective would have made itself apparent. Consider, for example, a Sherlock Holmes story frequently adduced as an example in the modern (as opposed to Tiresias') study of signs called semiotics, "The Speckled Band."[27] "The Speckled Band" is the last phrase uttered by a woman who dies under mysterious circumstances. No one can figure out what the expression means precisely. Does it refer to the polka-dotted headkerchiefs of the gypsies who are camped near the scene of her death? Or is this the name of a sinister

[26] Richard E. Palmer, *Hermeneutics* (Evanston, Illinois, Northwestern U.P., 1969), p. 13.
[27] See, for instance, Ju. K. Ščeglov, "K postroeniju strukturnoj modeli novel o Šerloke Xolmse," *Texte des sowjetischen literaturwissenschaftlichen Strukturalismus,* ed. Karl Eimermacher (München, Fink Verlag, 1971), pp. 65-67.

gang? Or a motley musical ensemble? Speckled band is a symbol that could have many meanings, but because Sherlock is able to reduce the ambiguities to the one correct meaning (a snake) he is able to solve the crime.

But this analogue between seer and detective is, of course, only apparent: both are primarily engaged in a hermeneutical task, but each operates out of a different theory of signs. The ground of meaning for the seer is in another reality; he translates from one ontology to another, from the language of Gods to the language of men. The ultimate source of significance for the detective is, however, to be found only in the one ontology, the language of men. He does not translate from another language, he *uncovers* (*de-tegere*) a meaning that is potentially present in a language *already known*. Thus the means of interpretation will be quite different for each.

The relevance of this distinction for *Crime and Punishment* will perhaps be clearer if we characterize it further along the lines suggested by Paul Ricoeur:

"The hermeneutic field is internally at variance with itself . . . according to one pole, hermeneutics is understood as a manifestation and restoration of a meaning addressed to one in the manner of a message, a proclamation, or, as is sometimes said, a *kerygma*; according to the other pole it is understood as a demystification, as a reduction of illusion . . . on the one hand, purify discourse of its excesses, liquidate the idols, go from drunkenness to sobriety, realize our state of poverty once and for all; on the other hand, use the most nihilistic, destructive, iconoclastic movement so as to *let speak* what once, what each time was *said*, when meaning appeared anew, when meaning was at its fullest. Hermeneutics [is] . . . animated by this double motivation: willingness to suspect, willingness to listen, vow of rigor, vow of obedience."[28]

If wisdom tales and detective stories have in common that they are both about interpretation, they differ in the fundamental way here characterized by Ricoeur: the wisdom tale, in that it usually seeks to explain a prior text, Holy Writ, or

[28] *Freud and Philosophy*, tr. Denis Savage (New Haven, Conn., Yale U.P., 1970).

the saying of an Oracle, attempts to "let speak what once . . . was said . . . when meaning was at its fullest"; its vow of obedience insures that its explanation will end by insisting on the mysteriousness (for human reason) of the mystery that occasioned it. The tale of Job would be best illustration. The detective story, on the other hand, is best "understood as a de-mystification, as a reduction," its explanatory aim is to show that mystery is an illusion. Any of the Father Brown stories would serve as clearest example of this tendency.

Now each of these hermeneutic narratives presupposes a different temporality. The wisdom tale attempts to wipe out time in that the mystery at the end of the plot refers back to the mystery with which it began: it is a language act performed in time that seeks to dramatize the timelessness of its subject; it is words about the One Word, the Logos. Its end, both as plot constituent and as telos, is an insistence on the primacy of the Beginning. It is a sequence about a moment that is privileged vis-à-vis its own time markers. Just the opposite is the case with detective stories, each of which is less a "black-mask mystery" than a black-box puzzle, a narrative self-destruct mechanism: the end of its plot is to wipe out its beginning. While, as mentioned earlier, the process, the middle of the story, is what interests the reader, from the point of view of the plot itself, it is the end that counts. The end moment is privileged, but only vis-à-vis the *particular* sequence that is the story's plot, not against sequence *as such*. Some of Sherlock's solutions may be more logically ingenious than others, but they all depend on sequence, indeed insist on it.

I dwell on these particular aspects of what must seem an obvious contrast because the two attitudes toward interpretation, the two temporalities they presuppose, and the two narrative structures we have been discussing are the determining features, constitute the terms of, the moment-sequence *dominanta* in *Crime and Punishment*. That is to say, if I may recapitulate, that the plot of *Crime and Punishment* is arranged around two moments, each of which is privileged in a different way, and each of which results in a different sequence. The first is the moment of Raskolnikov's crime that occurs in Book

One, and the sequence of punishment that flows from it in the following five books. The second is the moment of Raskolnikov's conversion in the epilogue, and the sequence of the "new story" with which the novel ends. The first has the formal properties of a detective story, the second of a wisdom tale.

II

The two clocks of a detective story are represented by two characters, the criminal and the detective. Now to the list of oppositions that is usually invoked to capture the duality of a typical Dostoevskian character (sinner-saint, proud-humiliated, etc.), we must in the case of Raskolnikov add another: he is both hunter and hunted. As happens in such twentieth-century metaphysical detective stories as Robbe-Grillet's *The Erasers*, Borges' "Death and the Compass," or Witold Gombrowicz' "Premeditated Crime,"[29] there is a mysterious collusion between detective and murderer; but in each of these examples what is essentially a subject-object dilemma is still neatly divided between two characters. In *Crime and Punishment* the split is internalized in the consciousness of a single protagonist, Rodion Raskolnikov.

He is the criminal, so much is obvious. But he is also victim: on the way to commit the murder he compares himself to a man on his way to execution (I,v); and as he confesses to Sonya later (v.iv), "I killed myself, not the old woman." What he means by this is that the man who murdered the pawnbroker *in that act* got rid of the self Raskolnikov conceived himself to be before the act of murder. Raskolnikov's identity is felt by him not to be continuous with itself before and after the crime: after discovering that the role of murderer made his old self a victim, in the first book, Raskolnikov is forced to take up a new role, that of detective of his old self's motive, in order to create a new identity, a new life for himself. If he can understand *why* his old self committed the crime

[29] See: Michael Holquist, "Whodunit and other Questions: Metaphysical Detective Stories in Post-War Fiction," *New Literary History*, Vol. III (1971-1972), pp. 135-56.

he will know the self whodunit; and insofar as he understands whodunit, he will know who he is.

The crime itself is performed in a fog of uncertainty; everything happens by chance. Raskolnikov acts as if in a delirium; he is constantly surprised to find himself in this or that place, holding the axe, running away. His dream-like state is dramatized by the narrator's subtle but insistent emphasis on the cut-off between Raskolnikov's hallucinatory uncertainties and the precise chronology of all his movements, which are charted from moment to moment: "Suddenly he heard a clock strike. . . . It seemed to him strange and monstrous that he could have slept in such forgetfulness from the previous day and had done nothing, had prepared nothing yet. . . . And meanwhile . . . it had struck six" (I,vi). As he dazedly makes his preparations he hears someone in the yard say, "It struck six long ago," and he says, "Long ago, My God," and rushes out. As he walks to the pawnbroker's apartment, "he saw that it was ten minutes past seven." And then, as he gets there: "here was the house, here was the gate. Suddenly a clock somewhere struck once! What! Can it be half-past seven? Impossible, it must be fast!" After he murders the second woman, Lizaveta, "a sort of blankness, even dreaminess, had begun by degree to take possession of him; at moments he forgot himself. . . ." As Raskolnikov later says (III,iii): "I remember everything down to the smallest detail, and yet if you were to ask me why I did something, or went somewhere, or said something, I don't think I could give a clear explanation."

The confusion of the crime itself is contrasted in the rest of the novel with Raskolnikov's acute attempts to analyze it. He isolates three different motives, each of which becomes the iconic attribute of a self who is presented as a suspect, only to be cleared in favor of one of the other motive-defined selves. In chapter iv of book v he reviews them all for Sonya. The first is robbery: "It was to rob her." He wanted the money for food, to save his mother from poverty, his sister from being sold to Luzhin. But he quickly dismisses this; he admits he buried the purse he stole without even looking into it: "if I'd killed simply because I was hungry . . . then I should be happy now."

The second motive is one that is much more deeply explored in the novel: "I wanted to make myself a Napoleon, and that is why I killed her. . . ." Earlier (III,v) we learn that Raskolnikov's old, pre-murder self had written an article; in it Raskolnikov "developed the idea that all the . . . law-givers and regulators of human society, beginning with the most ancient, and going on to Lycurgus, Solon, Mahomet, Napoleon and so on, were without exception transgressors, by the very fact that in making a new law they *ipso facto* broke an old one, handed down from their fathers and held sacred by society" (p. 249). While such ideas have obvious parallels in Nietzsche's essay on "The Uses and Abuses of History," Philip Rahv was surely right to point to the greater fruitfulness of a comparison with Hegel's conception of the world historical individual: "Dostoevsky gives us a parody-version of Hegel's theory of two types of men [the superior hero and the inferior mass he is to lead] by abstracting [the theory] from its historical logic."[30] Raskolnikov's conception of the murder as a world-historical act is absurd, as he becomes painfully aware. He does so under the shadow of yet another brutalized aspect of Hegel's philosophy of history, an aspect often expressed in Schiller's line, *Weltgeschichte ist Weltgericht*, "world history is the world court." That is, Raskolnikov not only advances as his most programmatically complete reason for *committing* the murder a motive derived from Hegel; he also *judges* his act by appealing to a debased Hegelian principle of interpretation: what succeeds is correct, what fails is wrong. As he says to his sister Dunia (VI,vii):

"I shed blood, which flows and has always flowed on this earth in torrents, which is poured out like champagne, and for

---

[30] "Dostoevsky in *Crime and Punishment*," as reprinted in the Norton Critical Edition of the Coulson translation of the novel, ed. George Gibian (New York, W. W. Norton, 1964), p. 612. Much that Martin P. Rice has to say about the underground man's "Hegelianism" would apply with equal or greater force to Raskolnikov. See: Martin P. Rice, "Dostoevsky's *Notes from the Underground* and Hegel's Master and Slave," *Canadian-American Slavic Studies*, 8, iii (1974), pp. 359-69.

which men are crowned in the Capitol and afterwards called benefactors of mankind. . . . I myself wanted to benefit men, and I would have done hundreds, thousands, of good deeds, to make up for that one piece of stupidity—not even stupidity, but simple clumsiness, since the whole idea was not nearly as stupid as it seems now when it has failed (failure makes anything seem stupid) . . . if I had succeeded I should have been crowned, but now I shall fall into the trap."

Let us recapitulate for a moment: it may be, as G. K. Chesterton had one of his characters say (in "The Blue Cross"), that, "The criminal is the creative artist; the detective only a critic." But even, as in Raskolnikov's case, when—or especially when—artist and critic are one man, a general ground for any specific interpretation is necessary. Raskolnikov committed the murder as in a trance, it is like a dream he must interpret. It is precisely for him the problem as Freud posed it: "The dream as a nocturnal spectacle is unknown to us; it is accessible only through the account of waking hours. The analyst interprets this account, substituting for it another text which is, in his eyes, the thought-content of desire, i.e., what desire would say could it speak without constraint."[31] Raskolnikov, dreamer and analyst, turns for the ground of his interpretation to history: the causes can be known only in their effects. There is nothing higher than history; there is no transcendent, so the truth can be known only retrospectively, in events, as a judgment of historical trial by combat. The shape of events will explain them. As Hegel said, "It was for a while the fashion to admire God's wisdom in animals, plants, and individual lives. If it is conceded that Providence manifests itself in such objects and materials, why not also in world history? . . . Our intellectual striving aims at recognizing that what eternal wisdom *intended*, it has actually *accomplished*. . . ."[32]

Raskolnikov's historicism is important to any understanding not only of his own motives, the thematics of the novel if

[31] Cited in: Ricoeur, p. 15.
[32] *Reason in History*, tr. Robert S. Hartman (Indianapolis, Indiana, New York, Bobbs-Merrill Co., 1953), p. 18.

you will, but also to its morphology. Since Raskolnikov uses historical method in his search for self, he inevitably acts like a detective, interpreting "the traces left by earlier events in terms of the same laws and principles as apply in the present." Since all that is real is rational, and all that is rational real, in Hegel's oft-misunderstood formulation, reason will suffice unto a solution. It is reason that tells Raskolnikov he has failed in his intention to transcend morality; therefore at the end of the novel he turns himself in—he has finally discovered that he is no more than a criminal. The true self has been found, and like the detective story whose temporality it shares, the novel thus can close.

III

But of course there is still the epilogue. In it, as Raskolnikov finds a new conception of time and selfhood, we discover that his Hegelian motive and its consequences are a false solution. Already in the novel proper Raskolnikov had hinted at a reason for his crime other than robbery or a secularized messianism. The murder was simply an extreme situation he sought to exploit in order to find out who he really *was*; as he says—in one of those terrifying Dostoevskian immediacies— "I longed to kill without casuistry, to kill for my own benefit and for that alone! I would not lie about it even to myself! I did not commit murder in order to use the profits and power gained to make myself a benefactor to humanity. Rubbish! I simply murdered; I murdered for myself, for myself alone . . . it was only to *test myself* . . ." (v,iv). But of course—given his historical bias—he can only conclude he failed the test. As late as the second chapter of the epilogue Raskolnikov "could find no particularly terrible guilt in his past except a simple blunder . . . he was ashamed he had perished so blindly and hopelessly, with such mute stupidity, by some decree of blind fate and must humble himself and submit to the 'absurdity' of that decree . . . the first steps of [the benefactors of mankind] were successfully carried out, and therefore *they were right*, while mine failed, which means I had the right to permit myself that step." Accepting history as the ultimate source of meaning, he can find no way to appeal its verdict, there is no extra-temporal supreme court; the sequence the moment of his crime has condemned him to is final: "An objectless and undirected anxiety in the present, and endless sacrifice, by which nothing would be gained in the future, was all the world held for him." Raskolnikov had sought to give himself definitive knowledge of his self in the murder; it was an attempt to create a secular *kairos*, a moment that would insure the validity of all his other moments. Among his other dualities, he thus has taken on the roles of both Christ and Lazarus, seeking to gain a new identity by his *own* actions, to bestow a new life through his own mediation. But instead of raising a new self, his old identity is executed in the murder. At the end of the novel, then, he is in the dilemma Hans Meyerhoff has described in connection with Oedipus:

"He is 'in fact,' that is, in terms of his own experience, two different persons—though in terms of the objective 'facts' of Nature and history he is one and the same. We say that Oedipus didn't know who he was, which is correct in that he failed to experience his life under the aspect of temporal continuity . . . the tragedy of Oedipus may still be seen in the light . . . of the fact that the break between his two 'pasts' was so severe and the consequences of this split in his personality were so disastrous that it was impossible to mend the broken pieces of the self."[33]

As Maurice Beebe has said, "Raskolnikov commits a murder not that he may be an 'extrordinary' man, but that he *may see* if he is one,"[34] and the novel up to its last three pages chronicles the failure of Raskolnikov's gamble in the lottery of selfhood. In those last three pages, however, he is granted another moment, another sequence, as he becomes a character in the wisdom tale with which the epilogue concludes.

It is Easter, time for rebirth. Raskolnikov has just come out of the hospital, where, in his illness, he has had one of those great Dostoevskian programmatic dreams that recapitulates

---

[33] *Time in Literature* (Berkeley and Los Angeles, U. of California P., 1960 [originally published 1955]), pp. 42-43.
[34] "The Three Motives of Raskolnikov," in Gibian, p. 634.

in symbols the meaning of his novelistic actions. He sits by the bank of "the wide, solitary river. From the high bank a broad landscape was revealed. From the other bank far away, was faintly borne the sound of singing. There in the immensity of the steppe . . . it seemed as though . . . *time had stood still*, and the age of Abraham and his flocks was still the present" [emphasis added]. Sonya appears and "how it happened he himself did not know, but suddenly he seemed to be seized and cast at her feet . . . *now at last the moment had come*" [emphasis added]. What has happened here, of course, is that Raskolnikov has undergone a conversion experience, and even in its small details it is strikingly similar to the source of this and many another example of the *topos*, the famous scene in the garden at the end of Chapter VIII in Augustine's *Confessions*: tears, distant voices, being thrown onto the ground, and inability to speak, this last trait especially significant in the conversion experience because it dramatizes the condition of infancy (*in-fari*, *infans*, he who does not speak) that is part and parcel of the rebirth that conversion symbolically makes possible.

But in order to be reborn, the old self must die. We are here touching on the main theme of *Crime and Punishment*, as Dostoevsky himself indicated in his notebooks to the novel: under the heading "The Main Idea" (followed by "Eureka!"), he writes: Raskolnikov sees in Sonya "perspectives for a new life and love . . . he finally comes to himself, victorious. From one point of view life has ended, from another, it is beginning."[35] This radical break in identity is present in almost all accounts of conversion (even when they are "secondary conversion") experiences: Augustine, the rhetor, dies, as the future Bishop of Hippo is born; Thomas Aquinas, after his experience, on the Feast of St. Nicholas in 1273, dies as a scholar: "All that I have written seems like straw to me . . .";

[35] *Prestuplenie i Nakazanie: rukopisnye redaktsii*, ed. V. V. Vinogradov, *Polnoe* (Leningrad, Nauka, 1973), Vol. 7, p. 138. It should be added, in all fairness, that Dostoevsky often gets carried away like this in his notebooks, which are peppered with *"samoe glavnoe's"* (the most important thing) even when this turns out to be far from the case in his final draft.

and he never wrote another line. In Raskolnikov's case this mystical suppression of self, the death of his old identity ("Love had raised [him] from the dead"), is just as decisive as was the death of an even earlier self, the one that died in the act of murder. Raskolnikov is a completely different person as the epilogue closes: "And what were all, *all* the torments of the past? Everything, even his crime, even his sentence and his exile seemed to him *now* . . . to be something external and strange, as if it had not happened to him at all."

And just as in the confessional mode of autobiography there is a break in the sequence of the self after the *kairotic* moment, so is there a change in the sequence of the telling. Augustine, again, provides a convenient example: to the moment of conversion, the tale of his life advances more or less chronologically, as an autobiography; but after the crucial moment in the Roman garden is recounted (and its immediate after-effects), the historical progression ceases, we are given no more biographical details for the fourteen years intervening between the mystical experience in Rome and the written account of it in the *Confessions*. Instead, the concluding chapters are devoted to a meditation on time and memory, and it closes with a reading of the book of Genesis. It, too, *ends* with an interpretation of a text that is about ultimate beginnings. After conversion, all else is felt to be anticlimactic, the ensuing series of discreet moments is already foreshadowed in that one moment. Augustine's first four books cover twenty-eight years, but the next five books treat only *four* years, climaxing in his conversion. The last four books abandon chronology altogether. What is significant is precisely the rupture between old and new identity, the meaning of the self in its discontinuity:

"It is the internal transformation—which furnishes a subject for a narrative discourse in which 'I' is both subject and object. . . . It is because past 'I' is different from the present 'I' that the latter may really be confirmed in all his prerogatives. The narrator describes not only what happened to him at a different time in his life, but above all how he became—out of

95

what he was—what he presently is . . . the deviation, which establishes the autobiographical reflection, is thus double: it is at once a deviation of time and of identity."[36]

This deviation in *Crime and Punishment* is experienced as a felt discontinuity between the narrative mode of the novel, on the one hand, and its epilogue, on the other. All readers of the book have sensed this disjunction, many objecting to the forced or tacked-on quality of the ending,[37] usually because they assume Dostoevsky was striving for a conventional narrative homogeneity. But if we assume on the contrary that he seeks to accentuate, to dramatize, the differences between the two parts of the book, the shape of the text assumes another kind of unity.

The whole novel is an account of Raskolnikov's various attempts to forge an identity for himself with which he can live. From the very beginning of the novel he has sought a means to justify his existence or, in the language of the text, to find a faith. Porfiry Petrovich underscores this thirst for validity: the investigator says: "Do you know how I regard you? As one of those who would allow themselves to be disembowelled, and stand and face their torturers with a smile—if they had found a faith . . ." (vi,ii). All Raskolnikov's actions—his article on new law givers (who found a new faith), the murder itself, and his attempts to understand it—are probes toward a moment that will give lasting meaning to the rest of his life.

He is like the underground man in that he seeks a plot in which to become a character, a shape that will endow each of his discreet actions with an end. But *unlike* the underground man he attempts to ground his identity, not in fictive plots, but rather in historical narratives. The six parts of the novel tell how Raskolnikov, who feels he is existentially out of place in the historical context of nineteenth-century Russian

---

[36] Jean Starobinski, "The Style of Autobiography" in: *Literary Style: A symposium*, ed. Seymour Chatman (London, New York, Oxford U.P., 1974), pp. 289-90.

[37] An example, chosen almost at random: "We as critical readers, cannot overmuch concern ourselves with such intimations of ultimate reconcilement and salvation" (Philip Rahv, *op.cit.*, p. 599-600).

society, tries to create a *new* historical sequence, as had Solon, Mahomet, etc. Like a tragic Baron Munchhausen, he seeks to pull himself out of the swamp of time by his own metaphysical pigtail. But he discovers that he is not a world historical individual; he is not a character in *that kind* of a history. It is only in the epilogue that he discovers the kind of narrative that is properly his own to live: it is not a secular history to which he belongs, but a wisdom tale.

Dostoevsky treats Raskolnikov as Stephan Marcus has suggested Freud dealt with his patients: "Freud is implying that a coherent story is in some manner connected with mental health . . . and this in turn implies assumptions of the broadest and deepest kind about the nature of coherence and the form and structure of human life. . . . At the end—at the successful end—one has come into possession of his own story. It is a final act of self-appropriation, the appropriation by oneself of one's own history."[38]

As narrator, Dostoevsky assigns values to the various characters according to the degree they are successful in merging their character with a plot that is adequate to it. Thus Lebezyatnikov is a gentle, naive person, a utopian socialist nevertheless who seeks to live out a scenario of tough-minded nihilism that results in such absurdities as his assumption that Sonya has become a prostitute as a protest against society. Marmelodov's drunkenness, his wife's insanity, are the consequences of biographical failures of emplotment: he cannot live the role of philosopher; she cannot live that of a grand dame. Svidrigailov is a gambler, possibly a double murderer (of his manservant and his wife), and a sensualist who violates young girls. Yet the story into which he wishes to insert himself, a parody of the golden-hearted prostitute cliché, is one in which, by forcing Dunia to marry him (at gun point), he will be saved, can settle down to a quiet life of domestic bliss. The consequences of failing to arrive at a workable assimilation of character and plot are severe—Svidrigailov cannot make his *happy* ending work, so is (self) condemned to death—the "correct" ending for the character he has played all his life. He

[38] Marcus, *op.cit.*, p. 92.

has lived the role of villain in a realistic novel, and because he cannot become the hero of a sentimental story, he dies.

Over against these failures stand those figures who have come to know themselves—or, in the terms we have been using, come to know the story to which their character corresponds. Porfiry Petrovich is able to sum up his whole life with conviction and modesty: "Who am I? I am a man who has developed as far as he is capable, that is all." He goes on to make the distinction between himself and Raskolnikov: "But you—that's another matter . . ." and suggests that Raskolnikov will "pass into a different category of men" (v,ii). It is the same distinction Raskolnikov will make in connection with Sonya: "You too have stepped over the barrier . . . you were able to do it. You laid hands on yourself, you destroyed a life . . . *your own* . . ." (IV,iv).[39] He recognizes that she has risen again, lives as a character in the Lazarus story she reads to him—even before he has been able to enter that same story himself, because he still sees himself in the light of historical narrative at this point in the novel. But after his conversion, the Lazarus plot will be his as well.

The deviation between "normal" lives and the one led by Raskolnikov is marked not only in a thematic distinction between his own old self and the new one he discovers, but in the difference between the formal properties of the detective story plot he lives in the novel and the formal properties of the wisdom tale, in which he becomes a character in the novel's epilogue. Thematically *Crime and Punishment* is the account of Raskolnikov's search for a story that will endow his life with validity. He first seeks such a narrative structure in a theory of history that is recognizably Hegelian and unquestionably secular. He kills in order to test whether he is, or is not, an instrument of historical change: since there is nothing higher than history itself, you can know its judgments only

[39] The theme of stepping over bounds is a central Dostoevskian concern, of course. For a sensitive analysis of the relationship between transgression (*perestupanie*) and crime (*prestuplenie*) in *Crime and Punishment* see: Vadim Kozhinov, "The First Sentence in *Crime and Punishment*," in *Twentieth Century Interpretations of Crime and Punishment*, ed. Robert Louis Jackson (Englewood Cliffs, N.J., Prentice Hall, Inc., 1974), pp. 17-25.

after having acted. Having committed the murder, he discovers he is in fact not a character in the drama of historicism. In order, then, to establish a continuity in his identities, to reassemble the shattered "I" destroyed in the outcome of the crime, he seeks the existential glue of another kind of story. But since historicism is the source of the murder—and of the confusion following upon it until Raskolnikov turns himself in—this part of the narrative is told in a way that employs many of the features of a detective story, since, as R. G. Collingwood has pointed out:

"There is nothing other than historical thought itself, by appeal to which its conclusions may be verified. The hero of a detective novel is thinking exactly like an historian when, from indications of the most varied kinds, he constructs an imaginary picture of how a crime was committed, and by whom. At first this is a mere theory awaiting verification, which must come to it from without. Happily for the detective, the conventions of that literary form dictate that when his construction is complete, it shall be neatly pegged down by a confession from the criminal, given in such circumstances that its genuineness is beyond question."[40]

Since an authentic self is the object of Raskolnikov's various attempts to explain why he committed the murder (if he understands *why*-dunit, he'll know *who*-dunit), it is clear that his first public confession—which ends the novel proper—is an unsatisfactory solution. A self-construction has *not* been "neatly pegged down by a confession from the criminal." Raskolnikov exhausts the detective story formula without achieving its benefit—a complete resolution of the mystery that sets the story going. If we invoke the metaphor with which we began, the two clocks of the plot fail to synchronize. Thus, after his trial, it is said of Raskolnikov (now in Siberia): "An objectless and undirected anxiety in the present, and endless sacrifice, by which nothing would be gained,

---

[40] R. G. Collingwood, *The Idea of History* (New York, Oxford U.P., 1956), p. 243. For an extended treatment of the analogy between detective and historian, see the anthology: Robin W. Winks, *The Historian as Detective* (New York, Harper and Row, 1969).

in the future—that was all the world held for him" (epilogue, II).

Raskolnikov has failed to find a self in the detective story into which his attempt to enter historical narrative has devolved; but another plot is vouchsafed to him, as we saw, in the epilogue's last pages—another time is broached. The last pages of the novel are not only *about* another time; they are told in a different time: the movement from the dream to the final word of the text is constituted in a manner that sets it off from the body of the novel insofar as it tells of years in sentences, while in the body of the text minutes are told in pages. This has disturbed such readers as Ernest J. Simmons: "Following the line of least resistance, [Dostoevsky] often ignored the time-sequence. In one of the notebooks he boldly declares 'What is time? Time does not exist; time is a cipher; time is the relation of being to unbeing.' "[41] Exactly—and that is why, far from "following the line of least resistance," Dostoevsky is at great pains to emphasize the difference between the time of the novel, whose hundreds of pages tell of only two weeks (the crucial part I tells of only three days), while the last paragraph of the epilogue covers the rest of Raskolnikov's life. Since Raskolnikov has found his self, he has entered what Dostoevsky always called "living life" (*Živaja' žizn'*): the relation between mere flux—unbeing—and the non-changing significance of the being he discovers in the moment of his conversion results in a diminished significance for chronology. This is not the historical or even psychological time of the Bergsonian *durée* variety—it is time understood precisely as "the relation of being to unbeing."

IV

If, as we have suggested, there is a disjunction between the temporal structure of the novel proper and its epilogue, does this mean—as many readers have felt—that there is a break in the unity of *Crime and Punishment*? The suggestion of this chapter has been, rather, that there is a bond between the parts, a bond that derives from the direction of time in the

[41] "The Art of *Crime and Punishment*" in Gibian, *op.cit.*, pp. 573-74.

two story types that define the novel, on the one hand, and the epilogue, on the other. The detective story properties shaping Raskolnikov's search for identity in the novel tend toward a conclusion that will resolve all the mysteries.

But it does not, because in the course of his investigation Raskolnikov has, in his obsessive honesty, raised the question of evil, and, as H. R. Niebuhr has said, "the mystery of good and evil in human life and in the world cannot be completely comprehended as stated in perfectly logical terms."[42] What the theologian here states is the ancient message of the wisdom tale: "Knowest thou the ordinance of heaven? Canst thou set the dominion thereof in the earth?" The movement of the epilogue is analogous to the wisdom tale in that it points back to the inadequacy of answers that precede its concluding insistence on *another* realm, *another* time: the "correct" answer is not a solution, but the reminder of another and greater mystery. Thus the historical movement of the novel is a necessary step toward the debunking of its assumptions in the epilogue. The underground man, who never found a plot, is therefore condemned to a dreary life of "bad infinity," an endless succession of empty moments. Thus the formal conclusion of the Dostoevskian plot that contains him is a note from the editor who says "the 'notes' of this paradoxalist do not end here. . . ." Whereas *Crime and Punishment* may conclude with a "new tale"—Raskolnikov has found a role for himself in the detective-story-become-wisdom-tale that defines the Dostoevskian plot containing him.

[42] "The Truth in Myths," in *The Nature of Religious Experience* (Douglas Clyde MacIntosh Festschrift) eds. Bewkes et al. (New York, Harper and Bros., 1937), pp. 124-25.

Chapter 4

The Gaps in Christology:
The Idiot

C*rime and Punishment* ends with the words: "But that is the beginning of a new story, the story of the gradual renewal of a man . . . of his slow progress from one world to another, of how he learned to know hitherto undreamt of reality. All that might be the subject of a new story, but our present story has come to an end." Now it is well known that Dostoevsky's next novel, *The Idiot*, was to revolve around a "genuinely good," a "truly beautiful" man. The main character was to be an exemplary Christian: indeed, something like a Christ figure.[1] But Myshkin's story is not that new tale about a transfigured Raskolnikov alluded to in the conclusion of *Crime and Punishment*. That novel's dominant motif is the Lazarus story, with its emphasis on rebirth, rising from the dead, whereas the central metaphors of *The Idiot* are execution and apocalypse, not a sudden beginning of life but rather its too abrupt *end*. We shall have occasion in this chapter to speculate on why this is so, but at this point suffice it merely to indicate formal distinctions between the plots of the two novels.

The narrative structure of *Crime and Punishment* derives from Dostoevsky's variations on and fusion of two pre-existing plot types, the detective story and the wisdom tale, each presupposing its distinctive temporality: what we have called horizontal time in the first case, and vertical in the second. Much of the novel's meaning derives from its contrast between the linear, merely human, cause-and-effect time for which the detective story is a structural metaphor, on the one hand, and the mysterious stasis of a transcendent world, on the other, for which the wisdom tale stands in as narrative marker. The resolution in the epilogue is dramatized as a

---

[1] For Dostoevsky's own account of his intention to depict "a wholly beautiful individual," see his letters to Majkov (January 12, 1868) and S. A. Ivanova (January 13, 1868).

movement between the two kinds of time. Raskolnikov's conversion experience is bodied forth as an abrupt shift to another narrative strategy, the significance of which is to recapitulate the drama of Christian redemption. The implication is that from now on for Raskolnikov there will be a balance between the two temporalities as he refers each moment of the rest of the linear progress that will be his life back to that one second of epiphany whose meaning will not change, that will insure his future against mere flux.

It is just such a moment that all the characters in *The Idiot* will seek, but that none of them will succeed in finding. Christian redemptive history in *Crime and Punishment* is used optimistically: the fusion of divine and human time is what Dostoevsky features in *Crime and Punishment*. However, the *split* between these two times constitutes the center of his next novel; indeed in all the rest of his novels *Heilsgeschichte* is treated less as a promise than as a paradox.

In contrast to *Crime and Punishment*, the lower layer in the palimpsest of *The Idiot*'s narrative structure is a single preexisting plot type. But it is one that contains in itself both temporalities present in the earlier novel. The plot of *The Idiot* is a series of narrative turns on the structure of Christ's execution and its relation to time before and after his death on the cross. Several executions are described in the novel, and the relationship of this symbol cluster to the crucifixion is made clear in the key role played by the younger Holbein's painting of Christ's corpse (1521).[2] The execution aspect of Christ's death is emphasized in reactions to the painting: "Some people may lose their faith looking at that picture," Rogozhin says (II,iv), because it shows a body so broken, so dead, that no resurrection seems possible from it. Ipolit, himself under sentence of premature death from tuberculosis, will say of Holbein (III,iv), "Here one cannot help being struck

---

[2] Dostoevsky had seen the painting in the Basle Museum in 1867, at the time he was feverishly attempting to get a conceptual grip on his new novel. His wife describes his excitement when first he caught sight of it, standing on a chair better to see it even though he could ill afford the fine that Anna Grigorievna was sure such a rash act would result in. See *Dnevnik A. G. Dostoevskoj: 1867 goda* (Moskva, Novaja Moskva, 1923), p. 366.

with the idea that if death is so horrible and if the laws of nature are so powerful, then how can they be overcome? How can they be overcome when even He did not conquer them. . . .?"

It is for this reason that executions figure so prominently in *The Idiot*. In each of the four books that constitute the novel a strategic place is assigned to descriptions or discussions of preordained death: Legros' death by guillotine in Lyons (I,ii; I,v); a firing squad execution, halted at the last moment (I,v); Dubarry's beheading (II,ii); speculation on the irony of execution as punishment for Ipolit, were he to commit murder since he is soon to die of his disease anyway (III,v; III,vi); references to the fourteen-hour agony of the nobleman Glebov, condemned by Peter I to impalement on a stake in Red Square (IV,v); and to the decapitation of Sir Thomas More (IV,vi).

The possibility that Christ's moment of execution was final, that it did not result in resurrection and thus did not insure the sequence of *imitatio Christi* for other men—as it seemed to do for Raskolnikov, for instance—is the primary metaphysical dilemma of *The Idiot*.

It is also the major structural metaphor for the failure of Myshkin's sojourn in Russian, that spark of lucidity which interrupts his long years of darkness in the Swiss asylum, the brief six months whose events make up the novel's major plot. An inspired moment that subsequently fails to change anything, that fails to usher in an expected new order, is not only the dominant pattern of Myshkin's career, but of the other major characters' lives as well: Ganya's attempted engagement to Nastasya Filipovna; Ipolit's attempted suicide; Nastasya Filipovna's several attempts to break with her past; Aglaya's attempt to marry the Prince, her conversion to Catholicism, etc.

Thus the significance of the Christ story in *The Idiot* goes beyond mere characterological parallels between the saintly progress of Jesus and Myshkin, parallels that, in any case, have been remarked often enough.[3] Far more important are the

---

[3] For a reading that takes this approach to an illuminating extreme, see: Romano Guardini, "Dostoevsky's *Idiot*: A Symbol of Christ," tr. Francis X. Quinn, *Cross Currents*, VI (Fall, 1956), pp. 359-82.

differences between Myshkin and Christ, the way Dostoevsky exploits the root contradictions of Christian historiography as symbols for basic conflicts in the lives of his characters. A Christ whose appearance did *not* unseat the realities that had previously shaped history is invoked as a metaphor for the sameness of lives lived on the other side of epiphanies that failed to change them. Just as blood and avarice, powerlust and violence, ruled human history before Christ, so do they appear to do so *after* his coming, and it is the possibility of this failure that is the highest expression of all those other epiphanies—those given and those sought for—in the novel that in the end leave the brute seriality of events uninterrupted.

It is not particularly surprising that Dostoevsky should turn to Christology. But the particular way in which he deploys it in *The Idiot* needs further clarification. In his ideologically charged journalism he extends Christian salvation history to interpretations of particular nineteenth-century political events.[4] He simply assumes that the possibility for the future redemption of the world coincides with a political boundary, and then goes on to use this doctrine as a jingoistic defense of Tsarist foreign policy. That is, he makes a direct parallel between two abstractions: the messiah and Russia. But in the fiction—and we shall have more to say on this—he relates the experience of Christ to the lives of individuals, and the novel's necessary emphasis on concreteness, detail, idiosyncrasy make such unmediated analogies impossible. The result, in the novels, is a radical analysis of *Heilsgeschichte*: not wish-fulfillment in the future, but a concern for how time itself works in Christian attitudes toward history. The paradox

---

[4] He was not, of course, the first to understand Russian history in the light of Christian historical models. Russian messianism goes back at least to the fifteenth century, when the term "Holy Russia" becomes prominent. "The meaning of the term must be sought in the analogy with the Holy Land. Palestine was holy because Christ had lived there, because it was the physical setting for the possibility of man's salvation. Thus Russia could be holy even in Christian times, if it had a unique and exalted role in the economy of salvation, if in it, and in it alone, Christ still walked in spirit if not in person." (Michael Cherniavsky, *Tsar and People: Studies in Russian Myths* [New Haven, Conn., Yale U.P., 1961], pp. 106-07). Such a condition in Russia was actually felt to obtain after the Council of Florence and the fall of Constantinople to the Turks.

that Prince Myshkin—Dostoevsky's Christ figure—is an *idiot* is better understood if we remember that Christ's interlude on earth is also, in Christian historiography, a paradox.

Since Christ's coming did not usher in the millennium for all men, no matter what it did for the inner lives of *individual* men, his messianic prophecy created problems in the years after his death that continue to plague believers and non-believers alike. Among others, consider the claim Christians make "for a Galilean prophet's brief activity, ending with execution under a Roman governor who ruled Judaea under Tiberius, [a claim that] contradicts the modern historian's principle of historical writing."[5] The historian conceives time as linear, using B.C. and A.D. as mere conventions for dating all events,[6] without assuming (or at least without instrumenting in his work) the uniqueness of the Incarnation: whereas for believers, that event effected a qualitative change at a given moment in history in the nature of *time itself*, so that things after it could never be the same again.

As the late French theologian Jean Daniélou, S.J., explains it: "The opposition is fundamental between the [historians' linear] conception and the Christian belief in a unique, irrevocable value belonging to the historical Incarnation. In the *Epistle to the Hebrews*, Christ is said to have entered 'once' . . . into the holy place, that is, when he ascended into God's heaven: something was there irrevocably gained. Nothing can ever again divide human nature from the Divinity; there is no possibility of a relapse; mankind is essentially saved. . . . The words 'past' and 'present' have here their full meaning."[7]

---

[5] Oscar Cullman, *Christ and Time: The Primitive Christian Conception of Time and History*, tr. Floyd V. Filson (Philadelphia, Westminster Press, MCML), p. 20.

[6] Or at least historians have done so since the eighteenth century, when the birth of Christ became a datum for enumerating backward as well as forward in time. Before such a practice came into usage, all systems dated time as a continuous, forward-moving series that began with "the creation," however or whenever one reckoned that to be.

[7] *The Lord of History: Reflections on the Inner Meaning of History*, tr. Nigel Abercrombie (Cleveland and New York, Meriden Books, 1968), p. 2. See as well: R. M. Grant, *The Earliest Lives of Jesus* (London, S.P.L.K., 1961), pp. 80-106.

The Gaps in Christology

A basic peculiarity of the Christian attitude toward time, then, is that in it, "the center of interest is neither at the beginning, as it was for the Greeks, nor at the end as it is in evolutionary theories, but in the middle."[8] Christ is conceived as an eruption of eternal order into the temporal sequence. The momentary simultaneity of these two strata of time, which Christ made possible, resulted in a cutoff between the "horizontal" segments of time we designate B.C. and A.D. Consequently, Christian thinkers very early on had to meet the objection that while Christ's coming may have altered the state of mankind's spiritual life, no change was apparent in the historical world.[9] It is this seemingly contradictory aspect of Christology that occupies Dostoevsky in *The Idiot*, where it is treated as the dilemma of unique persons, a problem sustained at the level of individual psychology rather than of systematic theology. That is, he re-enacts the life-death-and-transfiguration of Christ, *as if Christ were not the messiah, but as if he were an individual.* What in the Bible is a series of acts interpreted according to their exterior, universal meaning, is rehearsed by Dostoevsky as the actions of particular men, whose meaning is inner, particular.

II

In its thrust against generalization *The Idiot* most clearly defines itself as a novel. The power of the Christ story is in its promise not just to one man, to me, but to *all* men; the emphasis may be on individual salvation, but the means of redemption have been systematized. In its generalizing tendency the Christ story is mythic and therefore stands at the opposite pole to the novel, which is grounded in the specific,

[8] Daniélou, p. 7.

[9] It was to counter questions of this sort—questions that were exacerbated by Alaric's sack of Rome in 410—that Augustine systematized Christian historical doctrine in *The City of God*. He did not deny the apparent cutoff between Christ's coming and historical effect. Indeed, he made it the basis of his argument: the cutoff was there because of an even more essential division between *Civitas Dei* and *Civitas Terena*. For a treatment of Augustine that focuses on the meaning of this split for later historiography see: Erich Kahler, *The Meaning of History* (New York: George Braziller, 1964). See also Theodor E. Mommsen, "St. Augustine and the Christian Idea of Progress," *Journal of the History of Ideas* XII (June, 1951), pp. 346-74.

the particular. This is what Lévi-Strauss means when he says of myth that it "is the most fundamental form of inauthenticity," where authenticity is understood "as the concrete nature of the knowledge people have of each other . . . contrary to what might seem to be the case there is nothing more abstract than myths."[10] The novel, on the other hand, is preeminently *anti*-systematic. Its discourse more than any other is open to contingency, the particular and unique.

Lukacs has defined "the inner form of the novel" as "the process of [a] problematic individual's journeying toward himself,"[11] as a genre in which individuality is understood as the action of one "who must create an entire world through his experience,"[12] out of himself, since he exists in a world where nothing is given by an exterior system. If, in *The Idiot*, the Christ story is present less as a characterological parallel for Myshkin than as a key to an important aspect of the novel's inner structure (in this case, the pattern of failed epiphanies that characterizes the whole), the same may be said of the frequent allusions that are made to Don Quixote in *The Idiot* (Aglaya hides Myshkin's letter in a copy of Cervantes' novel [II,i]; the Epanchins, Kolya and Radomsky discuss likenesses between the Prince and "the poor Knight" [II,vi]; associations between Pushkin's "Poor Knight" fragment and Myshkin are made [II,vii]). At one level, surely, there is no doubt that similarities between Cervantes' hero and Prince Myshkin are being pointed to: their shared idealism, their championing of questionable "ladies," even their madness, although Dostoevsky gives this parallel a twist: while the Knight finally recovers at the end of *Don Quixote*, the Prince relapses into his former insanity. Myshkin is as much a black parody of *Don Quixote* as he is of Christ. But the presence of *Don Quixote* in *The Idiot* is more meaningful at a deeper level, as it dramatizes the thematic importance within *The Idiot* of that book's status as a novel. *Its genre is germane to its theme of Novel-ness.*

[10] Georges Charbonnier, *Conversations with Claude Lévi-Strauss*, tr. John and Doreen Weightman (London, Jonathan Cape, 1969 [although the talks were given originally in 1959]), p. 55.

[11] Georg Lukacs, *The Theory of the Novel*, tr. Anna Bostock (Cambridge, Mass., M.I.T. Press, 1971 [originally published in 1920]), p. 80.

[12] *Ibid.*, p. 83.

The Gaps in Christology

It has been written of *Don Quixote* that this "first great novel of world literature stands at the beginning of the time when the Christian God began to forsake the world; when man became lonely and could find meaning and substance only *in his own soul*, whose home was nowhere. . . ."[13] Cervantes' book is a novel in the degree to which it catalogues individuality more exhaustively than had ever been done before. It is no accident that it constantly undercuts the old chivalric romances, since its formal essence as a novel is opposed to the two formal tendencies of those romances that militate against individuality: their formulaic plots, making all stories the same; and their role-determined characterization (completely noble, completely vile), making all protagonists the same. The generic message of *Don Quixote* was that a new form had been found that was open to previously inexpressible idiosyncrasy.

Much as that novel dramatized the particularity of its universe through ironic contrasts with the system of Chivalry, so does *The Idiot* emphasize the contingency of its world by no less radically countering Christology. Christ's life, as a *system* of salvation, becomes a generality that can have only partial applicability in the lives of the particular individual's novel as a genre demands.[14] Insofar as Christ is conceived as a function of soteriology, he cannot figure in a novel, since he thus partakes of an absolute, and the novel, as D. H. Lawrence learned through his own painful experience in wrestling with the genre, is "incapable of the absolute . . . in a novel there is always a tom-cat, a black tom-cat that pounces on the white dove of the Word. . . ."[15]

[13] *Ibid.*, p. 103. Emphasis added.

[14] The Christ who appears in the Grand Inquisitor chapter of *The Brothers Karamazov* does so as a character in a legend, one of the many narrative forms that novel encapsulates. We shall have more to say on this subject when it comes up in Chapter 6. For a survey of other attempts to portray the Christ, see: Theodore Ziolkowski, *Fictional Transfigurations of Jesus* (Princeton, N.J., Princeton U.P., 1972). Ziolkowski recognizes that Dostoevsky, in *The Idiot*, "shared Nietzsche's awareness of the problematic psyche of the Saviour" (p. 104), but skirts triviality by adding that both "were exploiting the ancient *topos* that associates divine truth with madness" (*loc.cit.*).

[15] Quoted in Frank Kermode, *D. H. Lawrence* (N.Y., Viking, 1973), p. 27. Kermode adds about his subject, in words that apply with equal force to Dos-

That cat's name is contingency, and it counts among its victims not only the Word, but those who would speak it and only it. That is why Don Quixote haunts all subsequent novels: just as the Knight of La Mancha seeks to subordinate his life to the demands of Chivalry, so, in most later works, do the major characters thirst for a code, an absolute that will release them from their own contingency, even if the system is no more than a biography capable of knitting together the discrete moments of their lives into a continuous identity.[16]

It is this insistence on time as change, as that which problematizes unified identity in the novel, which led Lukacs to focus on temporality in his search for the genre's essence. For Lukacs the novel is the epic form of an age from which the Gods have fled. Such a view is particularly helpful, then, in understanding why corrosive time is so powerful a constitutive element of *The Idiot*: "... the bond with the transcendental home has been severed. ... Only in the novel, whose very matter is seeking and failing to find the essence, is time posited together with form...."[17] It could in fact be said that Dostoevsky's plots, the typical form of Dostoevskian time, are set up to do nothing else so relentlessly as to dramatize the absence of essence in chronology, the separation of moment and sequence. Thus the basic urge in Dostoevsky toward the novel as his dominant mode of expression, since the time Lukacs invokes is one of becoming, of identity in flux: "The greatest discrepancy between idea and reality is time, the process of time as duration. The most profound and most humiliating impotence of subjectivity consists ... in the fact that it cannot resist the sluggish, yet constant progress of time; that it must slip down, slowly yet inexorably from the peaks it has laboriously scaled...."[18]

---

toevsky, "It was in the novels that he wrestled with these transcendent systems. The novels do not have a design upon us; their design is upon the unqualified, unsuspected dogmas of the treatises and letters, which must be made to submit to life."

[16] The novel is in its essence radically anti-utopian; perhaps that is why all novels are, ultimately, *Bildungsromane*.

[17] Lukacs, *op.cit.*, p. 122.   [18] *Ibid.*, pp. 120-21.

The novel insists on the existence of the part by exhaustively demonstrating the inability of any whole to contain it completely. A creek may have a mean depth of only six inches, yet still contain isolated holes that are, say, ten feet deep. The novel always tells the story of that man who drowned in a stream with a mean depth of six inches. It always opts for the exception to the rules, whether they derive from the code of chivalry, from the code of society (as in most nineteenth-century English or French novels), or, as in the case of *The Idiot*, from the code of Christian salvation.

We are now able to speculate further as to why Dostoevsky chose (even before he had written it) as a title for this novel *The Idiot*: he does so to emphasize the subjectivity of his Christ figure. "Idiot" goes back through Latin *idiota* to the Greek word meaning private person (that aspect of a man *separate* from any collective identity) or layman, a man without professional knowledge (innocent of any *system* of knowing); the root for the word means "private," "own," "peculiar." Myshkin, then, as idiot, stands in for the isolated individual. In other words, he is *alone*, a would-be Christ figure who is denied the systematic time of *Heilsgeschichte*, a messiah who is a layman. He cannot have as an inhabitant of the novel-world that whole-part relationship that defines Christology, in which Jesus is a particular manifestation of the universal. Jesus' meaning is contained in the *telos* built into his biography; his life is lived toward resurrection, back toward his extra human, supra-individualistic state. The problem, on the other hand, for Myshkin is that he is only a subjectivity: his task is precisely to *find* a *telos*, to *achieve* a universality that can endow his particularity with meaning. Christ, by contrast, always exhibits the attributes of his role: he is the same yesterday today and forever, not only in his Godhood, but, for a believer, in his biography as a man as well. A Jesus who might, for example, be spiteful on occasion is unthinkable; he is always the same: supremely good. Thus he cannot serve as hero of a novel, the genre that more than any other flaunts variety in character, the rapidly shifting changes that dominate individual lives. Myshkin is saintly one moment, silly the next; now he is certain, now confused—and what is more, he *knows* there is no unity in his life.

When Keller, who has come to the Prince to unburden his soul, to confess and purge himself, admits that he has come *as well* to borrow 150 roubles, Myshkin recognizes this sincere desire for purity that is immediately undercut by a *no less* sincere desire to exploit others as a trait that defines the human condition. "You might have been telling me about myself just now . . . indeed . . . everyone is like that . . . for it is terribly difficult to fight against these double thoughts [*dvoinye mysli*]" (ii,xi). Double thoughts make unified sensibility, a non-dualistic identity particularly difficult to achieve. Myshkin may succeed in experiencing at one given moment a sense of wholeness, but the next moment will rob him of it. His attempt to live a unified existence is constantly exposed by the novel's relentless insistence on the multiplicity of identities that are merely human, merely personal.

III

Since the problem of identity is to find a common term for conflicting moments of plenitude and pettiness, self becomes a function of time, time that keeps going on, that will not stop, and that therefore continues to raise new contradiction, new knowledge of self, that must in its turn be integrated into a unity. A major expression of the dilemma is found in Myshkin's illness, epilepsy. There is a moment before the fit actually seizes him, "when suddenly amidst sadness, spiritual darkness and depression, his brain seemed to catch fire for brief moments. . . . His mind and heart were flooded by dazzling light. . . ." Myshkin senses not only that such a moment constitutes "the highest mode of existence" but that the special awareness such a moment grants him is awareness precisely of—self: ". . . the most direct sensation of one's own existence [remember that epilepsy is the sign of his idiocy] to the most intense degree" (ii,v).

But such a moment is followed, of course, by the onset of the fit. Although Myshkin says that he would give the rest of his life for the sake of his ecstatic second, suggesting parallels

112

with the Faustian temptation to say *"Verweile, doch, du bist so schön,"* he knows that such an option is denied him. He is constantly thrust back into a lower state, dramatized as convulsion. Using the parable of Mahomet's (another epileptic's) water pitcher to illustrate the most important aspect of what he feels at the onset of a fit, he adds, ". . . At that moment the extraordinary saying that *there shall be time no longer* becomes, somehow comprehensible." These words, taken of course from the Apocalypse of John, emphasize that the power of the moment expresses itself as timelessness. After it has passed, when the Prince lies grovelling on the ground in a helpless fit, when the falling sickness fells him, he collapses not only into epilepsy, but falls back into time again. Like Adam, he is cast out of Eden's eternal now into the flux of the world's becoming; or like Christ, who left the eternity of his godhood to fall into time as a mere mortal. The disease thus provides a metaphor for both aspects of the novel's key problematic: a feeling of wholeness that is then undercut, and the enormity of the distance between the two states, the unbridgeable space that constitutes the pain of time.

The constant collapse of privileged moment gives a special meaning to that other central metaphor of the book, the Apocalypse of St. John. It is present in Dostoevsky's text not because of the flaming end it prophesies. The horror consists rather in the discovery that there *are* no ends that give meaning, just as there are no beginnings. The terror is not that the Barbarians will come, but that they will not.

The cutoff that exists between moments that refuse to resolve themselves into a sequence is dramatized in *The Idiot* at different levels of narrative and in varying ratios of contradiction. The task in each stratum of plot and range of dissimilarity is to find terms appropriate to *particular* experiences, but that also, simultaneously, correspond to a general series. The problem is perhaps most familiar to historians, who must constantly answer the question: what is the proper perspective for explaining the relationships between events that are—in themselves—discrete, events that will seem, without such a view, unrelated? "Unfortunately, no law of history enjoins that only those years whose dates end with the figures '01' coincide with the critical points of human evolution. Whence there derive some curious distortions of meaning . . .[19] we appear to assign an arbitrarily chosen and strictly pendulum-like rhythm to realities to which such a regularity pattern is entirely alien."[20] The problem in the history of individual lives in *The Idiot* is that no essence can be found that will suffice to give shape to sequences that are therefore mere chronologies. Lives cannot be "periodized" because there is no point of view outside them to sanction the division of biographical eras.

The difficulty of finding a common term that will serve to connect otherwise discrete moments—conceived as an existential rather than historiographical dilemma—we have seen dramatized in the central metaphor of Myshkin's epilepsy: his inability to join health and illness, the moment of ecstacy that precedes his fits with the awful minutes he spends writhing on the ground in the grip of the epileptic attack itself. The unconsciousness he experiences between the onset of such fits and their aftermath is an epistemological as well as physical blackout, a symbol of his failure to find an identity that will connect the two experiences. There is no metaphysical copulative in the physical syntax of Myshkin's epilepsy.

The same pattern is present in the broken linearities that define biographical tasks for the other characters in *The Idiot*. The split between the "before" and "after" that Nastaysa Filipovna cannot connect is marked by her seduction. At the age of seven her father goes mad and she becomes the ward of Totsky, although he does not make any great changes in her life until, returning from a long sojourn abroad, he notices she has become "a lovely child . . . playful, charming, and intelligent, who promised to become an extraordinarily beautiful young woman" (i,iv). At this point Totsky puts the girl in the hands of a Swiss governess who teaches her French. While Swiss governesses were extremely common at this

[19] Marc Bloch, *The Historian's Craft*, tr. Peter Putnam (N.Y., Vintage Books, 1953), p. 182.
[20] *Ibid.*, p. 183.

time, the hint of Rousseau should not be missed, especially as the emphasis on a pedagogy oriented toward the simple, the natural, the Edenic, is taken up in the next step of Nastasya Filipovna's career as she is moved (after four years of such training) to another of Totsky's properties "in a more remote province," where she lives in a small wood house attended only by an old housekeeper and a maid. The house is filled with all the things to delight a young girl, and, in fact, the estate it is located on is called "as if on purpose [*kak naročno*] Otradnoe," a word that may be translated as joy or consolation, but that has as well, Edenic overtones.[21] It is while she is in this paradise that "Mr. Totsky himself put in an appearance. . . . Since then he seemed to have grown particularly fond of that remote little village in the heart of the steppes" (I,iv). The interval that Dostoevsky here marks with ". . ." is a typographical moment between Nastasya Filipovna's Edenic tick and the fallen tock of the remainder of her life. The full meaning of that break becomes apparent only when, as Totsky plans to marry a society woman, Nastasya Filipovna leaves the country and confronts her seducer in Petersburg: "Quite a different woman was sitting before him, a woman who was not at all like the girl he had known and had left in the village of Otradnoe only the previous July" (I,iv).

The Edenic parallel is pointed up later in the same chapter when it is said of Totsky, who is fearful that Nastasya Filipovna will not go along with his scheme to marry her off to Ganya Ivolgin, that he "did not quite believe her, even now, and was for a long time afraid that there might be a snake lurking beneath the flowers." This projection is one of the several inversions that mark relations between parents and children in *The Idiot*. The snake image is complicated further when it is recalled that the poem Nastasya Filipovna reads Rogozhin about Henry IV and Gregory VII is Heine's 1843 *Heinrich* (one of the significantly named series, *Zeitgedichte*).

[21] In fact, in some English versions it is translated as Eden, as in Magarshack, *The Idiot* (Penguin Books, 1955), p. 65. It should be added that *Otradnoe* was a fairly common name for country estates in nineteenth-century Russia. In *War and Peace*, for instance, the provincial seat of the Rostov family is also called *Otradnoe*.

The Gaps in Christology

In the poem, as the Emperor kneels before the Pope, he dreams of revenge, "an axe that will smite the serpent of my sufferings."[22] The association is doubled here: not only is an association of Rogozhin (and his knife) with Henry (and his axe) made, but Nastasya Filipovna's association with a long lost *Otradnoe* is present as well. The two major themes of their relationship—passion conceived as a power struggle, and the religious overtones of being a "fallen woman" (is she the cause of her own downfall, herself the serpent in her own Garden of Eden?), are both present in the Heine poem.

The rest of the five years remaining to Nastasya Filipovna after she leaves *Otradnoe* are spent not only in revenge, but in a frantic effort as well to recapture edenic time, to start afresh; failing to do so, she condemns herself to death, gives herself up to Rogozhin's knife. The search for a new point of origin that will efface her fall is best observed in the scandal scene that concludes the novel's first book. It occurs significantly on her name-day (she will gain the name of her true self), celebrated, of course, as her birthday (she will be born again). When Myshkin proposes to her she cries, "Oh, life is only beginning for me now!" And then abjuring the sequence inherent in a future shared with the Prince, she accepts Rogozhin, again stressing that she will start afresh. "I've spent ten years [since her seduction] behind prison bars and now it is my turn to be happy!" The scene ends as she dashes off into the night, having sloughed off her house and servants like the skin of another self, as she screams she will become a washerwoman or streetwalker (I,xvi). Of course she, like Myshkin, finds that her moment of decision does *not* serve to change the logic of the life she has sought to break out of (her prison, as she says).

There are many other parallels between her biography and that of the Prince, which is why Dostoevsky so laboriously points up at each of their meetings the sense they share of hav-

[22] The source for the quotation has been cited in: V. E. Xolševnikov, "O literaturnyx citatax u Dostoevskogo," *Vestnik leningradskogo universiteta*, 1960, No. 8 (Serija istorii, jazyka, i literatury), Vyp. 2, p. 136.

116

ing known each other *before* their first encounter. Both are orphans of ancient families, both have spent time in the country (he in Switzerland, she with a Swiss governess, both in a Rousseauistic state of innocence), and both regret being drawn into society. We learn of the Prince, as he stands amid the schemes that circle about him, that he has "an uncontrollable desire to leave everything here and go back to where he had come from, to some far-away solitary place. . . . He had a feeling that if he stayed here even a few days longer he would irrevocably be drawn into this world, and that this world would become his world thereafter" (II,xi). Myshkin is, in other words, afraid of falling into worldliness, and of course this is what happens as he becomes the center, the effective *cause*, of the intrigues that swirl in the rest of the novel, a condition for which his epilepsy—as a falling sickness—is the book's major metaphor.

Nastasya Filipovna's closeness to the Prince is underlined by her status as a "fallen woman," as, from the faraway place of her innocence and childhood, she plunges deeper and deeper into the world. She sees herself as a "fallen angel" (IV,viii) and constantly looks back to the past, an existential nostalgia that Dostoevsky emphasizes by constantly associating her with history. In the novel's most sustained and detailed account of her relations with Rogozhin (II,iii,iv) she tells the story of Henry IV's struggle with Pope Gregory VII ("You, sir haven't studied universal history, have you?"); there is also frequent mention of S. M. Solovyov's (the father of Dostoevsky's friend, the philosopher V. M. Solovyov) history, that Nastasya Filipovna has given Rogozhin to read. The significance of this choice consists first of all in its full title: *The History of Russia from the Most Ancient Times*. This is *her* iconic book just as *Don Quixote* is Myshkin's; it seeks to go back to the most primal origins, as she does. It also points to the crux of her problem, the difficulty of erecting continuous identity; just as Russia is orphan of the nations, so Nastasya Filipovna cannot find valid antecedents, as becomes clear in Dostoevsky's play with the history book and murder weapon.

117

As Rogozhin concludes his account of what happened to Nastasya Filipovna after she runs away from her name-day party with him, Myshkin picks up a knife lying on the table before him (II,iii). Twice Rogozhin takes it away from him, and yet the Prince picks it up a third time:

"Rogozhin seized it angrily, put it in the book, and threw the book [Solovyov's *History*] onto another table.

" 'Do you cut the pages with it?' asked the Prince, but rather absent-mindedly as though still too preoccupied with his thoughts.

" 'Yes, the pages . . .'

" 'It's a garden knife [*sadovy no ž'*], isn't it?'

" 'Yes, it's a garden knife. Can't one cut pages with a garden knife?' "

Rogozhin will kill her with this garden knife; but its first sheath is a history book—unfinished by Rogozhin (he has not cut all its pages). Thus it is that Nastasya Filipovna's death will come from the interrupted history of Russia. Long before the end of her life, *its* history had been interrupted by Totsky's seduction. Her constant attempts to "begin life anew" constitute a pattern of jerky biographical gestures that will not fall into a connected series, a history. She never succeeds in recapturing *otradnoe*, and so the two parts of her life are as marked off from each other as the opened versus the as-yet-uncut pages of the copy of Solovyov she gives Rogozhin. The reason for so radical a split in her biography is that she attaches a transcendent significance to her existence before the seduction: like the open pages of the book, it was full of meaning. On the other hand, the years after the seduction are as meaningless as the closed, still unread, uncut pages of that book. The inability to overcome this gap drives her on to ever more hysterical attempts to wipe out the *otradnoe* origin with a new beginning, until, in despair, she gives herself to Rogozhin's knife—a Garden-of-Eden knife that separates the open and closed pages of a history book. Like all the other characters, major and minor, in the novel, Nastasya Filipovna is cut off from the past, and as de Tocqueville, student of that other country that, like Russia, had an ambiguous history, wrote: "Since the past has ceased to throw its light upon the future, the mind of man wonders in obscurity."[23]

The darkness of the past is dramatized in *The Idiot* as the absence of true parents. This is why the parallel between individual biographies and Russian national history is so close in Dostoevsky: in each case the problem is to create a continuity without the benefit of antecedents. The problem of forging a continuous identity, connecting past and present in any given individual life, is exacerbated by the cutoff between past and present in the sequence of generations. The three major figures of the novel—Myshkin, Rogozhin, and Nastasya Filipovna—are all fatherless. The other characters must all in their own way confront the failure of the fathers. Burdovsky discovers he is not Pavlishchev's son, but he is able to be his mother's son, a consolation denied to Ipolit, who dreams of disowning (*otkazat'sja ot*) his mother (his father is dead) and going off to live with Kolya Ivolgin, who will also give up *his* family (I,xxi).[24] Aglaya, the center of the family for all the Epanchins, disowns her parents in the end by running off with a phoney Polish nobleman and converting to Roman Catholicism—in Dostoevsky's world, a fate worse than death.

The collapse of bridges between generations is marked in *The Idiot* by the failure of material inheritance. It will be remembered that money, which plays so enormous a role in the novel, always comes from the wills of a dead generation. Nastasya Filipovna's father dies in poverty, but leaves her to the guardianship of Totsky (who, as surrogate parent, leaves a sinister legacy indeed to his adopted child). Burdovsky

[23] Quoted in: Hannah Arendt, *Between Past and Future* (New York, Viking Press, 1961), p. 7.

[24] The old general is the most sustained example of the failure of the fathers. His constant insistence that he is related to those with whom he shares no blood, or that he knew other characters when they were still babies (hoping to signify, as with Myshkin, a connection between the generations), points to the debasement of such connections. Ivolgin is also important in the degree to which he points up the parallel between the two levels of past/present cutoff Dostoevsky is here working with, the generational (personal) and historical (national): he seeks to create the same specious connections between himself and Napoleon as he does with Myshkin.

seeks to establish the identity of his father in order to gain a part of his inheritance (II,iv); his problem is that of all the other characters: to discover the identity of his true parents. He differs from the others only in that he succeeds where they fail. Myshkin discovers his inheritance (135,000 rubles as we learn in IV,v) amounts to much *less* than had been anticipated (II,ix). Radomsky, instead of receiving his uncle's enormous fortune, is saddled with only his shame; the old man shoots himself after squandering thousands of rubles in public funds (III,ii). It is, of course, at a crucial point in Radomsky's career (he has just resigned his commission), that the awful truth is revealed—by that profound student of the consequences that flow from ambiguous legacies, Nastasya Filipovna.

Rogozhin's relationship to his dead father is especially complex. The father "had a great respect for the *Skopcy*," a sect of fanatical Orthodox Christians who castrate themselves (II,iii). Nastasya Filipovna (in the same chapter) says of the son that, "you'd have settled in this house, like your father, with those *Skopcy* . . . you'd have been converted to their faith in the end . . . ," a parallel that brings out the sterility of both generations. The father's sexless passion is the accumulation of wealth for its own sake. And while at first glance it would appear that the son's passion for Nastasya Filipovna is sexual, it soon becomes clear that it is actually another genus of greed. He is a miser who takes very seriously the grim joke of Nastasya Filipovna's sale of herself to the highest bidder in the auction that concludes the first book of the novel. Having bought her, he seeks to hoard her—because she possesses him. Unlike others in the novel, Rogozhin comes into his father's money, and the sum is as great as had been anticipated; but its effects are as calamitous as the failure of the others to collect their inheritance.

All the attempts to smuggle something across the border of generations fail, another of the novel's symbols for the condition of discontinuity. As Hannah Arendt has written in the title essay of *Between Past and Future*, "The testament telling the heir what will be rightfully his, wills past possession for a future. Without testament or, to resolve the metaphor, without tradition—which selects and names, which hands down and preserves, which indicates where the treasures are and what their worth is—there seems to be no willed continuity in time. . . ."[25] The absence of such a pattern is central to the whole fabric of the novel, dramatized in a wide range of discontinuities, each of which has its symbolic condition: execution, epilepsy, seduction. To this list of fractures in identity we must now add that of the failed inheritance.

Money plays so important a role in the novel because of its status as a metaphor for exchange, a potential means of communication, as something that passes between people—or in wills—between generations. Money is significant as a system of conventional markers for value. What is more, unless there is *agreement* as to its value, it is worthless. There is a sense in which money is nothing more than a symbol of values that can be exchanged between people who may differ on all other matters. There can be no solipsism in economics; like words, money brooks no Carollian Humpty Dumptys who would insist that a coin is worth what they say it is. This is one of the reasons why money constantly crops up in semiotics and linguistics. Saussure, for instance, uses it as a metaphor for a fundamental operation of language itself: "To determine what a five-franc piece is worth one must . . . know: (1) that it can be exchanged for a fixed quantity of a different thing, e.g., bread; and (2) that it can be compared with a similar value of the same system, e.g., a one-franc piece, or with coins of a different system (a dollar, etc). In the same way a word can be exchanged for something dissimilar, an idea; besides it can be compared with something of the same nature, another word."[26]

But in *The Idiot* the generation of the fathers has not passed on to the sons those principles by which the worth of things

---

[25] Hannah Arendt, *op.cit.*, p. 5.

[26] Ferdinand de Saussure, *Course in General Linguistics*, tr. Wade Baskin (New York, McGraw-Hill, 1966), p. 115. See also: Charles S. Peirce, "How to Make our Ideas Clear," *Philosophical Writings of Peirce*, ed. Justus Buchler (New York, Dover, 1955), p. 27, for a further turn on money (nickels versus five pennies) as a metaphor for decision-making that will involve doubt and belief.

may be determined. There is no common ground for value; thus money has the opposite effect from that of exchange. It serves instead as a symbol for the rupture between generations. It marks that bottomless canyon that "inheritance" has failed to bridge.[27] The inability of generations to transmit value from past to future is an extension of a pattern we have seen in the lives of the individual characters. They, too, cannot connect their own pasts and futures. In the lives of most of them there is a failure to sustain any of those moments which seem to define identity: Myshkin cannot will his moment of heightened awareness to his own future; thus he falls from ecstasy into epilepsy. Nastasya Filipovna falls from Eden into the world; Ipolit from a suicidal moment that would give his life significance to a "bad death" from a wasting disease. In these and other cases the future robs of its significance a past that was felt somehow to be privileged.

I V

The major symbol clusters of the novel—execution, the Holbein Christ, epilepsy, Don Quixote, money—swirl around a core that is common to them all: the failure of *kairos* to effect *chronos*. There is no wholeness that will remain unsplintered throughout its unfolding in time: the man who promises to change his life if not executed in the next second, continues—when spared—to lead the same existence as before, the meaninglessness of which was clear from the vantage point of that exalted moment before the firing squad (I,ii). The promise of Christ's life is denied in the painting of his death: the cycle of biological time is unbroken. The prince's moment of lucid self-awareness is wiped out in the epileptic fit that follows it. All the money, all the inheritances lead to a cutoff between past and present. No essence can withstand the battering of the moments as they pass by. The

[27] The disconnectedness of generations is one of Dostoevsky's on-going preoccupations throughout his life, leading (in his last years) to a fascination with the peculiar ideas of N. F. Fyodorov, who believed sons should work to raise—physically—their fathers from the dead. We will touch on Fyodorov in more detail in our final chapter.

structure of a single moment's promise broken under the onslaught of a series of other such moments following upon it, constitutes the novel's central pattern. Its most paradigmatic expression is in the failure of *Heilsgeschichte*: Christ did not change the course of history; his promise of peace has been eroded by all the wars ever since. It is the collapse of this messianic legacy in the past that underlies all the other failed testaments from father to son in the book. Without the Christian inheritance, at a time when the *imitatio Christi* breaks down, each man must find his own way, seek his own identity without the aid of preexisting models. He must, in other words, become an idiot in the root sense of that word—someone on his own.

Chapter 5

The Biography of Legion:
The Possessed

The Idiot ends in a Swiss asylum; *The Possessed*, Dostoevsky's next novel, concludes with two notes from that already dead citizen of the canton of Uri, Nicholas Stavrogin. Silence of madness, silence of suicide—so end novels that take their shape from characters unable to find coherent stories for themselves. The discontinuity of identity is in both cases dramatized as a temporal rupture, but a different kind of cutoff in time defines the conditions of each dilemma.

The Idiot is a catalogue of lapsed conversions, the constant devolution of inspired moments into meaningless sequences: Myshkin experiences ecstatic illumination and then falls into convulsions. In order to achieve a continuous self he seeks to weld vertical, unchanging time to the time of flux, the horizontal series of moment that ground his day-to-day existence. Failure to connect the two times, and the realities they ground, leads to madness.

Stavrogin's case is different: underlying his polarized selfhood is the opposition between historical progression, on the one hand, and logical series, on the other. The former implies development; yesterday, today, and tomorrow are interrelated by an evolution in the perceiving subject. Logical series, however, invoke "a kind of simultaneity, as in a sequence such as prevails among the parts of a syllogism, where the argument proceeds from the first premise, *through* the second premise, to the conclusion, *but not in a temporal sense*."[1]

The first sequence assumes becoming: I gradually learn who I am as the sum of actions performed between birth and death. Such a concept of temporal development conceives variety as a kind of freedom in the sense that I might have performed any one of several actions at any given point in my

---

[1] Kenneth Burke, *The Rhetoric of Religion* (Berkeley and Los Angeles, U. of California Press, 1970 [paperback ed.]), pp. 31-32. Emphasis added.

biography. In the end the sum of all these decisions will have constituted an identity that is uniquely mine: I am the shape of all my actions. Something like this assumption prevails in the self-definitions worked out by the majority of characters in *The Possessed*. Stravrogin, however, sees such identities as based on a deception, the precisely *self*-serving notion of an ego free to make choices the history of which will ultimately make it known. He conceives another and far less optimistic possibility. What if biography were shaped, not by actions freely chosen "from within," but rather by forces from without, such as the laws of biology or economy, extra-subjective systems with rules of their own? Biography in such a view would not be a process of becoming but simply the working out of patterns whose sequence was *already* immanent in the structure of, for example, the biological conditions of human physiology.

Stravrogin is thus similar to that other very "fancy and most sophisticated machine" who suspects he "is at the entire mercy of the input fed into him from a world impervious to his desire—the underground man: ". . . science itself will teach man . . . that as a matter of fact he possesses neither will nor uncontrollable desires . . . that he is nothing more than a sort of piano key or organ stop and that, in addition, these are the laws of nature and the world, so that whatever he does is not done of his own will at all, but is done of itself according to the laws of nature . . . as soon as these laws are discovered man will no longer have to answer for his actions . . . all human actions will then, no doubt, be computed according to these laws, mathematically, something like the tables of logarithms, up to 108,000 and indexed accordingly."[2]

Both Stavrogin and the underground man suffer from a trauma brought on by the discovery of structure, structure that stands over against psychology, which has no time in the sense of becoming. A convenient example of structural sequence may be seen in the operation of computers: they appear to work very rapidly, faster, it is significant to note, than the human brain, which depends on *developmental* thinking,

[2] *Polnoe*, Vol. 5, pp. 112-13.

because each time a computer is asked a question it effects a simultaneity not a duration. That is, it simply puts a formula for extracting an answer into contact with data that *already contains* the answer, but that will reveal it only to a question whose appropriateness, whose correctness, will be judged according to the criteria of the whole program, criteria that predate any specific operation. Thus the importance of programming in cybernetics, a priority expressed in the antic warning often printed at the head of read-outs, GIGO, shorthand for "Garbage in, garbage out," meaning that the output of the fanciest and most sophisticated machine is at the entire mercy of the input fed into it.[3]

Thus the answer does not grow or become; it simply, at a particular point, makes itself known, although it has been there from the beginning. It is a system, a structure, in the degree to which it is a logical series not a temporal unfolding. It is this logical kind of sequence that Stravogin fears may represent the determinants of his biography, rather than willed expressions of his own subjectivity, each of which expressions would then become a date on the calendar of his historical progress to selfhood.

The conflict between structure and history (the opposition of synchrony and diachrony, as it has come to be called) has recently emerged as the major dilemma for all the "sciences of man." Dostoevsky explores the implications of structure, the potential anti-humanism that disturbs so many opponents of the various Structuralisms now abroad. What is remarkable is that he should do so in a novel, that form which more than any other seems grounded in subjectivity and becoming. The biography of an individual comes closer to being the form shared by most novels, even when they otherwise have very little in common. In *The Possessed* Dostoevsky writes a new chapter in the history of the novel as a genre by putting the existence of individuality to question, just as he will in other

[3] Pierre Maranda, "Computers in the Bush: Tools for Automatic Analysis of Myth," *Essays on the Verbal and Visual Arts* (proceedings of 1966 annual spring meeting of the American Ethnological Society), ed. June Helm (Seattle and London, U. of Washington Press, 1967), p. 77.

novels put the existence of God into doubt. That is, Dostoevsky, by meditating individualism in this way, puts into question the humanism that has been one of the novel's most defining predicates.

Just as there was a Copernican revolution in the sixteenth century that robbed man of his central place in the universe, so it now increasingly appears there was a similarly decentering, if more diffuse, revolution in the nineteenth century. Such newly evolved disciplines as economics, linguistics, and sociology were based on a prejudice in favor of groups, the behavior of which could be studied scientifically (such and such a percentage of the population in France can be predicted to commit suicide next year) as opposed to individuals (but it is impossible to say of *this* man that he will kill himself). Just as the Copernican revolution led to a great search for physical laws in the seventeenth century, so the growing recognition that individuals were unavailable to "scientific" study (they could not—as individuals—be domesticated to predictability) has led to a search for laws in the social sciences.[4] This crisis in humanism—the suspicion that individualism may have been another reassuring myth of the kind that gave rise to earth-centered cosmologies—is reflected first in the underground man, but most fully developed in Stavrogin. They both share the suspicion that biography is more a logical than a temporal progression, a mere filling out of patterns that pre-exist the life of any given individual. But there are important differences in the way each resists the pain engendered by such a suspicion.

The author of the "Notes" retreats to an underground where desire may spin its narrative webs uninhibited, unchecked by the contending will of other persons or the brute ineluctability of outside forces. Fearing to be a mere part, a piano key among other piano keys, and—even worse, if his metaphor is pursued—to be manipulated by a yet *greater* other, he seeks to escape the keyboard of determinism. He at-

[4] See, *The Structuralist Controversy: The Languages of Criticism and the Sciences of Man*, ed. Richard Macksey, Eugenio Donato (Baltimore, Maryland, Johns Hopkins Press, 1970).

tempts to do this by establishing the validity of the part he conceives himself to be by severing it from the whole, cutting it away from the others with the blade of story. He resorts to a passive strategy in his duel with all that is not himself: he creates the illusion of manipulating the world according to his own desires by manipulating stories. He reveals a metaphysical dimension in what otherwise would be mere daydreaming.

Stavrogin does just the opposite. He *lives* his lust for uniqueness. He is the active principal of that hyperconsciousness broached in the underground man, who says, "All man needs is absolutely free choice [*samostojatel'noe xoten'je*], no matter what that freedom may cost or where it may lead him" (v,113). But such belief does not take the underground man very far: merely into other stories. The dichotomy Sartre has voiced in his dictum, "You must choose, live or tell," is neatly marked off, then, in the contrast between the underground man and Stavrogin: the former only tells, whereas the latter acts out his singularity by attempting to subvert the others themselves. The "themselves" being, of course, the other characters in the novel.

Instead of babbling on, as does the underground man, the teller—Stavrogin, the doer—is notably silent. While he is regarded by everyone in the novel as a phenomenon, someone remarkable, a being possessed of great and mysterious power, he never *says* anything particularly noteworthy in his own voice. Rather, in the characteristic scenes of the novel he sits mutely while some Peter Verkhovensky (". . . you wrote the rules yourself, so there is no need to explain" [II,6]) or Shatov ("I was the pupil and you were the teacher" [II,i]) or Kirilov ("Go look at [Kirilov] now—he's your creation" [II,i]) repeats back to him what he himself has *already* said on some previous occasion, something that changed the lives of those who were then his auditors. He need not tell who he is because all the others do it for him.

The nature of this distinctive relationship between Stavrogin and the other characters in the novel is what accounts for many of the formal properties that are peculiar to it in the

Dostoevsky canon. This should become quickly evident if we translate what is otherwise Stavrogin's metaphysical dilemma into the more immediately "literary" terms of plot and character. The plot, in the sense of *story*, in the novel is a fabric of various plots, in the sense of *conspiracy*, and thus all the characters are caught in a multiple web of exterior forces. They act out Stavrogin's suspicion that logical progression determines biography insofar as they reduce their selves to mere subfunctions of other characters, as do all those who knowingly follow one of Stavrogin's various leads, or who unwittingly submit to Peter Verkhovensky's machinations. Or they abandon the quest for radically unique identities by giving themselves over to a religious or political ideology, whose value is conceived to be that it is "bigger than myself," such as those to which Kirilov and Shatov surrender, but that also ultimately derive from Stavrogin. In either case they cease to develop from within as they divest themselves of the freedom Stavrogin conceives necessary to becoming. The existential nexus of self and other is dramatized by Dostoevsky in the architectonic relationship of character to plot.

What is the ratio between the two, the whole of the plot and the part—in the systematic as well as theatrical sense of that word—of any character in it? In Dostoevsky's previous work the ratio appears to be one in which character is primary. It is character precisely that determines plot in the sense that the actions of the narrative as a global unit correspond in their outline to the narrative progression that articulates the major protagonist. The slice of his biography we are given constitutes in itself the essential movement of the plot as a whole. Such characters can be told. Texts of the sort we have in *Notes from the Underground* or *Crime and Punishment* are dominated by one protagonist to the relative exclusion of other characters, a thematic reason for the *Icherzahlung* of the former, and of the latter as well until its pronouns were "shifted" to the third person in its penultimate draft. The underground man's stories or Raskolnikov's strivings seem to fix the ideational shape and formal properties of works that do not contain them so much as exist co-extensively with them.

129

If, in such works, it may be said that character is plot, then the narrative distinctiveness of *The Possessed* may be grasped by adding that in *it* the order of priorities is reversed and plot is character. This is not a mere play on words, as I hope to show by examining the thematic significance of such a structural inversion as it is present in the relation of Stavrogin to other characters in the novel.

In order to do this, we must begin by recognizing that the characters of the novel can all be assigned to one of two groupings. First, those who have experienced fundamental changes in their personalities *before* the action of the novel begins, but who nevertheless continue to change or have at least one more epiphany to experience in the present action of the novel. This group is the smaller of the two and comprises only Stepan Trofimovich and Stavrogin, the novel's two originating figures. A second and much larger group, comprising virtually all the other characters, has also experienced a radical conversion of one sort or another in the past, but the character that emerged from such an experience is the personality they *still* have in the novel's present.

The structure of the novel is essentially that of a temporal palimpsest; the few days in August during which the literary fête, murder of Shatov, death of Lisa and Stepan Trofimovich, take place, as well as the suicide of Kirilov—these constitute the present action of the novel, make up the narrative surface of the main plot. But just beneath it, constantly erupting through it, is the past action of all the characters who comprise the cast of the novel's present. There is a constant counterpoint between events that take place during that August in the capital city of the province containing the Stavrogin estate, and events that took place earlier in other places, such as St. Petersburg, Geneva, or even America, where Shatov and Kirilov spend three months together. The novel's first line is: "Before describing the extraordinary events which took place in our town . . . I find it necessary . . . to go back a little and begin with certain biographical details concerning Stepan Trofimovich Verkhovensky." This is the temporal recipe for the whole novel: its "extraordinary events" are conceived as the final act of dramas begun much earlier; in order to understand present actions you must know the past, the biographies, of those characters who perform them.

The two times of the novel's plot, its *Voregeschichte* and its narrative present, contain within them another two times, those I have alluded to above as logical sequence and historical becoming. The before/after contrast that gives the novel its essentially palimpsest structure dramatizes the difference between those characters who in the past took upon themselves an identity that is still operative in the present—and who therefore have become static selves, subfunctions of the belief system that gave rise to the conversion—and those other characters who continue to change within the present. The plot's before/after indicators serve as marks on the clock of selfhood, the test for whether or not development of identity has ceased in the case of any given character.

Since "identity" is such a vexed and modish concept, let me be more specific about what is meant by the word as it is used in what follows. The concept of identity, as Harold Rosenberg, among others, has suggested, implies that, "in the realm of action the multiple incidents in the life of an individual may be synthesized . . . into a scheme that pivots on a single fact judged to be central to the individual's existence and which, governing his behavior and deciding his fate, becomes part of his definition, though it is external to him. Here unity of being becomes one of unity of 'plot' . . . religious conversion supplies the most complete example, though it is only an example. Through conversion the individual gains an identity which revolves upon a fact which is both private in its unifying effect upon him yet extra-personal in its relation to his world. . . ."[5] The identity thus gained "repeats itself to the satisfaction of [a presumed] external judgment, symbolized by a role, and unaffected by any possibility of organic transformation."[6]

---

[5] "Character Change and the Drama," *Modern Literary Criticism*, ed. Irving Howe (Boston, Beacon Press, 1958), p. 78.

[6] Rosenberg, p. 79.

At more or less specific points in the past, each of *The Possessed*'s characters has taken on such a homogenizing identity. The more central a role the character plays, the more definite we can be as to when and how his conversion was effected. In the case of the minor conspirators such as Liputin, Virginsky, or Shigalyov we know only that at some point in the past they became utopian socialists of one sort or another. Less important than the particular brand of utopianism that characterizes each is the ideological rigor mortis of them all: Liputin, who reads Considérant and who "was a fierce believer in God-knows-what future 'social harmony,' who at night gloated ecstatically over fantastic visions of a future phalanstery"; Shigalyov, who says "I submit to you my own system of world organization . . . there can be no solution of the social formula other than mine . . . everything I say in my book is irrefutable, there is no other solution." And so on.

These characters do not *act* in the novel's present so much as continue merely to work out predictable patterns of behavior that are encoded in the ideology to which they gave themselves in the novel's *Vorgeschichte*. In the moment they surrendered to system—a system moreover devoted to eradication of individuality—they ceased to grow as person. Their conversion moment was the point at which, if we may once again invoke our image of the computer, they were programmed: all their subsequent actions then became mere simultaneities of a particular moment's exigency and a predetermined response to it that was already there in the original data. Such characters are not free personalities but mere role inhabitors working out the logic of functions assumed in the past. Vis-à-vis their "conversion," these characters live posthumously, where living is understood as the continuing process of a potential that becomes. Plot, in the double sense of Dostoevsky's narrative and their own designs, fix who, or what, such characters are.

The stasis that characterizes them is present as well in their own plots for everyone else. That is, those characters who have ceased to develop all have schemes for causing the *world* to cease developing. The case of Shigalyov is most obvious here: "Starting from unlimited freedom, I arrived at unlimited despotism," which means that when nine-tenths of humanity have been turned into something like a herd, history will cease, flux will have congealed into a collective stasis. Paradise on earth, to use his own phrase, will have been achieved, and there will be no more changes because they would necessarily be devolutions from a perfection so complete. As in the original paradise that Shigalyov promises his system will restore, there will be no time. "He looked as though he expected the end of the world not at some indefinite time . . . but with absolute precision—say the day after tomorrow, at exactly half-past ten" [I,iv].

This same tendency toward induced apocalypse is even more apparent in Kirilov. He is a kind of tragic Pangloss who believes, "Man is unhappy because he doesn't know that he's happy . . . all is good . . . He who blows his brains out for the [sake of a little girl who's been raped], that's good . . . [II,i]. And he who *doesn't* blow his brains out, that's good, too." In his insane logic it follows that "when all mankind achieves happiness, there will be no more time. . . ." He further decides that the example of his "freely" determined suicide will create just such a moment of happiness for all men, thus, *ipso facto*, time is about to cease: "He who teaches that all are good [as Kirilov does] will bring about the end of the world." And like Shigalyov, who knows to the minute when the world will end, Kirilov, too, is characterized by extremely precise calculations of time. At a merely physiological level he is able to awake at whatever hour he chooses before falling asleep: "I know how to get up when I *want* to. I go to bed and say to myself: 'At seven o'clock' and I wake up at seven o'clock; 'at ten o'clock,' and I wake up at ten o'clock."

But this control over time he is able to exercise within his own body he wishes to project onto the world at large. This confusion about the power of Kirilov's subjectivity to effect history is best seen in his attempt to make the time pattern forced upon him by his epilepsy a normative chronology for mankind in general. In order to see how this works it will be helpful to remember yet another example of Kirilov's preternatural sensitivity to time. When Stavrogin asks, "When did you find out you were so happy?" Kirilov gives the remarkable answer, "Last week . . . on Wednesday . . . during the night . . . I stopped the clock. It was twenty-three minutes to three." Such an act, whose ritual character is pointed up when Stavrogin says, "As a symbol that time must stop?" becomes comprehensible if we keep in mind that Kirilov's root obsession is to extend the moment of intense joy he feels just before the onset of one of his epileptic fits. Kirilov seeks not just to stop time, but to maintain the ecstasy he is granted for short seconds "once or twice every three months." He says, "There are moments, you reach moments, and time comes to a sudden stop, and it will become eternal" [II,i].

The pattern we have suggested as the key to the distinctiveness of *The Possessed*, the relationship between two kinds of time, one static, one of becoming, is best schematized in Kirilov. He is possessed by a dream of universal harmony outside time, a dream whose ideology supplants personality. He is as much a subfunction of his essentially religious scheme as the political conspirators are puppets of theirs. In the case of both there is no more becoming, a personal trait they erect into manifestos, all of which assign their highest value to stasis.

Such characters are obsessed with the task of saving themselves, but they seek to accomplish this by saving others. The concern of earlier characters, such as Myshkin, to extend a personal epiphany becomes in the later work a drive to realize a utopian vision. A problem that had been dramatized in almost exclusively psychological terms (the self) now takes on a political aspect as well (the others). The possessed fail to distinguish between their own fate, and that of all the others, between parts and whole, thus relations between them become inevitably political, but a form of politics that constantly collapses into a wild utopianism beyond the possibility of statecraft. The sense of such an earlier Dostoevskian character as Raskolnikov that there was too *little* system in his life (therefore he had to originate his own) is dramatized in *The Possessed* as a concern for too much system. Too much in the sense that the various schemes by which the characters who are possessed are cathected, over-determined, have a kind of voraciousness in that they insist on incorporating *everything* and *everyone* else into them.

The plot of each character has its own internal coherence, but in order for that coherence to maintain its fragile logic no changes, nothing *new*, can be permitted to enter it. Thus others must always be seen as already part, or potential parts, of the system of such selves, which is why so much emphasis is put on the question of who invents whom. Two examples of this should suffice. It is said that Mrs. Stavrogin invents Stepan Trofimovich: "She had invented him, and she had been the first to believe in her own invention. He was, in a way, a sort of dream of hers . . ." [I,i]. And Peter Verkhovensky, after abasing himself to Stavrogin, ". . . You are my sun, I am your worm . . ." then screams, however, "I invented you while I was abroad . . ." [VIII,viii].

Such statements point to the typical relation of the novel's protagonists to each other: *essentially that of an author to the characters he invents.* The question then becomes, as Peter's ambivalence about Stavrogin (as his idol, on the one hand, and his creature, on the other) suggests: are you part of *my* scheme, a figure in my plot, or am I a character in *yours?* And of course the central event in *The Possessed*'s present action is Peter's attempt to make sure that everyone keeps his place as a character in Peter's plot, from Von Lembke the governor— whose novel Peter symbolically appropriates (takes over Von Lembke's authorial powers)—to Fedka the convict. He is a much better author than Karmazinov, which is why Peter is quicker than the others to suspect that worth's pretensions. He gets Karmazinov to believe in *his* scenario: "I promised Karmazinov to start [the revolution] in May and finish by the first of October [VIII,viii]. Once again the propensity of those characters like Shigalyov and Kirilov, who have ceased to unfold in time, always to know *exact* dates and hours, can be seen in Peter's revolutionary calendar. But, more importantly, Peter's possession of Karmazinov emphasizes the superiority of Peter's inventions, which is why he emphasizes the *aes-*

thetic side of his conspiracy, his plot: "I love beauty. I am a nihilist, but I love beauty" [VIII,viii].

We have up to this point considered only one of the two groups of characters in *The Possessed*, those who experienced conversions in the period preceding the present action of the novel, who are in that present what they had already become. Each has a system to which he has given himself, an act of surrender marked by a crossing over from one time, individual becoming, to another, the purely logical sequence that defines each of the character's various systems, whether political or religious. For such characters, as we have seen, the clock of self has effectively stopped, which is why they can always be so precise about chronology. It remains only to stop the clock of the others, a desire to arrest time whose full intensity is caught in Kirilov's final moment, when he screams "Now"—ten times ["*Sejčas, sejčas, sejčas, sejčas . . . 'Raz desjat'* "] [III,vi].

There are, however, two characters who live a different temporality, both of whom continue to evolve within the novel's present, Stepan Trofimovich Verkhovensky and Stavrogin.

Stepan Trofimovich enters the novel as a caricature, a humbug who practices his "spontaneous" gestures before a mirror and who chooses his clothes for theatrical effect. He seems to belong to the camp of the ideologues. Indeed, it is he who has the Bible seller read the parable of the Gadarene swine from which the books get its epigraph and title. He even speculates, just before his death, that ". . . perhaps I [was] at the head of all . . ." the possessed characters, "Peter *et les autres avec lui*" [III,vii]. Like them, his life came to a halt in the past at a point where he gave himself up to systemic time, in this case the cloudy idealism of the Russian 1840's, whose muddled mix of Fourier, Feuerbach, Hegel, Schelling, and Schiller is parodied in the play Stepan Trofimovich writes, a play "circulated in manuscript among two literary dilettantes and one student," that has singing insects, even singing minerals, and that concludes when Jehovah runs off while athletes complete the Tower of Babel. For the last twenty years Ver-

136

khovensky has languished in the provinces, "a living monument of reproach," who lets it be thought he is in exile and under police surveillance as a consequence of his advanced views. He gives up an evolving biography insofar as *whatever* the time, for him it is still the 1840's. Even the dilletantish nature of his liberalism is a function of the identity he derives wholesale from that decade notorious in Russian intellectual history for its ideological poseurs, its inflated rhetoric, and political indolence, all of which are caught very nicely in Stepan Trofimovich's propensity for discussing over oysters and champagne, the oppression of the masses or his habit of concealing risqué French novels under heavy tomes of political economy. The 1840's have a very definite personality in the Russian tradition, and it is that personality which defines Stepan Trofimovich. His is not so much a life as it is a decade. He is similar to the other possessed of the novel not only in his arrested chronology but in the manner in which the implied relationship between plot and character in his life determines his relationship to others. Stepan Trofimovich's authorial role is explicitly that of playwright, as the cosmic drama with the chorus of minerals suggests. He is the author of that melodrama-become-farce he has succeeded in producing with the help of Madame Stavrogin as his angel, and the claret-sipping, whist-playing members of his club as cast. No wonder, then, that he has the physical appearance of the hack Kukolnik, author of patriotic melodramas.

But once all this has been said, it must be added that Stepan Trofimovich differs radically from all the novel's other possessed characters in that he switches from one plot to another. He is forced to live through an unexpected reversal and recognition scene in the tragi-comedy of his own biography, whose plot, which seemed to have long been over, concludes instead with a surprise ending. The schematic role played by the disavowal of his former life (which is specifically called a conversion [*on uveroval*]) in the architechtonics of the book is underscored by its appearance in the terminal scenes of the novel proper, the last act before the conclusion. By this time Shatov is murdered, Kirilov dead, the conspirators under arrest or fled—all the novel's various utopias have collapsed. At just that point, Stepan Trofimovich sets off on his last pilgrimage toward his second conversion, the only one that occurs in the present action of the novel.

Stepan Trofimovich stands out from the novel's other characters not only because he is the only one to experience a second epiphany that is specifically called a conversion: the specific form this rejection of his former life takes makes it a commentary on all the other lives in the book. We need not dwell on the obvious use to which he puts the parable of the Gadarene swine—which is Dostoevsky at his most didactic and mechanical. We might rather examine the time/space symbolism of the novel's penultimate chapter, which is called "Stepan Trofimovich's Last Pilgrimage [*stranstvovanie*]," a title that indicates the importance of such symbols. What happens is that after years of immobility, trapped in the quagmire of that existence forced on him by his first conversion to the cloudy doctrines of the 1840's, Stepan Trofimovich gets moving again. Throughout his wandering there are inserted little hymns to the larger meaning of the road, as for instance: "The highway—that's something that goes on and on [*dlinnoe–dlinnoe*], stretching endlessly ahead, like a man's life . . . there is an idea in a great road . . ." [III,viii]. He repeats this thought several times. Dostoevsky is here not merely invoking an ancient cliché for quest. Within the structure of *The Possessed*, the spatial category, *travel*, with its attendant temporal suggestion of *change*, must rather be seen as the opposite pole of *remaining in one place*, with its suggestion of temporal stasis. All the other characters in the novel have ceased to grow at one point in their pasts; they have become immured, unable to get out of the prisons of their own utopias. Utopia, as a convenient symbol for a space where there is no *time*, thus stands over against the road in the novel's central dialectic: the conflict of life as logical sequence as a utopia, and life as historical becoming, as a road. With this in mind it is perhaps not too much to say that Stepan Trofimovich is a time traveler, who journeys out of system into self. But of course the progress of the novel does not conclude at the end of Stepan Trofimovich's road. *Its* end, in more ways than one, is in Stavrogin's suicide.

The failure of all the novel's visionary schemes can be laid to a single cause, the implications of which only Stavrogin grasps. Utopian dreams of system give birth to nightmares of experience because there is no correspondence between the desire of the *self* and the reality of the *other*. In Stavrogin we see the effect of a discovery that was also made by the narrator of *The Dream of a Ridiculous Man* (but not understood by him), namely that the language of dreams cannot be expressed in waking speech because, while we dream alone, we can have language only with others. All the other characters make the mistake of assuming they can get everyone else to do the same thing, the thing they desire them to do: either by suasion, as does Shatov; by miracle, as does Kirilov; or by force, as do Shigalyov and Peter. They refuse to recognize that the others want something *else*. Thus the utopian figures in the novel do not recognize the otherness of others. Stepan Trofimovich says just before he dies, "The hardest thing in life is not to lie and not to believe your own lie" [III, vii]. All the possessed believe their own lies, their own schemes, so completely that they cannot conceive there may be other truths outside them.

Stavrogin's desire expresses the opposite impulse: he battles not for homogeneity but uniqueness. Even as a child he felt "an eternal and sacred longing" [I, ii], and throughout the novel he is characterized by the most intense striving, a quest that has as its goal an absolute ego. What he desires is a kind of parthenogenesis of self. Another contrast with *Dream of a Ridiculous Man* may help to illuminate the point, if we remember what that narrator's dilemma was: if there is a cutoff between order of the self and the order I share with others, how is one to valorize the difference, to which assign the privilege? The ridiculous man, a late-blooming Romantic, assumes that the vision he has in a dream, a vision that is exactly the same as the Greek archipelago that Stavrogin dreams, and that is inexpressible in speech, is *therefore* superior to what can be expressed. It is of a higher reality than that which is available to mere discourse. The fact that it is ineffable is precisely what confers on his desire its privilege.

Whereas Stavrogin, who is beyond the consolations of religion or messianic politics—and who is thus suspicious of the ineffable—reaches just the opposite conclusion. The difference between a unique self he desires to have but cannot express, on the one hand, and those things he *can* get into language, on the other—but which do not constitute an acceptable self—defines the defeat, not the triumph, of ego. Stavrogin's conclusion is that only what is available to words, words that gain their value from being shared, is real. The radical assumption he then makes is that he therefore has no self, or at least one that is *his* in the sense that it is free of systems exterior to it. All his "free" choices, the sum of which should reveal who he is, the singular being unlike any other whose emblem is his name, are, in fact, determined by forces from some *other* whole that uses him only locally, as a part, for purposes of its own. Stavrogin spends his life seeking a self, only to discover at the end of each of his various ego probes that he has once again merely articulated a pattern that was determined by one of the preexisting systems he had sought to transcend. He increasingly suspects that his life merely enacts patterns that are prior to it. He keeps discovering the power of structure to subvert his lust for a unique identity.

Stavrogin's life is easily chapterized according to the various biographical structures he discards, as, like the hermit crab (who has no carapace of his own and who therefore progresses from one shell abandoned by other animals to another such abandoned shell), Stavrogin moves from one conventional life-style to another. His early years are spent as a typical member of his class: private tutors, lycée in the capitol, a commission in the Horse Guards, balls, duels, a court martial and reduction to line regiment of infantry. After conspicuous bravery in combat he wins back his rank. It is all very Lermontovian. At this point he tires of doing the expected: he resigns the commission he has regained and gets involved in utopian socialism for a period. But then, in another biographical convulsion, he abandons politics and plunges into the back alleys of Petersburg, wears rags, and takes up with the dregs of the city. It is during this period that he marries the mad Maria Lebyadkina and rapes the child Matryosha. The two legacies from this period that will crop up in the present action of the novel are Peter Verkhovensky and Maria. They are anachronistic reminders of two periods Stavrogin has now gone beyond: Peter, because he becomes fixed in the political option Stavrogin explored in his first attempt to break with a past whose future he already knew, his flirtation with utopian socialism; Maria because she was the unknowing accomplice to a marriage no one can explain because it was part of Stavrogin's second strategy, which was to do precisely what, given his background, would seem most unexpected. The wedding occurred to dramatize Stavrogin's freedom; it was a demonstration of his uniqueness. The incomprehension of the others guarantees the act's singularity. It is an attempt to insure Stavrogin's ability to act against expectations born of convention.

He soon tires of the debauchery ritualized in his unconsummated marriage since the longer it is exploited as a weapon against systemic expectation, the more habitual and itself systemic it becomes. At this point he decides to go back home to Skvoreshniki for the first time since his days in the lycée, and once again his attempt is to explore another self, try on a different identity to see if it really is his. This time the role is that of his mother's son, which has the desired effect of defeating the expectations of the others, thus, momentarily at least, proving he is not a creature of their habits. The narrator reports, "I expected to meet some filthy tramp enfeebled by debaucheries and reeking of vodka. He was, on the contrary, the most elegant gentleman of all those I had ever met . . . I was not the only one to be surprised . . ." (I,ii). No wonder, then, that his face, in a passage that has become a favorite topos in Dostoevsky criticism, is characterized by hair that was "a little too black," his eyes "a little too calm and clear," etc. "People said his face reminded them of a mask" (I,ii) and of course it was a mask in the ongoing drama of Stavrogin's search for a role that will correspond to his own demands for self. But after six months, Stavrogin's quest takes a different turn as "the beast finally showed its claws."

What the novel's sometime narrator means by this melodramatic phase, which he repeats, is that Stavrogin commits in quick succession three acts that appear to be as incomprehensible as his marriage: he pulls the nose of a fellow club member; he repeatedly kisses another man's wife in the man's presence; and he bites the ear of the governor of the province. It will be noted that there is nothing of the heroic about these actions, heroism being only another set of predictable expectations. Stavrogin seeks to astound, to perform a deed that will be so unexpected that it can have sprung only from a self free of all constraints imposed by social expectations. The logical consequence of so intense a need to act out one's uniqueness is, of course, madness, and it is at this point that Stavrogin becomes the victim of "brain fever." But that spring he succeeds in regaining enough control to begin three years of pilgrimage, a journey that goes much farther than the one undertaken by Stepan Trofimovich, but that does no bring Stavrogin to his destination as had the old man's travels, even though Stavrogin visits such far places as Iceland, and such traditional sites for pilgrimage as Egypt and Jerusalem. As the years of wandering come to a close, Stavrogin goes through several avatars very rapidly, each of which once again leaves its own living monument that will confront him in the novel's present action. He helps to reorganize the socialist "organization" associated with Peter Verkhovensky, although he does not join, because he has gone into another phase, the messianic solipsism with which he infects Kirilov, on the one hand, and the messianic Russian nationalism with which he infects Shatov, on the other. Switzerland marks not only the geographical end of Stavrogin's travel, but its symbolic conclusion as well; it is the metaphor of his failed quest, the pilgrimage that failed to achieve its goal, thus the country, like the rainy country of which Baudelaire was king, of which Stavrogin is most properly a citizen.

The *Vorgeschite* ends and the novel proper begins its ac-

142

count of those few days in August which constitute its present action. It should be noted that as Stavrogin comes on the scene, so do all the bits and pieces of his past as they are present in the other characters who now congregate in the same province, those characters whose lives have been changed by Stavrogin in one or another of the various roles he has played: Shatov, who has become fixed in Stavrogin's religious ideology just as Peter had earlier been caught in Stavrogin's socialist politics, like an insect trapped in the amber that will preserve him in the crystallized juices of a tree that has long since itself perished; Kirilov, the book's other religious fanatic, works out his theory of salvation by suicide, a theology he, too, derives in complex ways from Stavrogin. The other characters who now stream into the provincial capitol, such as Lisa, Dasha, Shavtov's wife, Drozdov, etc., are all the helpless refugees of the battles that rage around them, the border wars between different utopias, all of which have one or another of Stavrorin's masks as their national symbol. He is a kind of Frankenstein monster, made up out of all the other characters. The present that the novel describes, then, is really a reenactment of Stavrogin's several parts, a theater of the self that dramatizes once again his own biography: an existential syllogism forcing him to conclude that all his failures to find a unique identity prove that such a thing does not exist. He is the sole spectator of the tragedy, since each disaster it chronicles—the murder of Shatov, the suicide of Kirilov, the flight of Peter Verkhovensky—all reenact the end of processes he has already concluded for himself and gone beyond.

The underground man, as I tried to suggest earlier, has difficulty *telling* himself; he cannot find a plot to contain his self, so the text that contains him does not end. Stavrogin ultimately cannot *act* himself, so the text that contains him concludes with his end in suicide. And as we know from its vexed textological history, Dostoevsky experienced great difficulty in telling Stavrogin, as, over the years of its composition, the novel changed from a religious pamphlet (Dostoevsky's own word for it) that would enlighten Russia's atheists, to political melodrama based on the trial of the

Nechaev conspirators. We have been arguing that Stavrogin's defining impulse is to avoid becoming a character in already existing plots, and the time has come to take up the question of that most fraught of all aspects in Dostoevsky's, as well as Stavrogin's, concern for plot in *The Possessed*, the suppressed ninth chapter of Part II, "At Tikhon's." The manifest reason the chapter was not included in the initial version of the novel that appeared serially in *The Russian Messenger* is that Katkov, the journal's editor, strenuously objected to it, fearing (probably correctly) that the censors would not pass the account of the little girl Matryosha's rape and suicide.

But another reason suggests itself, if our interpretation of the novel's basic conflict of temporalities is at all valid. Dostoevsky chose to excise the chapter in all versions of the book printed during his lifetime because it contains Stavrogin's confession, an attempt by Stavrogin to *tell* his radical individuality. Had the chapter been included, the overwhelming intentionality of Stavrogin's attempt to articulate his autonomy by living it instead of telling it, as had the underground man, would have been compromised. It is Stavrogin's one narrative gesture—though what a gesture it is! Thus it had to be excluded if his function as the active agent of the underground man's dilemma were to be maintained.

We may make sense of both decisions—Stavrogin's to erect a self in story and Dostoevsky's to suppress that story—if we see each decision as growing out of the same dilemma: the breakdown of certain conditions for establishing a coherent identity. "The beginning conditions of all narrative are the possibility of consecutive explanation and return: the fundamental text is *The Odyssey* or *Don Quixote*, where the Don's madness corresponds to the Greek hero's voyage away from home. The ideal course of fiction can be characterized as the return to a point of fruitful origination in the past from which the narrative subsequently begins to unfold and to which it can always return."[7] For instance, "in such a novel as *Tom Jones* . . . the foundling is discovered through a series of ad-

[7] Edward W. Said, "Narrative: Quest for Origins and Discovery of the Mausoleum," *Salmagundi*, No. 12 (Spring, 1970), p. 66.

ventures that make the birth intelligible: he is given paternity.
. . . Whether in a novel in Boswell's *Life*, or in the continuing
sequence of Swift's work, narrative is the redefinition of ego
into the emergence of a strong historical identity; as Meredith
saw, the Book of Life and the Book of Egoism, the novel,
gradually become synonymous."[8] It is just this equation of
comprehensible histories—of well-made stories and coherent
identities—that is at issue in *The Possessed* for both the author
and central character of the novel. Thus the suppressed chapter is important because of its absence: it points to the dilemma that "originating" actions of the sort Stavrogin seems
to tell in his confession, actions that explain all subsequent action, have become by the nineteenth century.

The theme of Dostoevsky's earlier novel *The Idiot* was—in
more ways than one—coterminous with its genre. That is, if
we accept Lukacs' definition of the novel, which for present
purposes may be reduced to an account of the quest for a coherent self in a world from which the gods have fled, then *The
Idiot* is a paradigmatic example of the genre: it is "about"
nothing so much as Myshkin's quixotic search for an identity.
The novel-ness of that work is underscored in its title, which
points to idiosyncrasy, uniqueness, the aloneness of men who
must originate themselves. Myshkin's structural origin is
Switzerland and madness, the country and condition he
comes from on the first page of the novel as well as where and
how he is left on its last page—an ironic twist on "the ideal
course of fiction . . . characterized as the return to a point of
fruitful origin in the past from which the narrative subsequently begins to unfold and to which it can always return.
. . ."

Three years later, in *The Possessed*, Dostoevsky takes up the
problem again, as can be seen in the relation of each book's
title to novel-ness: *The Idiot* suggests singularity, the unique
sense of character that made novels novel when first they
began appearing; whereas *The Possessed* suggests *many*. This
plurality is made explicit in the use Dostoevsky makes of the
parable of the Gadarene swine. A madman is brought to

[8] Said, p. 67.

Jesus, who casts out the several devils (the *Besy* who provide the Russian title) that possess the man, who thereby is cured. But this idiot's name is not Myshkin, nor any of those other names which stand for the stories their novels tell, such as *Don Quixote*, *Tom Jones*, or even *The Odyssey*: "And Jesus asked him, saying, what is thy name? And he said, Legion: because many devils were entered into him." The meaning of this passage for Stavrogin goes well beyond the obvious one of satanic infection. He fears that *his* name is Legion, because many *others* enter into himself, because he is not an autonomous identity. He spends his whole career seeking to prove he is himself a whole, and not a part, that his time is not one over which an exterior logic presides. It may be that it is not given to the caterpillar to choose whether or not it will become a butterfly; it may be that the acorn is condemned to become an oak. But Stavrogin will not content himself with a future that is already known. Thus he tries several different futures. The great boredom he feels, and that everyone notices as his iconic attribute, is the result of being trapped into a present moment of a biographical chain the future links of which are already all too clearly known. Thus he is a Prince Harry who will refuse to become a King Henry: that plot is known. Thus he is both Hamlet in the zigzagging of his career, which appears to others as indecisiveness, and a false Dmitry in that he is never what he appears to be and because in him the king's two bodies of man and role refuse to cleave together.

At the end of his life and his novel, Stavrogin says, "nothing has come from me but negation," a recognition that all his attempts to erect a self have merely been denials of the power other people and other extra-subjective forces have had in making him what he would not be. When in the end he discovers he is Legion, he is all the others in the novel who tell him, he commits suicide in a last attempt to be himself, as his short note makes clear: "No one is to blame I did it myself (*"Nikogo ne vinit', ja sam"*). But of course in the book's final irony he does not get the last word, which belongs rather to the society he sought to escape: "The verdict of our doctors

146

after the post mortem was that it was most definitely not a case of insanity." In other words, the act *could* be understood by others. The system of medicine can explain even Stavrogin's ultimate gesture of idiosyncrasy. He did not do it *alone*.

Thus *The Possessed* has as its theme as well as its structure the impossibility of its putative genre. Novel-ness, the search for a unique coherence, collapses into anti-novelness, the recognition that coherence can never be unique.

Chapter 6

The Either/Or of Duels and Dreams:
A Gentle Creature and *Dream of a Ridiculous Man*

I

A Gentle Creature would at first glance appear to be stitched together from all the most frequently recurring Dostoevskian clichés. It is told in the first person by a man keeping vigil beside the body of his dead wife. She is to be buried in the morning, but in the meantime the narrator meditates on the meaning of her death. He is a former officer, who, having refused to fight a duel, leaves the army in disgrace, vowing revenge on society. A self-confessed dreamer, he becomes a pawnbroker sustained by the vision of acquiring thirty thousand rubles so that he may retire to the Crimea and become a lordly philanthropist. A young girl comes to him in order to pawn a series of increasingly pathetic objects. Learning that she is about to be forced into an abhorrent marriage, he proposes himself as an alternative. Their marriage turns into a battle of wills between the two that ends when the girl commits suicide.

The typical themes of fatal duel (*rokovoj poedinok*, that central topos of Romantic poetry) between man and woman; the dialectic of pride and humiliation; suicide; lonely Faustian dreamers, etc., are all here. What sets *A Gentle Creature* apart—the reason why it is more than a stew of Dostoevskian formulae—is the prominence in it of the structural resistance the tale offers to its own apparent theme, the way the fact of the narrator's monologue, his *one* voice, undercuts his stated desire for harmony, *more* than one voice.

When the girl first appears in the pawnshop, she does so to get money to pay for a notice that will advertise her services as governess. The notice is to appear in a newspaper called *The Voice*. Now there was a St. Petersburg daily with this title, of course.[1] But it is named on the first page of this particu-

---

[1] In fact it was probably a story in *The Voice* that provided Dostoevsky the *donnée* for *A Gentle Creature*. See the account of the suicide of Maria Borisova,

lar story in order to announce the terms of the tale's dominant structural metaphor: the human voice, and the myriad kinds of silence it fills.

The most obvious use of voice in the story is as a weapon in the duel between the pawnbroker and his wife, a conflict that stands in as a microcosmic example of the struggle between him and society at large. When the girl comes into his house she does so because the attempt to maintain her own independence—by working as governess—has failed: no one has heard her call for help in *The Voice*. By proposing, by asking a question, the narrator *answers* her; she assumes that only the narrator has *listened* to her plight. Therefore, she is free to *talk* to him. He says, "She met me with protestations of delight. Told me in that chatter [*lepet*] of hers (her sweet chatter of innocence) about the days of her childhood, her babyhood, her old home, her mother and father."[2] The narrator adds, "But I poured cold water on her raptures. That was essentially what my idea amounted to: to her transports I answered with silence . . . I created a whole system."[3] Throughout the rest of the story the absence of words between the two is insistently emphasized: "She began lapsing into silence" (p. 391); "We went [to the theater] in silence, and in silence we returned . . . there were no quarrels, just silence . . . I became more silent than ever . . ." (p. 392); "And, I grew more and more silent, more and more silent" (p. 393). He tells her of his plan to move to Crimea, adding, "That was the reason for my proud silence, that was why we sat together in silence."

The titles of the two plays they see define the ironic distance between them: the first is "The Pursuit of Happiness" (*Pogonja za ščast'em*), the second, "Singing Birds" (*Pticy pevčie*). Because they are silent, *their* pursuit ends in tragedy—the full depths of which are revealed in a pathetic *song* (which, almost too schematically, is a love song) that she

---

which in many details, such as leaping out of a window with an icon clutched in her hand, parallels the death of the wife in the fiction: *Golos* (Oct. 2, 1876), No. 272.

[2] References are to *Sobranija sočinenija*, ed. L. P. Grossman, et al. (Moskva, Gos. izd. xud. lit., 1958), Vol. 10.

[3] All quotes, pp. 389–90.

sings in the period immediately prior to her leap out the window. The narrator hears her singing, which she has not done since the very first days of their marriage: "At that time her voice (*golos*) was still still strong and clear. . . . But now the song sounded so feeble . . . it sounded as if her little voice (*golosok*) could not manage it, as if the song itself were sick. . . . Such a poor little voice, and it broke off so miserably . . ." (p. 409). The wife then kills herself, a casualty in an imperialist war of aggression (she was to be a colony of his utopia), the course of which is charted in the more intimate terms of battle appropriate to a duel.

The duel metaphor in the story is so prevalent that it is possible to overlook its role as a mere subfunction of the larger and more important political mechanism. The narrator rejects society when he refuses to accept a challenge while in the army; his attempts to "revenge himself on society," a phrase that occurs twice in the tale (pp. 383, 387), then focuses on the girl as vengeance-object: "What pleased me was the idea of our inequality . . ." (p. 407). She wins an encounter with one of the narrator's former fellow officers who seeks to calumniate her husband and seduce her: the engagement is specifically referred to as a duel (*poedinok*, p. 398). The narrator, who has overheard this battle of wits, brings his wife home from the meeting with her would-be seducer (who, of course, challenges him to another duel [p. 399]). The narrator emphasizes ". . . all the way home not a word was spoken" (p. 399). But the wife looks at him "with a grim challenge in her eyes" (p. 400).

Now the Russian word for challenge used here—*vyzov*—has its root in *zov*, a call (plus *vy-*, the prefix indicating direction out); thus it is similar to the English expression "to call (someone) out," when challenging him to a duel. But in the pattern of voice and silence that Dostoevsky works out in *A Gentle Creature*, to "call out" has other meanings as well: it is not only challenge, but an *appeal*, which, needless to say, in this case the pawnbroker rejects—with his silence.

In desperation the girl—after an all-night vigil beside her sleeping husband similar to the one he will keep later beside her corpse—takes a revolver and puts it to the pawnbroker's temple. He awakes, but feigns continued sleep. "... A deadly silence had fallen, but I could hear that silence . . . the silence continued . . . at that moment a duel was going on between us, a duel of life and death . . . there was a dead silence . . . I opened my eyes quickly. She was no longer in the room . . . I had conquered and she was conquered forever. . . . But I never said a word to her. She understood without words" (p. 402). He wins the duel with his wordlessness, but in her subsequent suicide she responds with the even greater silence of death.

The primary plot of the story, then, tells the narrator's inability to effect his lust for a spectral wholeness, that condition in which his wife would *not* be separate from his will, in which he would be a benevolent despot presiding over the mini-kingdom of a Crimean estate where his subjects would also be indistinguishable from the unifying force of his will. The whole that he dreams is one in which the rest of the world would collapse its otherness into his self. The otherness of the world and of other persons expresses itself as resistance to the homogenizing impulse of his will. The world is for him those parts of the kaleidoscope that refuse to fall into the shifting patterns dictated by his holistic desire. Otherness is an affront to his solipsism: others thus are regarded not as others *as such* but as potential building blocks for the whole self his desire dreams. Others are not granted independent existence; they *are*, simply that they may become parts of the whole he is driven to constitute.

The insistence of the others that they do in fact exist independently of his desire is worked out in the form of a duel between the narrator's desire for a unity shaped by his will, and his wife's intention to be more than a mere part. Her death invokes the silence of an ultimate otherness, and thus announces the deeper intention of the struggle.

The battle of the two recapitulates the dilemma of post-Romantic consciousness: how to be a self at the same time one is part of the larger whole of society (thus the "family of nations"). How can one exercise his particularity, develop those

151

aspects of self which are uniquely his, if he must constantly subordinate his will to a collective whose claim on him is *merely* contractual, where the relationship of individual part to social whole is not felt to be organic, ineluctable? Dostoevsky in this story mourns the loss of *nature* as whole to which *society* might correspond as whole, with a resulting decline in the ability of any whole to insure validity of parts: the task of authenticity devolves onto the self. What Dostoevsky here registers as absence is that state when men were not separate from nature, therefore not separate from each other, "a state of unanimity which is independent of [any] decision."[4] The homogeneity of parts contained by the whole is expressed as a "state of unanimity . . . [which] is then brought to bear on the decision to be taken."[5] When this state, in which individual desires are in equilibrium, collapses, men seek to establish "society," where unanimity is a function of politics, and expressed in decisions reached *after* conflict. The result is not a virtual homogeneity but the uneasy truce that reigns between a majority that has won and a minority that has lost. It is in such condition that men discover separateness, and—for better or worse—that they have selves, which brings with it a discovery of loneliness as well. It is in the space of such a political separation that the drama of *The Gentle Creature* is played out. The narrator, rejected by society, refuses to keep up the pretense of unity with it. He declares a kind of war on the others that is enacted as a duel with his wife.

Early on in the tale, when the narrator names the sanction for his treatment of the girl, he says "I had a right" to do as I did, because, ". . . you have rejected me, you, that is, the people, have cast me out with contemptuous silence" (p. 394). Several things should be taken immediately into account here: it is people (*ljudi*) the plural of *person*, who reject him, not the folk (*narod*), a category that reduces differences between people to a degree that permits it to be expressed as a singular of its own. It should also be noted that the narrator

[4] Georges Charbonnier in *Conversations with Cluade Lévi-Strauss*, tr. John and Doreen Weightman (London, Cape Editions, 1969), p. 36.
[5] Charbonnier, *loc.cit.*

152

senses his divorce from the others as a silence—but a silence that has *voice enough* to convey contempt. When nature has ceased to speak, to be meaningful, the problem becomes interpreting the silence of the world. For the narrator, such silence is contemptuous. It is this "voice" that seeks to still the narrator's own voice in the concluding paragraphs of the story, when he throws back the challenge: "what are your laws to me? What do I care [*k čemu mne*] for your customs, your morals, your life, your government, your faith! Let your judges judge me, let me be brought before your court, to a public trial. . . . The judge will cry out, 'Be silent, officer!' I will shout to him, 'Whence comes your power, that I should obey you . . . what are your laws to me now? I will go my own way [*otdeljajus'*].' "[6]

The institutions that define the particular society that opposes the narrator are introduced at this point in the story so as to reveal the larger meaning of the conflict between him and his wife, a conflict implicit in all their actions, but frequently obscured by the insistently personal, seemingly only psychological, mechanism of the duel. The continuity between the struggle of the pair, and the struggle between society and those whose allegiance it would claim, is pointed up in the dynamic of silence at work in both. We have seen how the duel between the narrator and girl is fought with the weapon of silence. The same weapon is invoked in the larger struggle.

In the scene above not only is there an attempt by the judge to silence the narrator, but the court in which he does so is called in Russian "voice court," *glasnyj sud*, (from *glas*, or *golos*=voice), the public court in the sense that it is where the voices of the public may be heard. Just as the narrator had sought to drown out his wife, so does the court deny the space of discourse to him. What is more, the voice of society is precisely similar to his own in that it makes itself heard—as a ringing silence: "You—the people—have cast me out with contemptuous silence."

It is clear, then, that Dostoevsky pursues the conflict be-

[6] All following quotations from p. 419.

tween parts and whole at two levels: at the outset as a kind of matrimonial *corrida*, a duel between two people. After the girl's death, in the concluding paragraphs, the wider implications of the struggle become apparent as in the scene we have just examined: the battle between the two individuals has stood in for that between society (the needs of all) and its members (*my* needs). Without an extrapolitical unanimity preceding its actions, society fails as a meaningful whole: the marriage as artificial "whole" fails to bond its two parts.

The pawnbroker who has been rejected by society seeks to overcome the forces that lead to separateness in the world by creating a new unity in his relationship with the girl. He seeks to dominate her because he wants her to be identical with his will. It is the urge to such radical "togetherness" that accounts for his attempts to subjugate her, because the end of perfect union he imagines will redeem the *means* he uses. The end he conceives is utopian, as we discover in the last paragraphs of the story; "Oh, you don't know what a paradise I would have created for you! Paradise was in my soul, and I would have planted it all around you!" The edenic overtones of the vision are emphasized in the verb he uses here: "to plant" (*nasadit'*) paradise. Equally to the point are the recurring subjunctives, "I *would* have created," "I *would* have planted," which crowd this penultimate paragraph ("You *would* have loved me," "So we should have lived" etc.). The *distance* between the narrator's dream of perfect union and the reality of otherness is measured in all of them, as well as in the unresponsiveness of the wife's corpse, "She is blind, blind" she cannot *see* his vision; "She is dead, she cannot *hear*," now that he—the former proponent of silence—seeks most strenuously to use his voice.

That the dilemma of otherness is what the tale most centrally dramatizes becomes even clearer in the final paragraph. It begins with two rhetorical gestures, the double exclamations "Insensibility! Oh, Nature!" The Russian word here rendered as "insensibility" is *kosnost'*, which means in its most frequent usage, stagnation, or inertness, and it is related to the verb *kosnet'*, to grow hard, to stiffen. Thus it may be said that

154

it is the dead girl's stiffening body that sets off this last reflection. But nature is not invoked merely as the force that turns that which was the girl into an inert corpse. Nature is, rather, brought in here as a bitter metaphor for the power which, uncaring of subjectivity, resolves the particular (the girl, trailing all her own uniqueness and specificity) into the universal (death), that abstraction which drains all our selves of all their striving. To paraphrase Hegel, death is the homogenization whose price is all our particularities. Death is simply the most dramatic way nature flaunts the silence that is *her* otherness; what the narrator here mourns when he exclaims "Nature!" is the separateness, the otherness of men, as becomes clear when in the next line he evokes symbols that combine both silence and combat; " 'Is anyone on the field alive?' cries the Russian epic hero [*bogatyr*]. And I too cry out, I who am not a hero, *and no one answers*. They say the sun gives life to the universe. The sun will rise—and look at it, isn't it really a corpse? Everything is dead, and everywhere there are corpses. There are only people [literally, of course, "*Alone* only people," *odni tol'ko ljudi*] and around them, *silence*!" Society as a collective is dead (no one answers), nature as a unifying force is dead (the sun is a corpse), men are alone. And the silence that has been the narrator's iconic attribute throughout the story, his weapon and his goal, the state in which there is total communion—no *separate* voices, no other voices to oppose the homogenizing force of his will—is in the end present as the most unbearable proof of his aloneness. The dream of a unity so great that words would be superfluous, has become a nightmare of separation, a whole new dimension of aloneness.

II

The pattern of *A Gentle Creature* (1876) is one in which a utopian dream of unity turns into a nightmare of separation and loneliness. *The Dream of a Ridiculous Man* (which appears a year later, 1877) tells a nightmare of atomization that turns into a dream of new wholeness. It would appear that what we have, then, is another chapter in the familiar story of how

155

Dostoevsky first opens a metaphysical problematic (such as *Notes from Underground*) and then seeks to close it with an appeal to religious certainty (as in the epilogue to *Crime and Punishment*). It might be argued that these two short stories represent a gradually intensifying attempt to light up the stage, littered with bodies and utopian dreams, that was left so black in the conclusion to *The Possessed*, the novel with which Dostoevsky opened this last decade of his life. But a close examination will show that the two stories merely constitute another movement in the same dominant figure found in all the work from this period: They are further meditations on the lust for a whole that will sanction and contain all the parts: at one level, as a society that would have this unitary effect on discrete individuals, a history without time; at another level as a single self that would have the power to order and contain all the contradictions, the various selves, that are lived through in single life, a biography without becoming.

Both stories end with the key phrase from the Sermon on the Mount: in *A Gentle Creature* it is "Men, love one another" in the last paragraph. In *Dream* it is more insistently put in the penultimate paragraph: "The main thing is to love your neighbor as yourself—that is the main thing, and that is everything, for nothing else matters." What is important in each case is not the explicitly Christian association of these words, an association that is at any rate obvious, but the emphasis on *wholeness* they convey. The message is utopian at least as much as Christian in that it seeks to eradicate *differences* between selves, the pronouns "you," "I," "mine," and "yours," would collapse into a homogenized *One*. But it is just this thematic insistence on sharing that is undercut by the major structural property of both stories—the monologue. Monologue dominates the narrative in two ways: it first of all emphasizes the eccentricity, the *aloneness*, of the narrator; at the same time it dramatizes the variety *within his own voice*, the disparate states of consciousness he experiences, the parts of his own being that will not resolve into a pattern.

This is especially true of *Dream*, which is another of Dos-

156

toevsky's suicide fictions. The narrator begins to doubt his own existence (like the underground man he knocks against people on the street to convince himself he is *there*). Convinced that "nothing existed in my lifetime . . . that there had not been anything even in the past . . . there would never be anything in the future either," he falls prey to that *acedia* that is so prevalent in Dostoevsky: the condition in which the expression "it's all the same to me" assumes hegemony over all aspects of experience. He buys a pistol and one rainy night decides to shoot himself after rejecting a call for help from a little girl in the street. He falls asleep first, but *dreams* he completes the deed, is taken out of his coffin, and whisked off to another world. The planet he visits is the third and last[7] of those arcadian Greek archipelagos based on Claude Lorraine's painting *Acis and Galatea* that Dostoevsky uses in this decade. The planet is a version of Eden, "earth unstained by the Fall, inhabited by people who had not sinned and who lived in the same paradise as that in which, according to the legends of mankind, our first parents lived before they sinned, with the only difference that all the earth here was everywhere the same paradise" (p. 432). The narrator mysteriously corrupts this perfect society, and it falls apart into warring factions. "A struggle began for separation, for isolation, for personality, for mine and thine" (p. 437). The narrator weeps for their lost one-ness, implores them to crucify him, but when he is therefore treated as a madman, he feels he is dying and wakes up. He decides to preach the gospel of one-ness to all, even though he is treated as a holy fool (*jurodivij*). The tale ends with his statement that he has succeeded in finding the little girl who had appealed to him on the night of his projected suicide, and that he will go on.

While this conclusion may appear more optimistic than that of *A Gentle Creature*, it should not be forgotten that the "truth" that the narrator ends by preaching has the effect of isolating him as completely as had the eccentricity that originally drove him to near suicide. He has simply found another

---

[7] The first is the suppressed chapter of *The Possessed* (1871); the second is found in a *A Raw Youth* (1875).

cause for his separateness. *Before* the dream he was different because, "It's all the same to me," because he is haunted by a homogeneity that speaks no differences, that says, therefore, Nothing. *After* the dream the cause of his distinctiveness changes, is now grounded in the All, the "truth" that is vouchsafed him alone.

The plot of this tale may be best conceived, then, as an experiment in narrative framing techniques. The dream is framed by the narrator's account of his dilemma *before* his visit to the Edenic planet, on one side, and the account of his dilemma *after* the visit, on the other side. At first glance it would appear that the story has three distinct phases: one, the opening that ends with the resolve to commit suicide; two, the dream; and, three, the conclusion, in which the narrator speaks of his new-found happiness. The apparent sequence is a familiar Dostoevskian one of conversion, the tale of an event that sets off a lost "before" self against a found "after" self, as in *Crime and Punishment*, where another dream (the vision of plague) has much the same effect for Raskolnikov. But a closer look at "Ridiculous Man" reveals that the three narrative sequences that comprise its plot all tell *the same story*, and it is a tale of the narrator's megalomania and solipsism.

Each of the three movements simply charts a different strategy by which the narrator asserts his radical uniqueness. In the opening he is worse than the others: "They always laughed at me. But not one of them knew or suspected that if there were one man on earth who knew better than anyone else that he was ridiculous, that man was I" (p. 421). In the dream sequence he is also unique, the only inhabitant of the planet he visits who is not part of its unity, a unity so great that language is not necessary for the indigenous population to understand each other—or, as far as that goes, to understand the stars and trees. Here, too, he is worse than all the others, and his difference is so great he succeeds in corrupting the whole planet: "I only know that the cause of the Fall [*grexopadenie*] was I" (p. 436). He goes on to compare his deadly effect to that of trichina, the cause of the plague in Raskolnikov's dream. Having played the role of Satan in this

Eden, he then seeks to play its messiah: "I told them I alone was responsible for it all—I alone; that it was I who had brought them corruption, contamination, and lies! I implored them to crucify me, and [he is both Prometheus and Christ] I taught them how to make a cross" (p. 439). And, finally, in the third and concluding segment, he again makes claims to radical uniqueness: before worse than the others, now he is *better* than the others. ". . . they all laugh at this faith of mine. But how can I help believing it? I have beheld it—the truth . . ." (p. 440).

The story's plot is made up of the same solipsistic pattern dramatized three different ways. In each case the ridiculous man fails to recognize that the gap is absolute between his own fantasies and the constraints on them represented by other persons and exterior reality. He is like the pawnbroker in *A Gentle Creature* in that he seeks to subsume everything that is *not* his desire into the one pattern or relationship that *is* his desire. And of course the effect for both narrators is the same: their attempts to engulf others into themselves, to reduce variety to the unity of their own wishes, serve only to exacerbate their isolation, to increase the *distance* between themselves and the others. The instrument of desire in *A Gentle Creature* is the voice that seeks to still all others so that only it may be heard. In *Dream of a Ridiculous Man* the metaphor for an all-embracing unity is the dream itself, to which the narrator seeks to accommodate the to-him-intolerable variety of experience. That is, just as the pawnbroker sought to implement his desire by homogenizing the world into its ritual silences, so does the ridiculous man seek to absorb others into the dream world his desire has conjured in sleep.

It is then, appropriate, if we—very tentatively—invoke categories from Freud in order to understand the politics of the Ridiculous Man, since what is utopian in his scheme is precisely that he fails to distinguish between the phantom wholeness of his dreams, home of desire, and the waking world of the others, home of necessity. Reality in this view is merely anything that impedes the immediate and complete implementation of what is dreamt.

The Either/Or of Duels and Dreams

The relationship between desire and dreaming is recognized by the Ridiculous Man himself: he says very early on, "Dreams seem to be induced not by reason, but desire. [*Sny, kaz̆etsja, stremit ne rassudok, a z̆elanie*], not by the head by the heart . . ." (p. 427). He is a dreamer then, no matter how self-consciously, of *infantile* dreams. As Freud says, after enumerating a series of them, "The common element in all these children's dreams is obvious. All of them fulfilled wishes which were active during the day but had remained unfulfilled. The dreams were simple *wish fulfillments*."[8] He adds:

"Every one of these dreams can be replaced by an optative clause: 'Oh, if only the trip on the lake had lasted longer'—'If only I were already washed and dressed.' . . . But dreams give us more than such optative clauses, they show us the wish as already fulfilled; they represent its fulfillment as real and present . . . thus, even in this infantile group, a species of transformation, which deserves to be described as dream work, is not completely absent: a thought expressed in the optative has been replaced by a representation in the present tense" (p. 39 [573]).

What makes the narrator of this story typical of late Dostoevskian utopians is not only that he dreams the same dream as Versilov (in *A Raw Youth*) or Stavrogin (in *The Possessed*). It is rather that—like all the characters in *The Possessed*, not just Stavrogin—he refuses to limit to dreams the operation of optatives translated into the active voice; he seeks to put all his optatives into the present tense, to enact the utopian future as a political present. In my dream "I have beheld [the truth] and it was so utterly whole and complete that I cannot believe that it cannot exist among men" (p. 440). He has earlier said,

[8] Sigmund Freud, *On Dreams*, tr. James Strachey (New York, the Norton Library, 1952), p. 34 [224-26]. I will use this simplified version of Freud's conception of dreaming (first published in 1901 as *Über den Traum*), rather than the *Interpretation of Dreams*, simply because the formulations are more lapidary than in the earlier book. Since, however, many of the statements quoted are qualified in important ways in the more complete (and doctrinal) *Interpretation*, I am also listing [in brackets] pages in the Strachey tr. of *Die Traumdeutung* (New York, Discus paperback ed., 1962). Further references to these editions will be noted in the body of my text.

"they are making fun of me now by saying that it was only a dream. But isn't it it *all the same* [*Neuželi ne vse ravno*] whether it was a dream or not. . . . For once you have recognized the truth and seen it you know it is the one and only truth and that there can be no other whether you are asleep or awake" (p. 427) (emphasis added).

That is, he denies a contradiction between the opposing orders he names heart (desire) and reason (reality principle). This dichotomy is not only present in the narrator's insight into the source of dreams already quoted ("the heart, not the head") but it appears at other critical points in the narrative as well: he specifies when he "shoots" himself at the onset of the dream, ". . . I picked up the gun and, sitting in my armchair, pointed it straight at my heart," and he goes on to emphasize "at my heart, and not my head" (p. 427). As he hears the songs the inhabitants of the edenic planet sing, he says, ". . . I could never entirely fathom their meaning. It remained somehow beyond the grasp of my *reason*, and yet it sank unconsciously deeper and deeper into my heart" (p. 435).

The distinction between heart and head (or reason) so central to the story is the distinction between the order of dream and the order of waking experience, between desire and necessity. The whole story revolves around the dichotomy between the two orders presented as *two languages*, each with its own set of semantic operations and techniques of privilege.

We have seen that in each of the tale's three segments— *before*, *in*, and *after* the dream—the narrator is isolated from the others, misunderstood. In each case his alienation is presented as a problem in *language*. Before the dream, at a dinner with some companions, he is silent the whole evening until, as they begin to argue, he bursts out, "It's really all the same to you, isn't it gentlemen?" But far from being offended, "they all burst out laughing at me . . ." (p. 422). Within the dream he says, ". . . I could not understand their knowledge. . . . I knew too that they would never be able to understand me . . ." (p. 433); or, "While understanding the words [of their songs] I could never entirely fathom their meaning . . . they listened to me, and I could tell that they did not know what I was talking about" (p. 435). And after the dream, as he seeks to "preach" its message ("I made up my mind to preach from that very moment and, of course, to go on preaching all my life. I am going to preach, I want to preach"), *just as before*, everyone laughs at him, giving a new meaning to the tale's key phrase, "It's all the same." His preaching fails because he cannot translate the language of dream into waking language: ". . . those [shapes] I actually saw at the very time of my dream were filled with such harmony and were so enchanting and beautiful, and so intensely true that on awakening I was indeed unable to clothe them in our feeble words . . ." (p. 436). Or, "But how to organize paradise—that I don't know, because I can't put it into words. *After my dream I lost the ability to put things into words*" (p. 440) (emphasis added). Literally he says "I lost my words."

He cannot find words in the order of experience (which he calls "reason") for the "truth" he discovered in the order of dream (realm of "the heart" in his system) *because they are two different languages*. At one level the narrator knows this, as when he remarks on the peculiarity of dreams:

"Dreams, as we all know, are very curious things: certain incidents in them are presented with quite uncanny vividness, each detail executed with the finishing touch of a jeweler, while others you leap across as though entirely unaware of, for instance, space and time. . . . My brother, for instance, died five years ago. I sometimes dream about him; he takes a keen interest in my affairs, we are both very interested and yet I know very well all through my dream that my brother is dead and buried. How is it that I am not surprised that, although dead, he is here beside me, doing his best to help me? Why does my reason accept all this without the slightest hesitation?" (pp. 426–427).

What he refers to here is the indeterminacy of the dreamwork that Freud also describes, but in terms of language: "The alternative either/or is never expressed in dreams, both of the alternatives being inserted in the text of the dream as though they were equally valid . . . 'either-or used in *recording* a dream is to be translated by 'and' " (pp. 65 [353, 361, 372]).

It is this collapse of categories into each other, the ability to be free of the necessity of distinction and therefore liberated from choices that embody differences, that makes oneiric language superior (in the narrator's eyes) to waking speech, where meaning is precisely (as Saussure has shown) a function of difference, the either/or of phonemic and semantic units that exist in binary opposition.

Thus the primary condition of the narrator's edenic utopia—a whole that admits no independent parts, where men, animals, even stones and stars are all subsumed in a great sameness—is merely an extension of a fundamental trait of the activity of dreaming: the laws of utopia derive not from politics but from the dreamwork.

And just as utopian schemes comprehend a unity so perfect that actual politics, the art of resolving *differences*, become unnecessary, so in the dream is *its* work so homogenizing that there need be no negatives: not only does "and" substitute for "either/or"; "Ideas which are contraries are by preference expressed in dreams by one and the same element. *'No' seems not to exist so far as dreams are concerned*" (p. 63) (emphasis added). (See again pp. 353, 361, 372.)

The language of dream has multiple stratagems by which to elide cause and effect, linearity, logic, all those aspects of waking speech which insist on separation, difference. "The dream work is particularly fond of representing two *contrary* ideas by the same composite structure" (pp. 48, 49). This "condensation . . . is the most important and peculiar characteristic of the dream work" (p. 50 [312-39]). Thus the emphasis on sameness in society and nature that characterizes the narrator's edenic vision is simply a political metaphor for the brute impulse to sameness that is the root condition of dreaming. Eden, then, is a dream about dreaming.

But such a privileging of sameness for its own sake is what makes the language of dreams impossible to express immediately in speech, which is the narrator's utopian error, the reason he is misunderstood by others. Not everyone will share his desire; the world he wakes to is one in which contrary ideas will not lend themselves to an ideological condensation.

And yet he continues to deny the distinction between the two worlds and their languages: "But isn't it all the same whether it was a dream or not?" He seeks to implement not any *particular* aspect of his dream in waking experience, but rather the very homogeneity that is the distinctive feature of the oneiric world: "If only we all desired it, everything could be arranged immediately" (p. 441). (Dostoevsky is playing with *vse/vsë*: "*Esli tol'ko vse zaxotjat, to sejčas vsë ustroitsja.*")

The last line of the story (following upon the above quote) refers back to the little girl whose rejected appeal occasioned the dream: "And I did find that little girl . . . and I shall go on! I shall go on!" What we have is a literal example of how "A thought expressed in the optative has been replaced by a representation in the present tense." Thus the last lines of the story undercut this narrator, as do the editor's concluding remarks the underground man. Just as the conclusion of the earlier work highlighted the continued presence of a constantly recurring pattern (the underground man's attempts to reduce experience to story), so does the ending of "Ridiculous Man" dramatize the sameness of a pattern that has been repeated three times in the plot as a whole: the narrator's inability to distinguish between desire and experience. The first text highlights a gap between narrative strategies drawn from literary fictions, on the one hand, and on the other, lived experience. Featured in the second text is the cutoff between narrative techniques derived from the dreamwork and the rhythms of waking experience.

Chapter 7

How Sons Become Fathers:
The Brothers Karamazov

Novels continue to be new because no one yet knows what they are. The novel has not died but many conceptions of it have. Its birth was marked by painful attempts at self-definition, a struggle that continues to define the genre's vitality. Of the many critics who have come forward to say what the novel is, few have had their prescriptions pass into use. Two formulations, however, have recently been particularly influential: Georg Lukacs' *Theory of the Novel* (originally published in German in 1920) and Rene Girard's *Deceit, Desire and the Novel* (originally published in French in 1961). While each of these books is informed by quite different prejudices, they share some central assumptions. Both men agree that there are a few key texts that define the possible limits of the novel and they furthermore agree on what those touchstones are: Cervantes is the great originator, Dostoevsky the problematic *summa*.[1]

Both men distill out of the pressed titles in their canon a definition of the genre itself. They do so by focusing on the distinctive nature of novelistic plot, a narrative uniqueness that is most succinctly stated in yet another influential study, Ian Watt's *Rise of the Novel*. Early novelists, such as Defoe and Richardson:

"are the first great writers in our literature who did not take their plots from mythology, history, legend, or previous literature. . . . When Defoe, for example, began to write fiction he took little notice of the dominant critical theory of the day, which still inclined toward the use of traditional plots; instead he merely allowed his narrative to flow spontaneously from

---

[1] For both critics he comes *after* Proust in the normative development of the type. The absence of a Dickens or a Joyce in both canons is not the limitation some readers claim, since Lukacs and Girard use Balzac and Proust in their systemic slots to meet the same goals and objectives as might be raised by the English masters.

his own sense of what his protagonists might plausibly do next. In so doing Defoe initiated an important new tendency in fiction: his total subordination of plot to the pattern of the autobiographical memoir is as defiant an assertion of the primacy of individual experience in the novel as Descarte's *cogito ergo sum* was in philosophy."[2]

Lukacs and Girard share the assumption that biography, the story of an idiosyncratic person, is the determining model of the novel's narrative structure. But they disagree fundamentally as to the meaning novelistic biographies articulate.[3]

Lukacs says, "The outward form of the novel is essentially biographical. The fluctuation between a conceptual system which can never completely capture life and a life complex which can never attain completeness because completeness in immanently utopian, can be objectivized only in that organic quality which is the aim of biography." Thus the aim of the novelist is always "to make the individuality of a living being, with all its limitations, the starting point of stylization and the center of form. . . ."[4] This is the novel's outer form. Its inner form, according to Lukacs, is "the process of [a] problematic individual's journeying toward himself" (p. 80), the biography of one "who must create an entire world through his experience" (p. 83). But this search for an autonomous self is doomed to a failure that is "covered over by skillfully ironic compositional tact, by a semblance of organic unity which [nevertheless] is revealed again and again as illusory" (p. 77). Thus for Lukacs the novel always tells the story of a man who seeks to find an autonomous identity that is his own essence but who, since he lives in a world without a transcendence to ground it, is condemned to be only what at the end of his life he, or others, can interpret the course of his actions to have

[2] Berkeley and Los Angeles, U. of California Press, 1967 (6th printing), p. 15.

[3] The assumption of the central role played by biography in defining the novel is shared implicitly by Robbe-Grillet, whose attack on plots and the psychology they presume is perhaps best understood as an attempt to write a novel that is not condemned to repeat even so loose a pre-existing narrative archetype as that built into *any* life history.

[4] *The Theory of the Novel*, tr. Anna Bostock (Cambridge, Mass., M.I.T. Press, 1971), p. 77.

made him. As Walter Benjamin has said in an essay that owes
much to Lukacs, "The novelist . . . cannot hope to take the
smallest step beyond that limit at which he invites the reader
to a divinatory realization of the meaning of life by writing
'Finis.' "[5] This, of course, is a basically historical, roughly
Hegelian conception of identity: *Geist* will know itself only at
the end of its progress. It is the defining temporality of autobiography, where the last moment of a sequence is always
the point of metaphysical as well as narrative privilege.

Just the opposite obtains in what might be called confessional temporality, which—in Western tradition, at any
rate—always models itself on the pattern of Christian historiography, where "the center of interest is neither at the beginning . . . nor at the end . . . but in the middle."[6] The confession always tells a conversion experience, a point at which
the "I" who tells his life according to such a scheme became
"himself." All subsequent time has not affected the identity
that was gained when Augustine became a Christian, Gibbon
the historian of Rome, or "Detroit Red" became Malcolm X.
The Rome Garden, the ruins of the Roman Forum, Norfolk
prison, are all spaces where time ceased for these three confes-
sionalists.

Rousseau and Tolstoy, on the other hand, constantly seek
to grasp the existential prize contained in such a version of
narrative closure as they tell their life stories: at this point in
my development "I" became the one for whom the rest of my
history was merely an anticlimax, a specific working out, a
series of local applications of those patterns which were
forged in the crucible of my conversion. But they keep falling
back into autobiographical time, are never content with such
a moment, must always name yet another and *later* moment
when they took on their "essential" selfhood, an essence that
constantly eludes them. We begin to suspect that if they continued to tell their stories beyond the point from which they

---

[5] "Leskov the Storyteller," *Illuminations*, tr. Harry Zohn (New York,
Schocken, 1969), p. 100.
[6] Jean Daniélou, *The Lord of History*, tr. Nigel Abercrombie (Cleveland
and New York, Meridan Books, 1968), p. 7.

actually compose their narratives more and more such "decisive" moments would be named, none of which would really suffice to exhaust the telling self who continued to unfold in new and even-to-him unexpected ways. Such autobiographies seek to adopt the confessional mode as their norm, but constantly sprawl out of, live beyond a syntax whose semantic climax is in the middle. They are quests whose only end can be narrative "Finis" or biological death. "The nature of a character in a novel cannot be presented any better than is done in [the] statement which says that the 'meaning' of his life is revealed only in his death."[7]

Lukacs seems to be saying that both the inner meaning and outer shape of the novel are best understood as replicating a life that aspires to the fixed, whole, organic identity of the sort conversion experiences seem to grant, but that is condemned to the flux of mind and events that make an essential self unobtainable. There is no transcendent end to autonomous identity.

Girard also sees biography as the novel's basic narrative structure, but conceives a more optimistic relation to confessional temporality: "There are a hundred heroes and yet there is a single hero whose adventure spreads over the whole of novelistic literature."[8] This hero, much as the protagonist of Lukacsian biography, always seeks an autonomous self. While for Lukacs the novel celebrates the heroism (it is the genre of "virile maturity") of those condemned to failure in such a quest, making his an essentially tragic vision of the novel, Girard believes: "The novelistic dénouement is a reconciliation between . . . men and the sacred" (p. 308). He insists "The differences between novelistic conclusions are negligible" (p. 296) because "All novelistic conclusions are conversions . . ." (p. 294). For him, then, the novel's structure is biographical in its beginning and middle, but confessional in its ending. "The unity of novelistic conclusions con-

[7] Benjamin, p. 101.

[8] *Deceit, Desire and the Novel*, tr. Yvonne Freccero (Baltimore, Johns Hopkins U.P., 1965), p. 253.

168

sists in the renunciation of metaphysical desire" (pp. 293-94) for an autonomous self.

The obvious question arises, in the name of what service is this renunciation accomplished, and one of Girard's key metaphors may help us to understand: "The truly great novels are all born of that [final *askesis*] and return to it the way a church radiates from the chancel and returns to it. All the great works are composed like cathedrals . . ." (p. 310). As proof of his assertion that "the truth of [Proust's] *Remembrance of Things Past* is the truth of all great novels" (p. 310), he cites the endings of *Don Quixote, The Red and the Black*, and *Crime and Punishment*. Girard's view of the novel, then, is essentially Christian, assumes a transcendent presence that is free to abrogate becoming, that can give meaning to moments and make them ends outside the systemic confines of mere biology or architectonics.

But if we do not share Girard's transcendent view, an obvious difference between conversion and novel structure makes itself immediately apparent: the self so triumphantly proclaimed in such texts as those Girard cites is achieved at the very same point where essential self is *always* named, even in other novels where transcendence is not only unknown but denied: at *the end of the story*. We are free to ask what would have happened if the Don did not die after his return to sanity and the Church; what would happen to Julien Sorel if he were not executed immediately after his conversion; why must Dostoevsky say after Raskolnikov's Siberian epiphany, "Here begins a *new* story"? We are free to ask these questions as we are not free to do so with Augustine or Gibbon or Malcolm X, since in *their* stories the end of identity precedes the end of narrative. Girard wishes to confer the same interruptive capacity to forces at work in novelistic biography. The difficulties built into such a view become apparent as soon as we think of other novels mentioned by Girard: *The Possessed* does not conclude as a formal narrative structure with Stepan Trofimovich's conversion, but with Stavrogin's suicide. *The Idiot*'s structure can hardly be said to parallel "the way a church radiates from a chancel and returns to it"; Myshkin's end is the asylum, not the cathedral.

For both Lukacs and Girard, Dostoevsky has a uniquely important role in the history of the novel. Lukacs concludes his little book (in what might almost be read as a parody of the epilogue in *Crime and Punishment*) by confessing that with Dostoevsky begins a new story in the history of his topic: Dostoevsky "and the form he created lie outside the scope of this book. . . . Only formal analysis of his works can show . . . whether he is merely a beginning or already a completion" of the novel (pp. 152-53). Girard too concludes his book on the novel with Dostoevsky, whose works, even better than those of Stendhal or Proust, demonstrate that "Every novelistic conclusion is a *Past Recaptured*" (p. 297).

For Girard Dostoevsky is *the* novelist; Lukacs says "Dostoevsky did not write novels" (p. 152). Each of these statements about Dostoevsky's place in the history of the novel can be shown to make sense even though they would appear to contradict each other if we assume that both critics are thinking primarily not of Dostoevsky's total *oeuvre*, but of his last novel, *The Brothers Karamazov*. That is, all of Dostoevsky's mature work would seem—especially in the readings they have been given in the present volume—to have been written for no other purpose than to illustrate Lukacs' thesis that the novel essentially narrates a search for autonomous self that ends in failure. And yet Lukacs maintains that Dostoevsky is not part of the world he charts in his *Theory of the Novel*: "He belongs to a new world" (p. 152). If you exclude *The Brothers Karamazov* from consideration, it is not at all clear why this is so, since all the other novels are grounded precisely in the biography/confession opposition of which Lukacs makes so much. But there is nothing in Lukacs' recipes to account for the happy ending of *The Brothers Karamazov*. Since Lukacs' essentially Hegelian assumptions are so relentlessly oriented toward conclusions, Dostoevsky's concluding novel must nevertheless have a special significance. If it does not, in its privileged final position accord, with expectations, it raises questions about all the preceding works, which may be why Lukacs is right about all of Dostoevsky's novels except the last.

Girard is wrong about all Dostoevsky's novels except the last one. Two years after completing *Deceit, Desire and the Novel* he went on to devote a whole book to Dostoevsky, a volume whose sub-title *"du double à l'unité"*[9] states his thesis very economically, but describes a movement absent from all the texts that precede *The Brothers Karamazov*, including *Crime and Punishment*, whose epilogue, as we saw in Chapter 3, is an exercise in non-novelistic narrative. *The Brothers Karamazov* thus contradicts Lukacs' typology, while it is the preeminent example of Girard's. Each differs as to the typicality of *The Brothers Karamazov*, but both labor under its generic hegemony. The question arises, must we persist in the confession/biography distinction that both the Hegelian and Christian critics employ, even if each accommodates it in different ways?

I am assuming that there is a way out of the dichotomy, one that begins by recognizing the controlling prejudice of both critics (and many others less interesting, as well): they assume all novels have a recurring structure that is that of biography. They both see the novel as telling a man's life; where they differ—where most critics of the genre differ—is in their evaluation of how typical that life is when compared to an implicit model of biography each brings to his reading of particular works. Does the story of Wilhelm Meister, of Julien Sorel, or of Raskolnikov correspond to the normative biography of Hegelian man, whose paradigm is *Geist*'s coming to consciousness of itself, or to that other biographical prescription, Christian Man, whose narrative expectation, perhaps even more than his ethical expectation, is always an *imitatio Christi*? Each critic presumes a biographical master plot that preexists any specific novel, and the more closely the life of a novel's major protagonist accords with that ar-

[9] *Dostoevski* (Paris, Plon, 1963). The subtitle also gives an ironic twist to Tolstoy's oft-voiced complaint about novels: "They always end in a marriage!" For an extreme statement of the "unity school," see: Temira Pachmuss, *F. M. Dostoevsky: Dualism and Synthesis of the Human Soul* (Carbondale, Ill., Southern Illinois U.P., 1963).

171

chetypal story, the more of a novel it is. At the heart of systematic metaphysics and Christian theology is a normative anthropology, an image of the typical man each system would like to produce, an image of the best man that, when stripped of its ontology or ethics, always resolves itself into a particular kind of story, a distinctively shaped biography. From the point of view of novel theory, then, ideologies that give rise to world systems are of interest in the degree to which they presuppose proscriptive biographies that may serve, in turn, as norms for narrative.

Neither narrative paradigm we have been examining is adequate to the temporal shape assumed by *The Brothers Karamazov*, and not only because it is made out of multiple and varying biographies. Both Lukacs and Girard err in their judgment of the Dostoevskian canon as a whole because each (Lukacs implicitly, Girard explicitly) uses a misreading of this last novel as a norm for all the others. Lukacs cannot accommodate it because Alyosha, at the end, seems to have found a self not condemned to decline into the mere transience that characterizes the fallen world of the novel. Girard seeks to take Alyosha's epiphany into account, but because he ascribes it to a transcendence unknown to the *Romanwelt*, he, too, misreads *The Brothers Karamazov*.

II

If, then, neither the biographical model proposed by Lukacs nor that of Girard conforms to the narrative shape of *The Brothers Karamazov*, where might we seek an alternative structure that does? A hint is provided by the cluster of specific preoccupations that swirl about Dostoevsky during the period of the novel's inception. Let me briefly recapitulate certain well-known facts in the author's life in order to set up the pattern that I believe finds its most complex expression in the dominant biographical paradigm of the novel. First hints of the new work can be gleaned from letters written during the early spring of 1878, especially to those correspondents who might be expected to have special knowledge of children, such as the educational thinker, V. V. Mikhailov, to whom Dostoevsky announced (March 16) he was beginning a novel in which children of seven to fifteen years would play a large role. Interest in young people is present as well in several of the author's friendships during this period, especially that with the precocious philosopher Vladimir Solovyov, who was in his twenties at this time, young enough to be Dostoevsky's son. Many biographers have pointed out that relations between the two resembled those of Father Zosima to the novice Alyosha. In May of 1878 Dostoevsky's actual son, the youngest—and favorite—son, whose name would be given to that novice, Alyosha, died. Dostoevsky's wife, Anna Grigorievna, tells us the father was "particularly distressed . . . that the child had died of epilepsy—a sickness which had been inherited from him . . . in order to comfort [him] . . . I begged [Solovyov] to go with him to Optina Pustyn,"[10] the great monastery that brought pilgrims to Kaluga from all over Russia. They did indeed make this journey, which brought a new intensity to their discussions of God-manhood, an ontological reconciliation in which distinctions between God and men, Father and sons, would be wiped out.

What emerges during these years is a gradually deepening preoccupation not so much with children as such, which is obvious enough, but the relationship they bear to adults, to parents. It is not childhood conceived as a kind of utopian state of innocence that adults must regain[11] that concerns Dostoevsky in this last period, but rather children conceived as one term of an opposition the other pole of which is parenthood. He treats the two groups almost as an anthropologist might two different cultures: the simple, naive, direct tribe of children living on the jungle side of the chronological barrier; and the stern, masterful, adults, living on the European side of the border between generations, presiding over secrets the natives can only guess. The overriding

[10] Quoted in Konstantin Mochulsky, *Dostoevsky, His Life and Work*, tr. Michael A. Minihan (Princeton U.P., 1967), p. 574.

[11] For an analysis based on this assumption see: William Woodin Rowe, *Dostoevsky: Child and Man in his Works* (New York, New York University Press, 1968).

173

question of this last phase is how can so enormous a split ever be overcome, how can sons become fathers? This is the project—not how fathers may once again become sons—a point that is made with bizarre force when we take into account the reverence Dostoevsky accorded during these years not only to Solovyov's schemes for reconciling the two camps, but to those of N. F. Fyodorov as well. Fyodorov's peculiar philosophy has been summarized most economically by Konstantin Mochulsky: Fyodorov's book, *The Philosophy of the Common Task*, "reduces to a paradoxical proposition: the joining together of sons for the resurrection of their fathers. . . . One must do away with the struggles between governments, peoples, classes; a classless society, a single family, a brotherhood must be created. And then united mankind will be able to realize its great vocation. All living sons will direct their forces to a single problem—the [physical] resurrection of their dead fathers. 'For the present age' writes Fyodorov, 'father is the most hateful word, and son is the most degrading. . . .' "[12]

Dostoevsky's tendency was always to arrange his texts around the most clashing oppositions. But the major opposition that preoccupies his last years is of a different order from those which characterize his work up to *The Brothers Karamazov*. Between God and man, transcendent ego and the existence of others, there is so complete a cutoff that mediation becomes, at least in the narrative limitations of the novel form, an impossibility. But while father may be "the most hateful word" and son "the most degrading," there is nevertheless between *these* poles a possible movement denied the space between those oppositions which have obsessed Dostoevsky up to this point.

Throughout his mature career Dostoevsky sought to write a particular kind of biography, a project he always referred to as *The Life of a Great Sinner*. At times, in such works as *The Idiot* or *The Possessed*, the opposition generating the biog-

[12] Mochulsky, p. 568. More detailed information is contained in an unpublished Ph.D. dissertation by George M. Young, *The Philosopher of the Common Task: A Study of the Life and Thought of Nikolai Fyodorov* (Yale, 1973).

raphy seems to accord with that posited by Lukacs, between the desire for unique identity and the necessity of others; in *Crime and Punishment* the opposition is of the sort Girard has used to define his master biography, between man and the sacred. The first two examples end with the madness or death of their heroes, the latter with the birth of a new hero whose story cannot be told. Thus, up to *The Brothers Karamazov*, Dostoevsky would seem to have used precisely those biographical master plots put forward by Lukacs and Girard, *imitatio* of *Geist* or *imitatio Christi*, to structure his narrative. But in his last novel he was to go beyond the unbridgeable antitheses of such models, to find a way out of the narrative dilemma defined by the absolute hegemony of self (*The Idiot*), the absolute hegemony of the others (*The Possessed*), or the absolute hegemony of the Completely Other (*Crime and Punishment*). A man cannot become a God, absolute ego cannot become another, but a son may become a father, which is the progression of *The Brothers Karamazov*.

But once we make the unremarkable admission that *The Brothers Karamazov* is about growing up, why must Lukacs and Girard be eschewed in our attempt to grasp the narrative implication of maturation? After all, both critics implicitly suggest that the *Bildungsroman* is the essential form of the novel. They seem to ignore the fact, however, that since the emphasis is on education (even when not sentimental), most novelistic heroes are young—or if old in chronological age, act "childishly," as do Don Quixote or Père Goriot. What is told of them is best expressed in a phrase whose increasingly banal implications should not blind us to its still great utility: novels tell identity crises. Their heroes are similar to those exemplary figures described by William James in *The Varieties of Religious Experience*, especially in those chapters (that sound like a roll call of novelistic themes) such as "The Sick Soul," "The Divided Soul," and "Conversion," even though, as has been pointed out, he does not "make a systematic point of the fact that . . . his illustrations . . . are almost exclusively people in their late teens or early twenties—an age which can be most painfully aware of the need for decisions, most driven to

175

choose new devotions and to discard old ones, and most susceptible to the propaganda of ideological systems which promise new world perspective at the price of total and cruel repudiation of the old one."[13] Nor do Lukacs or Girard make much of the fact that almost all the novels they cite as examples of the genre could just as well have the title Dostoevsky gave his penultimate work, *The Adolescent.* The reason they do not, I think, is that each in his own way is concerned to establish a biographical norm grounded in uniqueness: I strive against History in Lukacs, against God in Girard, but it is always *my* struggle and it seems to take place in a lonely world without others.[14] We must add to Girard's insight, "Every novelistic conclusion is a Past Recaptured" (p. 297) that, in *The Brothers Karamazov*, at any rate, the past that the hero recaptures is not his own.

The Brothers Karamazov is about four young men, each of whom, before he is confronted by problems of metaphysics or theology, and the distances they imply, must first overcome the dilemma of his status as son, must cross the mine field between that condition and its opposite state, fatherhood. The end of biography in this last novel is not a transcendent ego or God, but fatherhood. And just as the other two *tele* presuppose a specific biographical structure, each of which assigns different weights now to beginnings, now to middles, now to ends, so does the goal of fatherhood (which, of course, must not be confused with mere paternity). Behind Girard's biographical myth stands St. Augustine, behind Lukacs, Hegel. It should come as no surprise that the figure who might be invoked as source for an alternative biographical structure more appropriate to a novel so singlemindedly about sons taking (or failing to take) the place of the father is Freud. I have in mind particularly his "just so story" as he

[13] Erik H. Erikson, *Young Man Luther: A Study in Psychoanalysis and History* (New York, Norton Library, 1963 [9th printing]), p. 41.

[14] It could be argued that I am being particularly unfair to Girard here, since he makes so much of "triangular desire," but this geometrical metaphor is a figure whose angles are not equal: God is always the apex and "the other" is a mere instrument between me and Him.

came to call it,[15] "the scientific myth of the father of the primal horde."[16]

III

Freud first told the story in *Totem and Taboo* (1912-1913) but came back to it many times,[17] each variant further extending its implications. In what follows, we will use successive versions of the legend as biographical templates for examining the careers of the different brothers.

The simplest account is the first. It was inspired by Darwin and such anthropologists as Robertson Smith and is Freud's attempt to make the dynamics of the Oedipus complex into the engine of history. At the beginning of time there was a primal horde, composed of a despotic father who held absolute sway over his sons and the females of the tribe. One day (*eines Tages*, a German fairytale formula) the sons, angered by their father's control of the women, rose up, killed the father and ate him.[18] But "the tumultuous mob of brothers were filled with the same contradictory feelings which we can see in . . . our children . . . and . . . our neurotic patients. They hated their father, who presented such a formidable obstacle to their craving for power and their sexual desires; but they loved and admired him, too. After they had got rid of him, had satisfied their hatred and had put into effect their wish to identify with him, the affection which had all this time been pushed under was bound to make itself felt. A sense of guilt made its appearance, which in this instance coincided with the remorse of the whole group."[19] In order to propitiate the dead father, who "became stronger than the living one had

---

[15] *Group Psychology and the Analysis of the Ego*, tr. James Strachey (New York, Bantam, 1960), p. 86.

[16] *Ibid.*, p. 69.

[17] Especially in the following texts: *On Narcissism* (1914); *Group Psychology and the Analysis of the Ego* (1921); *The Future of an Illusion* (1927); and *Moses and Monotheism* (1937).

[18] The impulse to add "all up" has been stifled in my account, but would not let itself off without at least getting into a footnote.

[19] *Totem and Taboo*, p. 143.

been . . . they revoked this deed by forbidding the killing of the totem, the substitute for their father; and they renounced its fruits by resigning their claim to the women who had now been set free. They thus created out of their filial sense the two fundamental taboos [against murder and incest] . . . which correspond to the two repressed wishes of the Oedipus complex."[20]

This story has two parts, each of which is characterized by different meanings for son and father. In the first, the sons are helpless, the father all powerful; in the second, the sons become fathers, but not of the sort against whom they were forced to rebel. The new father tries to be different from the old parent, to be better in the sense that he permits more freedom to his own sons, thus eradicating some of the worst effects of the either/or condition of the son/father dichotomy that obtained in the primal condition. A complete biographical model may be adduced from the legend by focusing on the progression of a son who has gone through both stages, one who kills the father and then eradicates the need for his own murder by liberating the children he sires from the oppression he himself knew as a boy.

The Brothers Karamazov is built on just this biographical paradigm, although only Alyosha fully completes its movement, with all the other characters in the novel sorting themselves out according to how many steps and implications of the master plot they actually articulate. As we move from the most distorted versions of the primal horde myth, in Smerdyakov and Ivan, to its most fully realized expression in Alyosha, we shall also move from the simple account of the legend outlined above to some of its later and more far-reaching versions.

In order to read the novel this way, we begin by assuming the Karamazov family as we first encounter it to be in something very like the initial condition of the primal horde. That is what all the talk about "Karamazov-ism" means. Rakitin says to Alyosha, "Your house stinks of crime . . . in your family sensuality has reached a point where it becomes a de-

[20] *Loc.cit.*

vouring fever. So these three sensualists are now constantly watching each other—with a knife stuck in the leg of their boots . . ." ("A Seminarist-Careerist"). Old Fyodor Pavlovich is the complete tribal despot, depriving his sons of power, money, and women, better to prosecute his own lusts:

" 'So far as I'm concerned' he went on, becoming animated all at once, as though growing sober for a minute as soon as he got on to his favorite topic, 'so far as I'm concerned—oh my children, you, my little sucking pigs—so far as I'm concerned there has never been an ugly woman in all my life . . . for me ugly women don't exist. . . . What's so wonderful is that so long as there are peasants and gentlemen in the world—and there always will be—there will also be such lovely little scullery maids and their masters—and that's all one needs for one's happiness!' " ("Over the Cognac").

The sons all feel their dependence on him, that is what in the end the Karamazovism in themselves they all admit but despise comes down to, but Fyodor Pavlovich has a different way of exercising his power over each of them. The first reason each son has for hating him is grounded in his treatment of their various mothers. While Dmitry has one mother, Ivan and Alyosha another, and Smerdyakov still another, they have all been treated the same way by Fyodor Pavlovich. Primitive patriarch that he is, he begins by stealing them from their families or by raping them; he then soon abandons them in pursuit of yet other women. He gets Dmitry's mother, Adelaida Miusova, to elope with him; she discovers he has taken her dowry, does not love her, and after bitter quarrels she runs off with another man to die in a St. Petersburg attic, "leaving the three-year old Mitya to be taken care of by her husband. Karamazov at once turned his house into a regular harem. . . ." Sophia Ivanovna, the mother of Ivan and Alyosha, lasts longer but fares worse. Fyodor Pavlovich also gets her to elope with him: "her air of innocence made a deep impression on the voluptuary . . . 'those sweet, innocent eyes cut my heart like a knife at the time,' he used to say, sniggering loathesomely." After eight years of living in the harem

179

she dies, half demented. "After her death, almost exactly the same thing happened to the two boys as to their eldest brother Mitya: they were completely forgotten and abandoned by their father . . ." ("Second Marriage and Other Children"). Stinking Lizaveta is raped by the old man as she lies sleeping in a bush and her son, whose mother's name Fyodor Pavlovich assigns to him, is condemned to bastardy. He more than any other of the sons dramatizes the effects of their father's rule over them; thus he is quite literally his father's servant, a bastard and an epileptic. It goes without saying that it is he who actually accomplishes the act of which all the other sons merely dream when he murders the old man.

Thus each of the sons has in his mother a reason for hating his father. But the old man goes out of his way as well to show the power he has over his children in a manner calculated to dramatize the particular helplessness of every one of them, thus engendering the unique rage of each. Smerdyakov he openly insults, constantly reminding him of his status as bastard and servant. Ivan he affronts intellectually by the banalities he constantly reduces the philosopher's arguments to; emotionally—as the great oppressor of children—he offends, since for Ivan as he makes clear in the prologue to his Legend, the worst crimes are those against innocent children. Alyosha, the novice, is attacked through his devotion to the church: Fyodor Pavlovich twice vows to take his youngest son out of the monastery, to reclaim him from the surrogate father he has found in Zosima. Not only does the elder Karamazov boast to Alyosha how badly his mother was treated; he adds that he took her favorite icon away, but not before spitting on it. Alyosha, the gentle one, when he hears this story "flushed, his eyes glowed, his lips quivered . . . just as had his mother when she appeared to be on the point of killing Fyodor Pavlovich" ("Over the Cognac"). Dmitry's case fits the Freudian paradigm most neatly, as the father's power is dramatized in the property and the woman he denies the son: " 'She [Grushenka] won't, she won't, she won't, she won't marry him for anything in the world!' the old man cried, starting with joy . . ." ("The Sensualists").

180

Thus Fyodor Pavlovich acts out in a particular way the general role assigned him in the primal horde legend: he has "prevented his sons from satisfying their directly sexual impulsions; he forced them into abstinence and consequently into the emotional ties with him and with one another which could arise out of those of their impulsions that were inhibited in their sexual aim. He forced them, so to speak, into group psychology. His sexual jealousy and intolerance became in the last resort the causes of group psychology."[21] The situation as the novel opens is, then, one in which the father tyrannizes over four sons who all labor under the weight of their *Karamazovščina*, which in their case is both a dominant character trait and a political condition. The indignities they share together at the hands of their father force them into a primary group, "a number of individuals who have put one and the same object in the place of their ego ideal and have consequently identified themselves with one another in their ego."[22] They begin with this bond of oppression, which is why they all can be so intimate with each other immediately, even though they have been isolated from each other. They come from completely different backgrounds, and have not actually talked together until that point where the novel begins. All the brothers will seek to find different ways out of the dilemma, thus creating four versions of the Freudian master biography, each of which is defined by how well or poorly it charts a complete movement from group to individual, son to father.

III

Smerdyakov represents the most truncated version of the biography. He remains trapped in its opening steps, cannot get beyond the climax constituted by his own act of patricide. As a very small child he already conceives the world in the opposed terms of group/leader; in his case in terms of the church, precisely one of the two groups[23] Freud proposes as

[21] *Group Psychology and the Analysis of the Ego*, p. 72.
[22] *Ibid.*, p. 61.
[23] The other is the army, a choice of examples perhaps secretly dictated by Freud's admiration for Stendahl. It is tempting to speculate that the two "ar-

exemplary: "As a boy he was fond of hanging cats and bury-
ing them with ceremony. He used to dress up in a sheet, to
represent a kind of surplice, and chant and swing something
over the dead cat, as though it were a censer" ("Smerdyakov"). When his father treats *him* as an animal (Balaam's
ass), Smerdyakov looks for a new leader and seems to have
found him with the return of Ivan to the household. "Smerdyakov had often been allowed to wait at table before. . . .
But since the arrival in our town of Ivan he had begun to appear at dinner almost every day." He gets into arguments,
and, as Fyodor Pavlovich points out to Ivan, "He's doing it
all for your benefit. He wants you to praise him" ("The Argument"). He murders his father less out of a desire for his
own revenge than as a desire to be the good servant of another
master, his half-brother Ivan. When he discovers that Ivan is
unwilling to grant his approval to the deed, Smerdyakov,
abandoned by one master, one father, in whose presumed
service he had killed his other father, commits suicide. He is
trapped in group psychology because he lacks the means to
break out of adolescence: that very quality of passion, of sex-
uality, that impels all the other brothers. He is always described as a "eunuch" or "castrate." Thus, since he cannot become a father, he is condemned always to be the helpless son.
And when Ivan, the father he has chosen, rejects him, it is a
metaphysical bastardy (all is *not* permitted) more unbearable
than that which defined his relationship to the first parent. He
commits suicide not out of fear of capture, but from the despair of a twice-abandoned orphan.

Ivan, Smerdyakov's *alter ego* in the technical sense of that
term, also fails to advance beyond the status of oppressed son.
He, too, hates the father: "I detest him so much. If it had only
been him, I'd have left long ago" ("The Brothers Get Ac-
quainted"), and he, too, finds himself in the frustrated sexual-
ity of the horde's initial state, loving Katerina, one of his elder
brother's women. Thus he has the passion denied Smer-

---

tificial" groups, the Red and the Black, play so prominent a role in novels
because novelistic heroes always seek their own identity, thus necessitating
such a group against which to match their uniqueness.

dyakov, but the "children" he sires do not yet suffice to
achieve for him the status of father: the eunuch patricide, he
rejects; the Grand Inquisitor, he invents; and the devil, he
dreams. He brings about the death of the old despot, but cannot enact the further steps of Freud's normative biography:
the reasons why we see in his *legend*; the consequences we see
in his *nightmare*.

The confrontation between Christ and the Grand Inquisitor
is as much a disquisition on parenthood as it is an exercise in
theology. Ivan is obsessed with other examples of his own
condition as oppressed child. He collects anecdotes telling of
particularly brutal crimes against children; as a prologue to his
legend, as his rationale for it, he recounts some of these to
Alyosha, adding, "I'm not talking of the sufferings of
grown-up people . . . let them go to hell, but these little ones,
these little ones . . . there are lots of questions, but I've only
taken the children. . . ." It is the suffering of children that
leads Ivan to hand back his ticket to God, the reason for his
"Rebellion" that gives the Proem chapter its title. We see
here, not for the first or last time, an equation between the
psychopolitics governing the relations of Fyodor Pavlovich to
his sons, on the one hand, and that of God the father to his
human children, on the other. The filial oppression that
sparks rebellion against old Karamazov is transformed into a
metaphysical cause for revolt against God.

The Legend pits two theories of parenthood against each
other. Christ appears in the story not in his Second Coming,
"No, he only wanted to visit his children for a moment"; his
only act, other than his final kiss, is to resurrect a seven-
year-old girl, a metaphor for the view that fathers must de-
liver children from the killing effects of paternal oppression.
"You want to go into the world . . . with some promise of
freedom," says the Inquisitor, who understands what is at
issue very well. He holds the opposite view. It is clear that the
miracle and mystery he invokes are mere subfunctions of the
third element in the triad that defines him, authority. He, like
that patriarch of the other legend, the leader of the primal
horde, wants to insure that children remain children; he forces

183

them into group psychology: "the absolutely essential thing is that they should [worship] *all together*." He goes on to say of even those who rebel against the authority for which he stands, "they are little children rioting in class and driving out their teacher. But . . . they will pay dearly for it." His system is grounded in a static dichotomy between group and leader, children and father: "There will be thousands of millions of happy infants and one hundred thousand sufferers who have taken on themselves the curse of knowledge of good and evil. . . ."

This is the vicious circle in which Ivan finds himself; it is why he cannot himself move from the one condition (son) to that of the other (father). He is incomplete; he is trapped in the initial stages of the normal progression Alyosha's career will completely articulate, a point that is made when Alyosha criticizes the incompleteness of his brother's story. Ivan has let his Inquisitor have the last word, "Tomorrow I shall burn you. *Dixi!*" But under Alyosha's questions he adds, "I feel that in defending my theory I must appear to you as an author who resents your criticism. Let's drop it." But Alyosha asks, "How does your poem end?" forcing Ivan to add the detail of Christ's kiss, an unexpected ending ("the old man gave a start") as much for Ivan as it is for his Inquisitor, which is underscored when Alyosha kisses him as they part, a true act of plagiarism, not a technical *imitatio Christi* so much as an endorsement of the parental principle for which Ivan's Christ stands in.

Ivan's incomplete biography is dramatized as well in the encounter with the spectre he fathers, the devil. The devil longs for an end to the responsibility of his own freedom, wants to be one of the eternal children for whom the Grand Inquisitor would be natural parent: "My fondest dream is to be reincarnated, irrevocably and for good, as a 200-pound merchant's wife and to believe in everything she believes. My ideal is to go into a church and offer a candle from a pure heart. . . ." Like the underground man, he cannot find a story to live as his own biography; "I am the X in an indeterminate equation. I am a sort of phantom of life [*prizrak žizni*] who has lost all his ends and beginnings, and who has finally even forgotten what his name is." Which is exactly what happens to Ivan, whose end is an indeterminate "brain fever." He cannot get beyond the dilemma of desiring his father's death: "Who doesn't wish his father dead. . . . They all wish their fathers dead. One reptile devours another . . ." ("A Sudden Catastrophe"). Thus his story ends in confusion: "shouting something incoherent, he went on screaming while he was being carried out." Like his devil he "has lost all his ends and beginnings."

Now it has often been said that the shape that stands over against Ivan's ideas and the incomplete biographical progression they dictate is to be found in the chapters on "The Russian Monk" that follow closely on the Grand Inquisitor section of the novel. Dostoevsky, in some of his attempts to explain away the power of the Grand Inquisitor, assumed this position as well. And at first glance there would appear to be much to support such a view, especially if we maintain our biographical prejudice, since it is here that we get the most distilled version of "the life of a great sinner" in the *Vita* of Zosima. The elder's life appears to be told according to confessional narrative norms: not only does he experience a conversion, but so in the same story does his brother Markel and his friend, the mysterious visitor Michael. His biography is laid out according to the strictest norms of hagiography. There are two sections; the first called "Biographical Data," tells how he went astray as a young man, becomes a dissipated soldier (". . . they behaved badly, and I worst of all"), but then experiences a mysterious grace: "I felt as though my heart had been transfixed by a sharp needle. I stood there as though I had lost my reason, and the sun was shining, the leaves were rejoicing and reflecting the sunlight, and the birds—the birds were praising the Lord . . . I covered my face with both hands, flung myself onto the bed and burst out sobbing." He conflates hagiographic tradition with literary clichés when next morning he nobly refuses to answer his opponent's fire in a duel. But the chronology of his life—as it always does in a true confession—effectively ends at this point. He has found the end—as both conclusion and *telos*—of his development, in contrast to Ivan, whose biography lacks an end. The second part of Zosima's biography is not told chronologically then, but consists in the "Discourses and Sermons of the Father Zosima," much as Augustine's life ends with his conversion, and what follows is a discourse on time and the book of Genesis.

But to oppose Zosima's biographical scheme to that of Ivan's would be to fall into the trap that leads so many critics to identify Stepan Trofimovich's conversion rather than Stavrogin's suicide as the conclusion of *The Possessed*. The story of the novel does not cease with the story of Zosima. Even more, there are elements in the plot that contains Zosima's life which suggest that it is included not as a definitive example of biography, but rather as yet another model of life history that must be superseded. I have in mind first of all those demurrers on the part of the novel's narrator as to the close fit between Alyosha's written account of Zosima's life, on the one hand, and that life as it was actually lived, on the other. At the beginning of Alyosha's manuscript the narrator warns:

"This account of Zosima's life was written down from memory . . . a short time after the elder's death. But whether it was all the conversation on that evening or whether he added to it from his notes of his former talks with his teacher I cannot say for certain. Besides, the elder's speech in his account seems to go on without interruption, just as though, in addressing his friends, *he had been telling his life in the form of a story*, while from other accounts of it there can be no doubt that it all happened somewhat differently. . . . Moreover there can be no question of an uninterrupted narrative on the part of the elder. . . . Nevertheless I have preferred to confine myself to the elder's story according to Alexei Karamazov's manuscript. . . ."

And as the manuscript comes to an end, the narrator points to the confessional aspect of the *Vita*: "I repeat, [the manuscript] is incomplete and fragmentary, the biographical data, for instance, covers only the elder's early years," or, in other words, only those years up to Zosima's conversion.

Two things should be noted about the narrator's reservations: first, that the life is suspiciously coherent, *told*; second, that it is nevertheless not complete. It is shaped along the lines of a traditional biography, "literary" in the sense of that word invoked by the underground man, but only up to a certain point. It is precisely Zosima's death that raises questions about the *Life*: the traditional ending of the *Vita* is reversed. The saint's corpse not only fails to smell of the obligatory roses; it raises a stench that forces the shocked monks to open all the windows. This conclusion of the life is in contradiction with the canonical norm of the *Life*. Dostoevsky is at pains to point out that the stinking corpse is not to be read as a judgment on how Zosima lived his life. But it *is* a judgment on how that life was told. The reason why the confessional biographical model is so spectacularly flouted, and why it is breached precisely at the end, is that Dostoevsky is abandoning it as a possible paradigm for the life of his hero Alyosha, whose progression will not be that from sinner to saint, but from group member to individual, son to father.

Before we go on to Alyosha, however, a few words should be said on the subject of Dmitry's relationship to the normative biography we have been charting. He comes as close to living through all the functions of the primal son's narrative as anyone except Alyosha. He, like Ivan and Smerdyakov, desires the death of his father, openly threatens him with murder, and challenges that other father, Captain Snegiryov, to a duel. But the rebellious son almost becomes the loving father himself after his arrest. As he lies dozing during the interview at the Mokroye tavern, he dreams of poverty-stricken mothers and a starving, freezing baby, the image of which causes him to ask "Why are they so black with misfortune, why don't they feed the baby?" ("The Evidence of the Witnesses".) Thus, just after learning of his father's death, Mitya dreams of assuming a kind of paternal responsibility and one, moreover, that is set off from Ivan's concern for children.[24] The starving baby is called "*ditë*," a peasant dialect word that marks the difference between it as an object of

[24] A point suggested to me by Victor Terras.

compassion and the more proper "child" (*rebënok*) whose fate
obsesses Ivan. The dream is as well contrasted to Ivan's
nightmare in its effect: Dmitry's "heart blazed up and rushed
forward to the light, and he longed to live. . . ." In the end,
however, it is not given him to experience full parenthood in
the sense that word takes on in the course of the novel: his *ditë*
is still a dream as he plans to escape to America. He is not yet
ready to take on responsibility of this sort, one that includes
responsibility for the death of his own father. As Alyosha tells
him ". . . you are not ready and such a cross is not for you . . .
such a cross is too much for you" ("For a Moment a Lie Becomes the Truth"). Zosima has bowed down to Dmitry and
not to any of the other brothers because it is Mitya who will
actually be judged for the crime of which they are all guilty:
patricide.

But Alyosha has won the right to judge whether or not his
brother is "ready," because he is at a further point in that
biographical progression which structures the whole novel, a
point he knows Mitya has not reached. Alyosha treats his
brother like a son, because Alyosha has become a father. In
the "scientific myth" we have been using as a narrative guide,
it is assumed that after the murder of the despotic father, the
sons, "the persons who were united in this group of brothers,
gradually came toward a revival of the old state of things at a
new level. . . . It was then, perhaps, that some individual, in
the exigency of his longing, may have been moved to free
himself from the group and take over the father's part [which
is how Alyosha in the end relates to Mitya]. He who did this
was the first epic poet; and the advance was achieved in his
imagination. This poet disguised the truth with lies in accordance with his longing. He invented the heroic myth. . . . Just
as the father had been the boy's first ideal, so in the hero who
aspires to the father's place the poet now created the first ego
ideal. The transition to the hero was probably afforded by the
youngest son. . . ."[25] This, then, is the achievement of the
youngest Karamazov: he creates a heroic myth or, more precisely, recreates a myth, since he is, as Ivan has accused him of

[25] *Group Psychology*, p. 87.

being, a plagiarist. The liberating story Alyosha comes to tell is, of course, the life of Christ, not as a theological consolation (or not merely as such) but as a—literally—*viable* model of biography, a narrative that rationalizes, mediates the transition from son to father.

Alyosha has been made to suffer by his father. Moreover, he is implicated in the other brothers' desire for their father's death, a point made most unambiguously when Ivan asks what should be done with a general who turned his Borzoi hounds on a naked little peasant boy, clearly a metaphoric recasting of the relations between Fyodor Pavlovich and his sons: "Shoot him!" Alyosha said softly, raising his eyes to his brother with a pale, twisted smile ("Rebellion"). But Alyosha is less completely an orphan than his brothers. Like the youngest son of Freud's legend, he has been spared the worst of his father's excesses, not by a protective mother, but because he has another father, in fact a *pater seraphicus*, in Zosima. The elder is a much more complicated figure than is often assumed, and in many ways presides over his followers as does the primal despot: "An elder is a man who takes your soul and will into his soul and will . . . you renounce your will and yield it to him in complete submission and complete abnegation. . . . Thus, the elders are in certain cases endowed with boundless authority" ("Elders"). He has, in other words, precisely the kind of power sought by Ivan's Grand Inquisitor; but Zosima, like Ivan's Christ, believes fathers should use their power to liberate sons so that they in their turn may become fathers: ". . . this is not the place for you in future . . . as soon as [I die] leave the monastery." In other words, cease being a mere brother, part of a group; become an individual, a father—which is what (after the death of both his own fathers) Alyosha does. His children are not the phantoms of Ivan's nightmare, nor even the spectral "*ditë*" of Mitya's dream. They are, rather, the band of boys who play so large a role in the novel.

These boys have frequently offended the sensibility of sophisticated readers: as one has recently written, "It is a doubtful proposition that one can achieve the Kingdom of

189

God on earth by converting mankind into boy-scouts, and that is why those chapters of *The Brothers Karamazov* [dealing with Kolya Krasotkin and the others] read like an unintended parody."[26] But if we assume a non-transcendent significance in Alyosha's Christology, he and the boys rather seem to be a happy parody of the Karamazov family, thus a narrative inversion of the political structure built into the two legends of the Grand Inquisitor and of the primal horde. That is, Alyosha's *imitatio* need not be read as necessarily grounded in Christian theology. Ideas about God, if Freud is correct, are rooted in ideas about fathers: ". . . at long last the decision was made to concede all power to one God only. . . . Only then was the grandeur of the primeval father restored; the emotions belonging to him could now be restored."[27] There is a psychological truth about fathers and sons contained in Christianity, particularly as it is present in *The Brothers Karamazov*, that seems to get back to a meaning in Christ's biography that loses nothing if it is stripped of the privilege that religions traditionally claim. Perhaps that is why Alyosha admits "I don't think I even believe in God" ("The Engagement") or what Dostoevsky meant in his famous letter to N. D. Fonvizina (March, 1854): "If anyone could prove to me that Christ is outside the truth, and if the truth really did exclude Christ, I should prefer to stay with Christ and not with the truth." That is, even without the claim of transcendent truth, Christ has a primary significance for Dostoevsky, one that he spent his whole career meditating, but that finally becomes clear in his last novel.

Christ is important not for the narrative scheme he usually is invoked to justify—the confession or Saint's life, which is explicitly rejected in *The Brothers Karamazov*. To read the whole novel as articulating this pattern leads to the undemystified contortions into which critics as different as Girard or Berdyaev get. De-mystification, on the other hand,

---

[26] Czeslaw Milosz, "Dostoevsky and Swedenborg," *Slavic Review*, XXXIV, ii (June, 1975), p. 318.

[27] *Moses and Monotheism*, tr. Katherine Jones (N.Y., Vintage Books, n.d.), pp. 171-72.

need not inevitably result in the biographical pattern of a lapsed Hegelianism that Lukacs sees the novel—and, as we have seen, Dostoevsky's previous heroes—condemned to, since the Christ story, conceived as the most schematic map of the mediatable distance between son and father, does not require the assumption of absolute ego. The movement is not between disjunctive states in the same essential self, the either/or of radical Romantic identity, but rather between different functions within an unchanging structure of relationships.

Thus, when Alyosha at the end of the novel speaks of resurrection, we need not take this to mean the same thing as is meant in Christian soteriology. It points to a model for how sons may become fathers; it makes of Christ a hero story. Alyosha, like the son in Freud's legend who becomes a poet, achieves that poet's goal: "The myth, then, is the step by which the individual emerges from group psychology. The first myth was certainly the psychological, the hero myth. . . . The poet who had taken this step and had in this way set himself free from the group in his imagination, is nevertheless able . . . to find his way back to it in reality. For he goes and relates to the group his hero's deeds which he has invented. At bottom the hero is no one but himself. Thus he lowers himself to the level of reality, and raises his hearers to the level of the imagination."[28]

Thus Alyosha, after leaving the family presided over by his father and the group presided over by his elder, becomes such an individual by means of the mediating Christ story, his example (the hero is no one but himself) and words ("I will find a place in my heart for you all and I beg you to find a place for me in yours") convey to the new family he fathers on the last page of the novel. By doing so he changes the significance that attached to his name. He has given his father's name a new meaning, his own meaning, which is why the last sentences of the book round off his biography: "Hurrah for Karamazov!"

[28] *Group Psychology*, p. 88.

Afterword

Dostoevsky's role in the history of the novel is determined by his use of the novel to interrogate history. The growing privilege that attached to history from the Renaissance through the Enlightenment peaked in the nineteenth century, an age in which the modern conception of its study was born. It is, of course, a gross oversimplification, if perhaps a necessary one, to say that before Niebuhr and Von Ranke each nation or each religion compiled a past that took into account "what had really happened" only insofar as the facts provided a sanction for the present. History, on the other hand, is not like this; it is not so much a different subject as it is a different attitude toward the same data that occupies the past. But it differs from the past in that it is open to the *multiplicity* of what has gone before, even when the details of which it is aware not only do not aid in comprehending the present, but actually contradict current pieties. So that when it is said, as it so often is, that the nineteenth century is the apogee of historical consciousness, one of the things we are expressing is the corollary truth: it is also the age in which various pasts began their dissolution. As J. H. Plumb has put it, "Once historical criticism developed, the Christian explanation of the past could not maintain its supremacy. It slowly collapsed under criticism, but . . . just as surely [so] did the interpretations which replaced it—the concept of progress, the manifest destinies of competitive nationalism, social Darwinism, or dialectical materialism. History, which is so deeply concerned with the past, has, in a sense, helped to destroy it as a social force, as a synthesizing and comprehensive statement of human destiny.[1]

The Russians occupy an anomalous position in this dialectic of history versus the past. When, in the decades when Dostoevsky was coming to consciousness, leading Russian intellectuals lamented the absence of a distinctively Russian literature, as did Belinsky in a piece he subtitled an elegy, he meant

---

[1] *The Death of the Past* (Boston, Houghton Mifflin, 1971), p. 136.

193

that Russian literature had no past of the sort we have been discussing. When Chaadaev wrote that the Russians have no history he, too, was expressing the thought that the Russians had no past. They had only a relative poverty, when compared to the rest of Europe, of uniquely indigenous myths about what had gone before that might be used to explain and comfort what was now. In an over-schematization whose only justification is its utility, it might be said that while in West Europe history was at work destroying the several pasts that were present, there was in Russia the felt absence of a past that history could demystify. This might help to explain the unusually receptive audience for Hegelianism in Russia, where attempts were made to fuse history and the past by finding a past in history. Dostoevsky in his correspondence and in his journalism actively participated in this attempt to use the facts of Russian history to erect a Russian past, a past that served as well, of course, to indicate and underwrite the Russian future.

But it was always in the novels that Dostoevsky permitted himself, or was compelled by his prior allegiance to the demands of the genre, to put his assumptions to the most radical test. The suggestion of this book has been that Dostoevsky is important *in the way* he is important because of the courage with which he sustained doubts about received ideas on the nature of personal identity and because of the conceptual rigor he displayed in the articulation of those doubts. Just as he raised questions about what a novel might be, so did he problematize what his age was still unembarrassed enough to call "Man." And both these aspects of his achievement are tied together: the metaphysical concern for the end of Man is realized in the most formal attributes of the structure of his novels, the narrative shape. And this is so because he was among the first to recognize that the question of what a man might be could not be separated from the question of what might constitute an authentic history. Each question is, in its own way, a dilemma of narrative.

At a time when Europe was desperately countering the encroachments of history on older and more comfortable con-

194

ceptions of the past by erecting new systems whose claims to superiority were still derived from secularized theodicies, exclusivist interpretations of previous events—and the Russians more desperately than others because of their peculiar relationship to European models of history that excluded them—at such a time Dostoevsky raised the even more disturbing prospect that history might not be able to generate *any* past.

Dostoevsky raises questions about the nature of Man because he refuses to take as a given the historical prejudice without which such a conception was unthinkable, that story which had its predictable end in European culture as surely as all fairy tales, diverse though they may be, end with the formula, "And they lived happily ever after." It was so widely held an assumption (even by non-Europeans) in the nineteenth century that all of history conduced to create a West European norm that such otherwise completely opposed figures as the Parliamentarian liberal Buckle, on the one hand, and such a radical revolutionary as Marx, on the other, could *both* appeal to this sense of the world's past and the implicit future it promised. In both cases, and in many others less influential, the past was conceived as being Europe's, and its product, just as surely as if it had been an equation, was Man, the name nineteenth-century ideologies invoked in the same structural slot that had previously been occupied by God: the name for their highest aspirations and the justification for their most unspeakable crimes.

Dostoevsky attacks Buckle (in *Notes from the Underground*) and the revolutionaries (in *The Possessed*) because they share a fundamental—and ultimately sinister—misconception about the nature of the relationship between narrative and meaning. Dostoevsky is not interesting because of his moral stance (he is "good" because of the way in which he can be accommodated to a single ideology), but because of the acuity and intelligence with which he analyzes the enabling assumptions behind all ideologies: their assumption that significance is a function of morphology, that the shape of events, their very ordering, exhausts their meaning—the validity of their claims

195

is guaranteed by a narrative sequence of concepts. Dostoevsky is among those (Neitzsche was another) who recognized that there was a fundamental contradiction between
religion and ideology: while both attempted to substitute a
past for a history, religions were more logical in that the story
of which they were a part had a transcendental author. Meaning was less in events than it was in the One who directed
their unfolding in time. The end and the End of *Heilsgeschichte*
was outside *Geschichte*. Ideologies, on the other hand, wanted
to have their past—and history, too. Conceptually rapacious,
they were naive as religions had not been. Ideologies sought
to use the engine of religious historiography without at the
same time having recourse to the fuel that made that engine
work, a transcendence outside time whose very separateness
from events insured their meaning.

It is arguably the case that it was Nietzsche's meditation on
The Uses and Abuses of History for Mankind that later caused
him to announce, in *Zarathustra*, the death of God. Not only
had God died in history, but perhaps *because* of history, or at
least that kind of history that was "for Mankind." An animating impulse in the Dostoevskian novel, at any rate, is such a
concern, care for the possibility that the death of one past may
be the death of all pasts—we must be prepared to entertain the
prospect that not only God has died, but that Man, his presumed successor, has perished as well. And both have done so
for the same reason. In an age in which it becomes increasingly clear, as it did in the nineteenth century, that history is
tied neither to Man nor to any other particular object, that it is
a method, not a justification, a method, moreover, with no
necessary content, then those forces which have used the past
as source for their claims to unique privilege must come
under attack.

I have tried to suggest that the generic role of the novel in
this drama of demystification was to provide a refuge for the
concept of the individual. Man may have been threatened in
the world, but the existence of *a* man, such as Rastignac or a
man such as Pip becomes—*that* existence was indubitably
there, flourishing in the novel, a kind of protected zone, a

sanctuary for the individual. The message of the novel was that history as such might not have a proper subject, but there was a kind of history that nevertheless did require—if not Man—at least a man, and that was biography. The novel was a place where the illusion was maintained that there was a correspondence between the shape of the events in a man's life *and* their significance, an illusion made possible by the characteristic coincidence in the novel of fictional story (*fabula*) and pseudo-biographical plot (*sjužet*). Freed of brute contingency by reason of its status as fictive construction, its power to endow the appearance of contingency with biographical meaning was thereby secured. What was an increasingly difficult to maintain relationship between history and exclusive meaning in theology or political ideology was inwrought into the generic distinctiveness of the novel—or at least until Dostoevsky.

Dostoevsky's peculiar role in the history of the novel, I have tried to show, consists in the way he built those radical doubts about the existence of God and Man that were abroad in the world into his novels. The gift of comfort that the novel had always proffered, the illusion of individuality, was withdrawn as Dostoevsky put the biography of a man to the same kind of question that had undermined the biography of God and Man.

Index of Names

Alleman, B., 56
Apollo, 85
Aquinas, St. T., 94
Arabian Nights, 57
Arendt, H., 119fn, 120, 121fn
Aristotle, 54, 55fn, 65, 57; *The Poetics*, 54-57
Aristotelean, 55, 59, 70
Arnold, M., 72
"Arzamas," 11
Augustine, St., 167, 169, 176, 186; *Confessions*, 17, 94; *City of God*, 107fn

Baader, F. von, 8
Bakhtin, M., 75; *Problems of Dostoevsky's Poetics*, 76
Balzac, H. de, 36, 65, 69, 165; *Père Goriot*, 69
"Baron Munchhausen," 97
Baudelaire, C., 142
Bayley, J., 76
Beebe, M., 93
Belinsky, V. G., 10, 12-14, 28, 193
Ben-Amos, D., 82fn
Benjamin, W., 167, 168fn
Benkendorf, A. K., Count, 7
Berdyaev, N., 190
Bergson, H. (durée), 100
Berthoff, W., 47fn
"Beseda" (Discussion Group of Lovers of the Russian Word), 11
Beztuzhev-Marlinsky, A., 12
Billington, J., 6fn
Bloch, E., 79fn
Bloch, M., 114fn
Bloomfield, M. W., 34fn
Boileau, N., 5
Borges, J. L., 88
Boswell, J., 145
"Brown, Father," 87
Buckle, H. T., 48, 59, 195
Bulgarin, F., 7, 8
Burke, K., 124fn
Butkov, Ya., 42
Byron, Lord G., 65

Cervantes, M. de, 108, 109, 165; *Don Quixote*, 108-110, 117, 122, 144, 146, 169, 175
Chaadaev, P. Ya., 14-16, 18, 20, 27, 28, 194; *The Philosophical Letters*, 14, 19; *Apologie d'un Fou*, 18
Chancellor, Sir R., 3
Charbonnier, G., 108fn, 152fn
Charles X (of France), 25
Cherniavsky, M., 10fn, 105fn
Chesterton, G., K., 91
Collingwood, R. G., 99
Considérant, V. P., 132
Cornford, F. M., 51
Cullman, O., 106fn

Daniélou, Cardinal J. (S.J.), 106fn, 107, 167fn
Darwin, C., 58, 59, 177; Darwinism, Darwinian, 58, 63
Davydov, A. I., 8
Debreczeny, P., 9fn
Defoe, D., 165, 166
de Man, P., 34
Derzhavin, G. R., 4, 12
Descartes, R., 64
Dickens, C., 36, 165fn

Eikhenbaum, B., 13
Eliade, M., 17fn
Erikson, E. H., 176fn
Euclid, 33

Fanger, D., 23fn, 42fn
Ferdinand VII (of Spain), 24
Feuerbach, L., 136
Field, A., 4fn
Fielding, H., *Tom Jones*, 144, 146
Fonvizina, N. D., 190
Forster, E. M., 51, 77, 78; *Aspects of the Novel*, 77fn
Foucault, M., 49, 52, 53, 61
Fourier, C., 136
Freud, S., 91, 97, 159, 176, 181, 183, 189, 190; *Group Psychology and the*

199

201

Index

Library of Congress Cataloging in Publication Data

Holquist, J. Michael.
  Dostoevsky and the novel.

  Includes index.
  1.   Dostoevskiĭ, Fedor Mikhaĭlovich, 1821-1881—
Criticism and interpretation.   I.   Title.
PG3328.Z6H6   891.7'3'3   77-3668
ISBN 0-691-06342-7